Jean Cameron

Anne Hutchinson, Guilty or Not?

A Closer Look at Her Trials

PETER LANG
New York • Washington, D.C./Baltimore • San Francisco
Bern • Frankfurt am Main • Berlin • Vienna • Paris

Library of Congress Cataloging-in-Publication Data

Cameron, Jean.
    Anne Hutchinson, guilty or not? : a closer look at her trials / Jean
Cameron.
        p.   cm. — (American university studies. Series IX, History;
vol. 146)
    Includes bibliographical references.
    1. Hutchinson, Anne Marbury, 1591–1643—Trials, litigation, etc.
2. Trials (Heresy)—Massachusetts—Boston. 3. Trials (Sedition)—
Massachusetts—Boston. 4. Puritans—Massachusetts—History.
5. Antinomianism. I. Title. II. Series.
KF223.H86C36   1994   973.2′2′092—dc20   93-17290
ISBN 0-8204-2227-4   CIP
ISSN 0740-0462

Die Deutsche Bibliothek-CIP-Einheitsaufnahme

Cameron, Jean:
Anne Hutchinson, guilty or not? : A closer look at her trials / Jean Cameron.
- New York; Berlin; Bern; Frankfurt/M.; Paris; Wien: Lang, 1994
    (American university studies: Ser. 9, History ; Vol. 146)
    ISBN 0-8204-2227-4
NE: American university studies / 09

The paper in this book meets the guidelines for permanence and durability of
the Committee on Production Guidelines for Book Longevity of the
Council on Library Resources.

© Peter Lang Publishing, Inc., New York 1994

Printed in the United States of America.

Contents

I would like to dedicate this book to the memory of my father:

Robert Horton Cameron.

ACKNOWLEDGEMENTS

I cannot begin to acknowledge all those to whom I am indebted for their insights and support. There are a few, however, to whom I would like to say a special thank you.

I would like to thank Ernest Bormann, J. Vernon Jensen, Fred Lukermann, and Rus Menard, for their helpful suggestions. In addition, I do not want to forget Herb Cederberg for leading me in the direction of this book. I wish to give special thanks to Roland Delattre, who gave me encouragement and good critical suggestions, to David Linde, for his assistance with biblical quotations, and to my editor, Heidi Burns, for her careful eye and good judgment.

To Suzette Fearing, Jean Hockman, and all those whose help has been so valuable, who have made the process so much more pleasant, who have said and done just the right things when I needed them, an especial thank you.

And finally, I would not forget my husband, Bob Linde, for all his patience and sensitivity, and for those helpful tips, and my mother and my children, for their enthusiasm. Thank you to you all.

Any deficiencies, of course, are my responsibility alone.

In addition, I would like to thank the presidents of the institutions of the Associated Colleges of the Twin Cities (Augsburg College, Hamline University, Macalester College, The College of St. Catherine, and the University of St. Thomas) and to the libraries of those institutions for sharing their collections with me.

Chapter One

Opposed to the Law: The Questions

Anne Hutchinson's story is well known to students of seventeenth-century America. The setting: the infant colony in the cruel wilderness; the group: upright Puritans; the symbolism: individualism, bloody but unbowed. Anne Hutchinson, after coming to Boston in 1634, was tried for sedition in 1637 for holding meetings in her home where sermons were discussed, and her theological ideas were disseminated. She was said to have accused most of the ministers of Boston of not being under the requisite "Covenant of Grace," and had been able to convince a large part of the people of Boston that she correctly assessed the ministers' spiritual estate. Tried in a civil court for maligning the ministers, and found guilty of sedition, she was sentenced to banishment, then underwent an ecclesiastical trial and was excommunicated. She left the colony for Rhode Island and died at the hands of Native Americans in New York a few years later.

The saga has long held a place of importance for scholars of the period because of its significant themes: the leaders of the colony were ready and willing to rush to summary judgment of one of their community for holding religious beliefs they did not consider tolerable, yet their assumption of the need for freedom of conscience kept bringing the case back to haunt them. Hutchinson's story, of a lone individual versus the authorities, has carried its captivation for Americans, and the significance of those themes in the history of America explains its freshness today. But the story needs some updating. It now is clear that the picture is more complex than had previously been thought, and there are new pieces to be added to the puzzle that will change the picture considerably.

The account as we have known it tells us that at her civil trial for sedition Hutchinson had almost out-foxed her accusers with her knowledgeable and carefully phrased answers, and her penetrating questions to the men accusing her. Then, somehow, just when she had conclusively deflected all their efforts against her by masterful legal maneuvers, retorts, and questions of their every point, she made a stupid blunder, told them she had received revelations from God, and the game was up. This is how the story has been presented. In her ecclesiastical trial, it appears that she insisted upon raising silly, unreasonable questions, until her pastor, John Cotton, and the other ministers lost patience with her, and finally were forced to excommunicate her.

In addition, we have read that the Reverend Mr. John Cotton, her pastor, whose preaching she so craved that she left England in order to be able to hear him preach, tried his best to help her at the trials, but to no avail: she gave the game away herself. Even those who have suspected that Cotton could have done more for her have excused him for not being more aggressive on behalf of someone who was so clearly confused or misguided. In any case, it would seem, while by our standards there is no question that such trials should not have happened, with Puritan standards and expectations, the verdicts were a fair outcome given the evidence. Had she just kept herself from making outrageous statements, she would have been fine.

However adding some new pieces of the puzzle reveals that contrary to what has commonly been assumed, Hutchinson was not proven guilty—by Puritan standards—of the charges leveled against her, in either trial. There are reasons to state that Hutchinson was well within the accepted standards of Puritan doctrine in the statements she made at her civil trial, and that the questions she raised at her ecclesiastical trial were reasonable ones, which could have been answered satisfactorily by John Cotton. The new puzzle pieces that change the picture are: a closer examination of her statements, in light of accepted doctrine; a look at the impact of the original languages of the Bible on her ecclesiastical trial, and the philosophical milieu in which some parts of the Bible that she questioned were written; a careful tracing of Bible verses quoted without citation by Hutchinson; and a closer examination, with comparisons, of both of the trials. The sum of these inquiries is to shed new light on the trials, add to a fuller understanding of her claims and questions, and to lead to the finding of "not guilty."

A brief review of the facts will help to give some context about the events of the Antinomian Controversy (or Crisis), as historians often refer to the story. Further, a word is in order about the information in existence about the trials. Fortunately records of the events make a careful study of the proceedings possible. Transcripts of the trials written at the time are readily available. David D. Hall has collected the relevant materials into one handy volume, and many of the references in this study bear witness to the debt scholars of the trials owe him. The two existing versions of transcripts of her civil trial, a longer one found in the history of New England written more than one hundred years later by a great–great grandson of Anne Hutchinson, and a shorter one found in writings of John Winthrop, who was present and took part in the trials, agree very well with one another in content, so that a comparison of them enables scholars to be confident in the accuracy of their presentation of the proceedings. There are also two versions of the church trial, only one of which is in transcript form. The other is a synopsis written by John Winthrop and found in his journal. The wording in these does not agree as well, although the substance is quite similar. These records give scholars a good sense of the proceedings of the events during the trials.[1]

In 1630 John Winthrop led a group of settlers to North America, as part of a new colony to be set up by the Massachusetts Bay Company. John Cotton, one of the great Puritan ministers of the time, had been asked to come along as part of the venture when the colony was first set up. However he did not emigrate until 1633. His parishioner at the church of St. Botolph in Boston, England, Anne Hutchinson, was so anxious to continue to be able to hear him speak that she then took her family and followed him to the new Boston in 1634.

It became apparent in the year 1636 that a large number of people in the colony were attending meetings at Hutchinson's home to discuss the Sunday sermon and listen to her expound upon it. She maintained that only Cotton and her brother-in-law, John Wheelwright, were preaching the correct understanding of the doctrines, and finally both the ministers and the civil authorities became alarmed. Ministers reported to Governor Winthrop and others that they were being maligned, and that their efforts to discuss the issue with Cotton had not been successful. The ministers' concern had to do with the doctrines of justification and sanctification. Cotton and Wheelwright were teaching the Calvinistic doctrine that God had preordained justification, or election to eternal salvation, for a select few, and those few would, after having received justification, show evidence of their election by their pure behavior, or sanctification. The rest however were propounding the newer doctrine that sanctification preceded, and could even lead to, justification. Cotton was finally persuaded by the ministers to agree to this understanding of the doctrines. There was more, though; there were some who would intimate that sanctification was not only evidence of justification, but was instrumental in leading to justification. For those who believed as Cotton did, this was heresy, and Anne Hutchinson believed that such heresy was what she had been hearing from the ministers in the Bay. She called it "preaching a Covenant of Works," rather than a "Covenant of Grace;" and to her it was anathema.

This is where the ministers had the largest dilemma. Many of them had indeed preached that sanctification presaged justification, and therefore could be taken as evidence that justification would follow good behavior. It is obvious upon some reflection that good behavior was to be encouraged in the colony, so that it was not only a theological concern but also a social concern to have one influential minister and an equally influential lay person claiming that good behavior could not possibly lead to justification, which was given freely by God, and therefore counted for nothing in the scheme of salvation. The ministers were upset with Hutchinson, who was known to be Cotton's pupil, for teaching that his doctrine was more "pure" than theirs, and the civil authorities recognized that such beliefs threatened the social cohesiveness of the colony.

In December of 1636 a meeting of the ministers and Hutchinson was held to discuss sermons of Cotton's and of John Wilson's, the preacher of the church in Boston where Cotton was the teacher. Wilson was one of the ministers singled out by Hutchinson as not correctly preaching a covenant of grace, and he was especially upset about it, as would be expected, given his relationship with Cotton. Answers were sent back and forth, but this only led to much commotion in the colony. Hutchinson's followers began to travel to other churches in the area and raise questions after the sermons. While the practice of raising questions was common, apparently their questions and their demeanor were becoming untactful to say the least.

In January the situation had become so tense that a fast was held to ask for God's guidance in the matter, but Wheelwright, asked to preach an extemporaneous sermon, delivered a long and carefully crafted one full of hellfire and damnation for those under a "Covenant of Works," and tensions continued to increase. In March of 1637 Wheelwright was brought before the General Court for having preached that sermon, which was considered seditious. He was found guilty, but sixty or so persons signed a petition that said they felt his doctrine was correct and that the proceedings of the court had been flawed. In May when the General Court was held to elect a new governor, Winthrop was reelected, which increased the political power of the ministers, because Governor Vane, whom he ousted, had been a follower of Anne Hutchinson.

A synod was held in late summer where the ministers could discuss the problem with Cotton, at which time he was able to convince them that his beliefs were in accord with theirs, and that his church members' beliefs did not differ from those of the other ministers in any substantial way. In November, after several of her followers had been tried and disenfranchised or banished, Hutchinson was tried. The proceedings were on shaky legal ground, as she was able to point out. But after two days, when she saw that they could prove nothing against her that would indicate seditious behavior, she told the court that she had had a revelation from God. She said that God had opened the scriptures to her and let her know she would overcome her adversaries, and God would protect her from them. With little ado this was interpreted to mean that she had been hearing voices, and expected God to perform a miracle in her behalf. This constituting heresy, she was found guilty, and was banished summarily, although it was customary to allow time for reflection upon ones behavior, and others such as Wheelwright had been allowed time to think over their misdeeds before sentencing.

Hutchinson was kept at Mr. Timothy Weld's house until March when she underwent a church trial, and was found guilty there as well. During the church trial Cotton led the questioning of Hutchinson with vigor, and finally horrified her by telling her that her ideas would lead to serious social crimes. Once the church leaders had decided that she held heretical views, they voted to admonish her, and Cotton admonished her, telling her that she had spread evils among the congregation. She was told to come back one week later, where more discussion of her beliefs was held, and she was sentenced to be excommunicated, with no concern expressed by Cotton, although several of the others were squeamish about such a severe sentence. She went with her family to Rhode Island, where Roger Williams was willing to receive dissenters of many stripes because of his insistence on the separation of church and state. Five years later she and her family moved to New York and were killed by Indians of the area. Those, briefly, are the facts of the case.

Several aspects of the case become clearer with a more thorough look at the trials. One is that her civil trial for sedition turned upon her statement that she had received a number of revelations from God and her declaration that God would protect her from her prosecutors. Governor Winthrop, who presided at the trials, chose to assume that she meant that God was speaking directly to her. However, a close reading of the trial records—taken by Timothy Weld, who was not a friend of hers—make it clear that she was not claiming that God spoke directly to her, but that He spoke to her through the scriptures. Also, the record shows that she was not looking for a special miracle from God to save her from them, but rather that she relied on God's protection.

Another aspect of Hutchinson's trials that has gone without careful study is John Cotton's part in the trials. This may be because few scholars other than her biographers have written about both trials. Edmund Morgan, like most, zeroes in on the first one, the civil trial, where Hutchinson declared that she had received an immediate revelation. One, J. F. Maclear, has written about the church trial.[2] Because scholars have concentrated on one or the other of the trials the situation has been created that even when John Cotton's change in behavior at the second trial has been noted it has only been mentioned in passing. This in turn has served to diminish the impact of his behavioral change from the first to the second trial. It then had the further effect of lessening the perception of the impact of his behavior at her trials.

However, a comparison of the two trials reveals that John Cotton behaved altogether differently at the two trials. He said little in her defense at the civil trial, merely suggesting that her statements about the ministers had been exaggerated by them. At the church trial, however, he was quite strident and aggressive with her. Looking at both trials together brings out the extreme contrast in his demeanor toward her. At her civil trial nothing was heard from him until asked by the court to address the veracity of the reports of the other ministers. (To be fair to him, it is not clear whether or not he was present up until that point in the trial.) When called upon to testify, his answers, which, if accurate, demonstrate that the ministers had been exaggerating her statements to them, appear to give as little information as possible. Finally, when she spoke of having had an immediate revelation, his efforts in her behalf were feeble. He hardly tried to point out to the court that her statement meant nothing more than what all Puritans could say, that they believed God spoke to them through His Word. When asked, he did explain that her claim that God would deliver her from them was not heretical since she was not claiming that God would provide a miraculous deliverance for her, but again his explanations in her defense were quite restrained.

His actions six months later at the church trial, in contrast, show a hostile attitude and aggressive behavior toward her. Some of his statements uttered to her in frustration have been interpreted to mean that he was attempting to help her, but that was not the case. In fact he refused to answer questions she put to him. He did this by professing that she had no reason to dispute the Bible verses she found confusing. He and the other ministers purported not to understand her questions about the difference between the meanings of the words, "soul" and "spirit" as used in some places in the Bible, and why some places asserted that the spirit would die. He glossed over her very reasonable questions of doctrine, although as the Greek and Hebrew scholar that he was, he knew the answers. This left her looking as if she were being unreasonable in her questioning and stubborn in her refusal to accept statements of the ministers that did not address her questions. Even when another minister, probably Mr. Davenport, who was staying with Cotton at the time did give some explanation to Hutchinson, neither Davenport nor Cotton explained the significance of her questions to her. They did not explain that there are two words in Greek, *psyche* and *pneuma*, and two in Hebrew, *nephesh*, and *ruach*, which in both cases are translated as soul and spirit respectively. Nor did they tell her that these words have different meanings in the original languages, with the English word, "soul" translating what is often referred to as the "immortal soul," and "spirit" translating what was intended to mean, breath, or animating life force. They also neglected to tell her that because there are the two very different words in the original languages of the Bible, these separate meanings of the words are therefore reflected in the English translations.

Her questions were not just hair-splitting: she had recognized something of substance in her reading of the verses in question. She had read her Bible carefully, and consequently had found passages that reflected Epicurean philosophy, and the differing meanings of the words, and wanted to know why the Bible said in one place that a spirit will die, and in another that a soul will live. Cotton knew why, yet at the church trial he did not tell her, and even chided her for asking frivolous questions. His strong assertion at her ecclesiastical trial that there was no reason for her to question the passages has led those who have studied the trials to assume that his assertion was true, when in fact his actions constituted a clear betrayal of Anne Hutchinson.

Cotton, the most highly respected theologian in the colony, did not use his knowledge or his prestige to aid her. At the last, Cotton capped his antagonistic performance at her church trial by telling her she was corrupt and that her ideas would lead to such societal evils such as men's sexual sharing of women. He left her to be found guilty and to be banished and excommunicated. We do not know what arguments were made to John Cotton during the time between the civil trial, where Cotton did provide what little defense she had, if in lukewarm fashion, and the church trial some six months later. But whatever they were, by the time of the church trial he had been persuaded to abandon her completely, and to come out aggressively against her. Furthermore, after the trials Cotton completely reversed his theological position—the position that he had held for more than twenty years, and which had brought him to the high regard in which he was held in both old and New England. There seems to be no other explanation except that he felt it prudent to allow himself to be persuaded by the other ministers, to completely overturn his understanding of the juxtaposition of sanctification and justification. In doing so he was also persuaded to abandon Anne Hutchinson altogether.

With these comparisons of the two trials in mind, it becomes obvious that Cotton bears heavy blame for the outcome of Hutchinson's trials. It would appear that he acted in the way he did because of the threat that he faced, as her pastor, of being banished along with her. His fears of being linked too closely with her ideas were exacerbated by the fact that just a few short years before, Roger Williams had also expected Cotton to agree with him, just as Hutchinson was expecting him to do. Cotton's theology was becoming much too closely linked to that of seditious and heretical individuals for Cotton's political health. In addition, Williams had had correspondence with Cotton since having left the colony. Although Williams had left Massachusetts in 1636, his continuing castigations of Cotton were infuriating to Cotton, and caused Cotton to engage in polemics against Williams for years, with his son carrying on after him. This further strain on Mr. Cotton does not seem to have been taken into account by any study of the Hutchinson chronicle, even where there has been mild criticism of Cotton's behavior at the trials.

The questions Hutchinson raised at her church trial concerning the words, "soul" and "spirit" have been ignored or glossed over by those who have studied the trials. These questions have been mistakenly assumed by scholars to be "this nice theological distinction," not to be taken seriously.[3] Only one scholar has dealt with questions she raised about these words at her church trial. J. F. Maclear has expressed the belief, which he admitted was "conjectural" that these questions reflected the "mortalist heresy" found somewhat later in New England.[4] The mortalist doctrine was that the soul dies upon the death of the individual, and according to some, is resurrected later, or in other versions of the belief, remains dead. Maclear is evidently the first scholar who has recognized the import of the questions and their centrality to the church trial, although his conclusions about their significance are incorrect. He does note, however, that she reiterated that she was merely questioning the meaning of the words and their different usage in the Bible, and denied that she held any heretical beliefs, and few others have recognized the significance of her claims.

One argument made to explain the guilty verdicts against her has been that the fact that she was found guilty in such circumstances perhaps says little about the Puritans anyway: a society that would hold such trials in the first place should naturally be expected to find anyone guilty for arbitrary reasons. This is to assume, however, that the Puritans who found Anne Hutchinson guilty had no concern with following proper procedure or keeping to the rules of evidence, but that they were willing to hold trials that were nothing more than a sham in order to rid themselves of dissension in the community. The Puritans would not agree, however, nor should they. For, while the legal procedures in Massachusetts were not codified, the leaders of the Massachusetts Bay Colony knew very well that they had to meet certain minimal standards of proof in order to find a defendant guilty.

further, they realized that they had to be careful to observe their own accepted legal procedures in order to do so. New Englanders followed a combination of English common law and new laws that they felt it proper to pass as a result of their circumstances in the new country, and they took their judicial procedures seriously. Proper procedure in trials was of great consequence to them, as they believed God demanded it. So, the stance that Anne Hutchinson was found guilty only because her prosecutors were negligent about the rules of evidence also will not stand.

Yet another explanation for the outcome of the trials has been articulated by some scholars. They have held that since her influence in the community had grown so strong, Winthrop, Cotton, and all the others were justified in doing whatever was necessary to save the cohesiveness of the community. Samuel Eliot Morison states that position most strongly when he says,

> Morally and socially, the Hutchinsonian leaders were of the best in New England—and their triumph would have led to no antinomian orgies, as their subsequent conduct in Rhode Island proved. But their success would have divided New England into a multitude of little jangling sects... What good would the triumph of Anne Hutchinson have brought to New England? Not toleration, which found no place in her system of theology; light perhaps, of a lunar sort; but no love or beauty, or civility.[5]

This attitude is one that may seem tempting, especially if one holds that the community must take precedence over any individual. But it must be rejected as a defensible posture for the New England leaders to have taken toward Hutchinson. Winthrop and Cotton in particular were themselves very sensitive to the charge that later was raised against them that they acted illegally in hounding her "for conscience sake," rather than for actions she had committed. They knew what scholars have glossed over: that the cohesiveness of the colony could not have been bought at the expense of righteousness on their part. To do so would have been to lose the whole purpose for which the colony had been founded. The leaders would no longer have had real authority to rule, as their authority required God's blessing as well as that of England, and of their freemen as well. Without any of these, it would have been impossible to rule a cohesive Christian commonwealth.

The issue of the Anne Hutchinson and her threat to the colony became one of power: the power that the leaders of the colony felt slipping away from them as they worried about the possible break-up of the community, and in addition, the ministerial power that John Cotton wanted to keep. The question of what should be done about dissenters such as Anne Hutchinson had become an issue of power for Cotton. For if the cohesion of the community was threatened, Cotton was personally threatened. Cotton was threatened by attempts by Thomas Shepard and probably Thomas Hooker, ministers who had reason to be jealous of Cotton's preeminence in the colony's ministry, to pose serious questions about the direction of his theology. Further, Roger Williams' articulation of the logical direction of Cotton's theory of correct church organization threatened Cotton, which made Hutchinson's claim that all her theology had come from Cotton all the more damaging to him.

The fledgling colony at the time of the Antinomian Crisis believed itself militarily threatened by the Pequot Indians, economically threatened by the facts of its new environment: harsh winters, rocky soil, new crops to learn to raise, the continued pressure of a too early exhaustion of initial provisioning, new trades to learn. It was threatened politically by the possibility that the homeland which had issued their charter might send a governor repugnant to them or void the charter altogether. In addition, there were stresses on the little colony both social and political as the colonists attempted to define their social organization and concomitant political structure, as well as to define the bounds of acceptable social deviance.

Most telling of all, perhaps, the doctrinal organization of the churches, the most dominant social structure of the colony, was being defined. This meant that the theological issues that served to hold together the community had to be carefully defined, and defined in such a way as to maximize the integration of the theological dogmas and social structure. The ideas of church organization that the leaders of the colony had brought with them from England were under siege from separatists in other colonies, and from Roger Williams with his own well articulated separatist message, and then from Anne Hutchinson, with her forceful questioning of doctrine and individual liberty to express irregular opinions.

For all these reasons the leaders of the colony were or felt themselves to be seriously threatened by Anne Hutchinson's outspokenness, believing that the future of the colony was at stake, and took the strongest steps they could, save only the death penalty, to quiet her. They made clear to her pastor and mentor, John Cotton, that he could not defend her without coming under suspicion himself, and so he turned against her, even to the point of dishonesty in his dealings with her at her church trial. The battle that came to be called the Antinomian Crisis was fought with theological weapons but it was not entirely a theological battle. The field was poorly chosen, surrounded by thickets of hostile Indians and enclosed by an ocean that could bring political damage, but could not be used to usher away dissidents. The mighty warrior, Cotton, was assailed by daunting foes like

Shepard and Hooker, whose words were as revered as Cotton's, and bloodied by Roger Williams, who demonstrated the ultimate ends of his logic. The ground was uneven, as Hutchinson was articulate; and her thrusts and parries of the questions were masterful. So, like many other fighters before him, Cotton gave ground where necessary, finally joined the enemy camp, and sacrificed his protege in order to save his position and his power.

The doctrines that were to become a Puritanism truly forged in and belonging to New England, and the legal circumstances surrounding the trials, will set the stage for an in-depth look at the problems addressed in Hutchinson's trials. It will become clear that the events that led to and formed the trials of Anne Hutchinson fashioned the change that was to become New England Puritanism. It is undeniable that Anne Hutchinson forced the good fathers of Boston to take a stand on what doctrine would be the future of New England and what would not. Without a challenge such as she posed, change might have come more slowly, as John Cotton could have continued to preach an older, even *passé,* Calvinism, and Hooker and Shepard would perhaps have accepted more shades and stripes of opinion within their domains: perhaps.

Notes

1. The title refers to the beliefs that Hutchinson and her followers were reputed to have held: that they did not have to worry about obedience to the law. In fact at a later date one of her erstwhile followers did make such a claim. The word, "antinomian" comes from the Greek words, *anti* and *nomos,* meaning "opposed to the law."

2. J. F. Maclear, "Anne Hutchinson and The Mortalist Heresy," *New England Quarterly*, vol. 54, 1981, pp. 74–103.

3. Philip Gura, *A Glimpse of Sion's Glory: Puritan Radicalism in New England, 1620–1660*, (Middletown CT: Wesleyan University Press, 1984), p. 91.

4. Maclear, p. 76.

5. Samuel Eliot Morison, *The Founding of Harvard College*, (Cambridge, MA: Harvard University Press, 1935), pp. 175, 179.

Chapter Two

Curse and Damnation: Puritan Theology

To find the roots of the story of Anne Hutchinson's trials, it is necessary to examine the reformation of the Anglican Church in the sixteenth century. The movement that came to be called "Puritanism" is at the heart of the tale, and her trials were also a test of New England Puritanism. The test for her community was to define how much individual freedom could be allowed within a congregation—or a society. It was a question of the necessary freedom of the individual and her involvement in her salvation, versus the community and its need for conformity in order to survive. The question was resolved in theological terms as a result of Hutchinson's trials. The decision of an individual—especially, but not only, an untrained individual—to determine correct interpretation of doctrine for herself came to threaten the stability of the New England Puritanism, and the society of which it was such an integral part.

The Puritans, who felt that the Anglican Church must be further "purified," were inheritors of the Reformation. They agreed with the Genevan reformer, John Calvin, and indeed held him in the highest esteem. Their theological preferences were Augustinian, rather than Thomist, and were in contrast to the Roman Catholic and Anglican portion of the Church.[1] They interpreted humankind as totally fallen from grace after Eve and Adam's sin. They did not believe that there was the possibility of human initiative toward redemption. God, being perfectly good, could not tolerate any imperfection or disobedience, therefore as humankind had sinned in the persons of its mother and father of all, every person was completely unable to reconcile with God. Thus, there was then no chance to return to the desired, prelapsarian state; there was no possibility of persons even making an effort toward reconciliation with God, as no fumbling, deficient effort on the part of such imperfect beings could be acceptable to the perfection demanded by God. No matter how much one might desire such restoration, no human effort, no good works, no change of heart, nothing could effect one's own salvation. Indeed, one did not have free will, as the will, along with the mind and heart, was corrupted. Anglicans and Roman Catholics, differing equally in their understanding of human nature and the nature of God's plan of salvation, saw humanity as having a free will which could contribute to the process of regeneration and reconciliation. The sinner could choose to trust in God's grace and magnanimity, thus participating in the salvation process. Puritans felt that it was precisely this belief in the possibility of effort on the sinner's part that had led to abuses within the church. They were concerned both with perceived abuses of the theology and practices which grew out of a logical extension of the theology, to which imperfect human beings had taken it. These abuses were what had necessitated the earlier beginnings of the Reformation, and which called for a continued, thorough reform of the church. For, while the English Church had been reformed during the marital merry-go-round of Henry VIII, under his daughter, Elizabeth, it had finally not gone far enough in the proper direction, to the thinking of the Puritans. It had retained some of the "trappings" of the Roman Church, and it had not traveled far enough along the road to a completely pure doctrine.

For the Puritans, who took their Calvin seriously, no one could contribute in the least toward reconciliation with God. As Calvin had put it in his *Institutes of the Christian Religion*, "Nay, rather, however we may have been redeemed by Christ, until we are engrafted into his fellowship by the calling of the Father, we are both heirs of darkness and death and enemies of God."[2] And in another place, "We see therefore, that all our salvation comes from God: he begins, he continues it, he brings it to perfection: a man may ascribe nothing to himself herein, no not so much as one drop."[3] This belief became in many instances a major source of anguish for the Puritans. The matter of salvation was an individual decision, but an individual decision that had been made by God before the foundation of the world; He had provided for the salvation of some individuals. He had sent His Son, Jesus Christ, to die on the cross and be resurrected as a substitutionary sacrifice for the sins of humanity. Further, God in His infinite wisdom and chosen before all time to redeem some fortunate few, meaning that He had not merely known in advance who would accept the message of the Gospel of Christ, but that He had chosen, elected, some to salvation, and allowed others to receive the damnation that all deserved. In his articles discussing predestination Calvin wrote, "as he [God] adopted some for himself for salvation, he destined other for eternal ruin."[4] Nor was this choice made by God merely a function of His having known ahead of time

who would be of a mind to have faith in Christ. Calvin stated unequivocally in his commentary on the Epistle of St. Paul to the Romans: "The fore-
knowledge of God here mentioned by Paul is not mere prescience, as some
inexperienced people foolishly imagine, but adoption, by which He has
always distinguished His children from the reprobate."[5]

The Puritans were entirely comfortable with this Calvinistic doctrine
of predestination: that those chosen for redemption were chosen at random,
based on no logical or rational system—and were not chosen based upon
any goodness, inherent or executed, of their own. They concluded that
humankind, having no innate goodness, had no reason to expect any compas-
sion or forgiveness form God. Therefore it seemed entirely reasonable to
them that God should make a decision to save or to damn some poor sinner
based only upon His inscrutable wishes and upon no discernible reasoning
whatsoever. Because there was no goodness involved, God was extending
His mercy and grace to a few undeserving sinners; those who were not
chosen for grace therefore had no cause to complain, as they were only
receiving that damnation which was their just reward for their sins. This
was the Puritan doctrine of predestination, and no one was to hold it more
stringently and logically than were seventeenth-century Puritans. One case
in which they differed from Calvin had to do with what is called, "double
predestination" or "reprobation." That was the view expressed by Calvin
that God had also decided before all time who would be damned. Logically
of course it follows that if God decided some should be saved, the rest,
whether specifically cited or not, had been damned by God. However,
Puritans did not agree that this was the way to understand predestination.
John Cotton, writing in defense of his method of organizing the churches,
and also of his treatment of Anne Hutchinson, refers to his having defended
the doctrine of predestination "from such harsh consequences as seemeth to
be derived from thence" from his first years at old Boston. He says, "I
then began publicly to preach, and in private meetings to defend the doctrine of God's eternal election before all foresight of good or evil in the
creature: and the redemption (*ex gratia*) only of the elect: the effectual
vocation of a sinner *per irresistibilem gratiae vim*, without all respect of
the preparations of free will: and finally, the impossibility of the fall of a
sincere believer either totally or finally from the estate of grace."[6] God
had thus predestined the elect, but not the damned.

It is also interesting to note, that although Puritans have come to be
seen as those who held the doctrine in all its terrible, unquestionable, logic,
the doctrine of predestination was not new at the time of the Puritans, but
had in fact grown out of orthodox theology of the established Church of
England. The Edwardian Articles of Faith of 1552 and 1562 included this

statement: "Predestination unto life, is the everlasting purpose of God whereby (before the foundations of the world were laid) he hath constantly decreed by his counsel, secret unto us, to deliver from curse and damnation those whom he hath chosen in Christ out of mankind, and to bring them by Christ to everlasting salvation."[7]

John Calvin's logic as understood by Anne Hutchinson is important because her thinking has always been considered extremely antinomian. That is, it was claimed at the time, and has been accepted ever since, that she held that those who have assurance that they are among the elect need obey no laws, and have complete freedom to act as they please. Those who have been given assurance by God that they are of the elect, according to this view, need worry no more about their everlasting condition, and can make their own decisions about which laws to keep. This thinking is drawn out of St. Paul, where he speaks of freedom of the Christian person. The extreme idea grew out of the letters of St. Paul to the Galatians and the Romans, where he discussed the idea that those who are among the elect, or Christians, need no longer walk under the threat of the law, because they are now under the Gospel of Christ, and therefore not subject to the law. Martin Luther and other great reformers wrote at length of the wonderful freedom that the Christian could experience, no longer trying unsuccessfully to live a life in perfect obedience to the law. This was of course liberating to those who had felt themselves constrained by their inability to keep all aspects of the law.

However, Luther, Calvin, and all other theologians cautioned that the true Christian would out of love and the exhilaration of the gratitude owing to Christ strive to live in as perfect obedience to the law as possible, always increasing in goodness. Those who were antinomian, however, were said to feel no concern for this righteous behavior, because, having been justified before God they now had no need to pay heed to the law at all. Since they had been chosen before all time for salvation, the reasoning went, they could now flaunt the law and live as they pleased. Those who believed that they have such freedom certainly would not decide to obey a law out of a belief that doing so would in any way effect, or for that matter, affect, their salvation.

Ultimately of course the threat antinomianism held for the community was that the person so assured of salvation would obey no laws, even those intended merely to regulate society, and therefore society could no longer exist. Anne Hutchinson was accused of holding such extreme notions of the doctrine of predestination, and the pejorative term antinomian is still used to describe her and her followers, although she and her followers claimed the term did not fairly characterize their thinking. Her brother-in-law,

John Wheelwright, was one of the two ministers whose preaching she felt was orthodox. He wrote a spirited defense of himself in later years, because, although he had, by that time, been certified by his church as being wholly orthodox, he still felt the sting of having been charged with such a serious heretical position.[8] Yet even those scholars who agree that Anne Hutchinson held the same doctrinal views as her minister, John Cotton, who was able to convince the ministers of his orthodoxy, assume that both of them held positions that were at the extreme end of the theological spectrum of the day, and that the other ministers of the Bay Colony were the mainstream of Puritan thought. However, what became the orthodoxy of Puritan thought in Massachusetts was not simply an extension of what had been orthodoxy in England. The doctrine that came to be the orthodox one in New England actually was shaped during the antinomian crisis, and the annealing fire that hardened it burnt most brightly during the arguments that carried the day in Hutchinson's trials.

The Anglican Church had much earlier been able to come to terms with the doctrine of predestination by softening and blurring its effects, but this unyielding Calvinistic doctrine was to prove more and more of a problem to New England Puritans, even as theologians wrestled with it. In his well-known essay, "The Marrow of Puritan Divinity," Perry Miller reminds the reader of what has been demonstrated through John Cotton's writings: that "the New England leaders did not stem directly from Calvin; they learned the Calvinist theology only after it had been improved, embellished, and in many respects transformed by a host of hard-thinking expounders and critics."[9] In New England a difference in interpretation of Calvin's theory of predestination led to Anne Hutchinson's trials and mistrust by the rest of the clergy of Massachusetts Bay of her pastor, the learned John Cotton. Yet, it was the ministers of New England who were the innovators.

Thomas Hooker, Thomas Shepard, and the other ministers in New England were the thinkers who were plowing new ground. They took the position that sanctification, or righteous conduct, rather than "confidence in God by the work of his Spirit," was the hallmark of the person who was among the elect. The perfectly godly life that could only be lived by the truly regenerated was designated, "sanctification," as it too was a gift from God to the chosen few. For while nothing could be done by any individual to ensure or effect any part of her salvation, Calvinist Puritans did believe that God used human understanding as a vehicle to aid in His conversion of the individual. Conversion was necessary to complete the earthly part of the process, and took place as the person came to realize with fear and trembling that she was a lowly sinner, and that only God's grace could save her. She would proceed through several steps, and, for those fortunate few, would finally come to a realization that she was among the elect, or justified. She could do nothing to affect her spiritual estate, and one must be careful here to separate works however passive done by the individual from proper appreciation for God's plan.

The distinction is crucial. Conversion, while passive on the part of the individual in the sense that she could do nothing to secure it but could only receive it, was however worked by God through the rational part of the receiving individual. The difference of opinion that caused the trouble in Massachusetts dealt with the doctrines of sanctification versus justification. Puritans insisted that each person should hope to have received justification before God, and should seek salvation, praying that God would have bestowed it upon her. Calvin had been adamant that nothing one could do could in any way change what had been planned from before one's existence. He said that only those who had been regenerated, "with our hearts formed to obedience to the law" could truly perform good works.[10] In another place he went so far as to state that, "attention to one's own righteousness nullifies the promises."[11] But Calvin too realized that even the person who had only begun to recognize God's goodness would be eager to live a life of goodness in so far as was possible. One strong evidence of justification was the righteous behavior that resulted from regeneration: sanctification. After one had begun the process and had become aware of one's thorough imperfection, and of God's terrible perfection, one would naturally desire to live a life pleasing to this awesomely good Creator: even before justification. Yet it was necessary to remember that the life of good works could really only be led by the ones whom God had elected. As Calvin put it, even those who appeared to be living holy, regenerated lives might not in reality be Christians, because they had not received the gift of faith. He said that, even though some people might appear to be "admirable," still, "by the pollution of their hearts they defile God's good works."[12]

William Ames was considered to be one of the seminal theologians of English Puritanism, and was a fellow at Christ's College Cambridge for a short time. He was forced to move to Holland in 1610, where he became one of the leaders in the Puritan movement, fighting against Arminianism, or the idea that human endeavor enters into the conversion process. Ames was often cited by the Puritans, and his arguments with Arminians shaped Puritan theology for the New England group before they came to New England. A friend of John Winthrop, he wrote him that he hoped to come to New England, but he died in 1633.[13] Although Ames was a friend of Thomas Hooker, his theology with relation to predestination and human endeavor was strictly Calvinistic. He explained justification in terms that might have dripped from the pen of Calvin. "Justification is the gracious judgement of God by which he absolves the believer from sin and death, and reckons him righteous and worthy of life for the sake of Christ apprehended in faith. Romans 3:22, 24." And of the idea that justification, or conversion happens in stages he wrote, "The change, of course, has no degrees and is completed at one moment and in only one act. Yet in manifestation, consciousness and effects, it has many degrees; therein lie justification and adoption."[14] Either John Calvin or John Cotton, or of course Anne Hutchinson would have agreed most heartily with Ames' sentiments concerning justification. Hooker and the other ministers of the Bay Colony were the ones who changed their theology to fit their circumstances. Sanctification, according to Ames, was the change that occurred in the person after grace had been given to the believer. It was the gradual change in the person's behavior that took place after—and only after—conversion.[15]

Aware of the need to keep justification and sanctification completely separate, John Cotton preached what he read in Calvin: that one must be careful not to interpret sanctification as clear evidence of justification, but only as one testimony pointing toward justification. Anne Hutchinson was pleased with Cotton's preaching when she lived in England, because she agreed with the clear-cut differentiation between sanctification and justification. The doctrines that dealt with God's gift of salvation and the condition of human beings before the fall were designated a "Covenant of Grace" and a "Covenant of Works." The Covenant of Works was a description of the pact God had originally made with Adam, that if he did not disobey God's commands, he would be allowed to live eternally. The "Covenant of Grace" however came into being after Christ's resurrection, and referred to the new covenant God had made with humankind, that by virtue of Christ's substitutionary atonement, some would be saved, according to His plan.

Another problem of the predestination doctrine with which Puritans had to deal was the question of how to discern who was among the elect. Those who had been adopted as sons of God, as St. Paul styled it, or given the gift of faith, needed a sure method to decide whether or not they had been selected by God for salvation. Calvin and the rest of the clergy taught that the person who had been granted justification could know in their hearts that they were among the elect. However, they recognized that this method was not without its dilemmas. How could the person who felt in her heart she was a child of God be certain? And what, indeed, would certainty mean? Calvin answered the question by stating that the person

possessed of faith would be sure, with "a full and fixed certainty," but even
if she had doubts, somehow she would know before her end came, and
certainty would triumph.[16]   That uncertainty was of great importance,
because Satan would continuously try to "sap it by covert devices."[17] It
should be remembered here that Puritan theologians, with their chiefly
scholastic education, thought of God the Father in intrinsically medieval
terms.   So, although the center of the salvation question was the new
covenant sealed by Christ's sacrifice, the person of the trinity responsible
for the decision about election was the Father. Included in this emphasis on
the doings of the Father were medieval notions of how God the Father
would behave, which colored their understanding of the problems of
salvation.   God was understood by the highly educated clergy to be "an
eternal, independent essence, or being, or spirit..."[18]   But because of the
emphasis upon the uncertainty of election, he was presented to the flock as
a sort of crafty loan officer, constantly reminding his clientele that he
could not only call their loans at any time but that he would be capricious
in doing so.   There was just enough rationality in this God's purported
thinking patterns to be consistent with human fathers' logic, yet enough
unpredictability to remind people that He is inscrutable, as in this example
of God's rather impenetrable behavior, from a sermon of Urian Oakes,
published in 1673.

> But we must say, *cum toto theologorum Chrono* (as Judicious *Ames*
> speaks) that God in such forms of speech, that he may commodiously treat
> with man, both *induere se homine*, put on Man (as it were) or vest himself
> in the condition and properties of man, and propose his counsels to us in
> such a way wherein we may best apprehend them, and they may be most
> familiarized to us... The great God in this *querimonicus* form of speaking
> resembles himself to a Father.[19]

That being entirely clear, the faithful souls in the pews were more
likely to think of God as a stern, incomprehensible father than as a benefi-
cent creator-being. The most telling instance of God's vagariousness was
the notion of his having foreordained, for no logical reasons, the salvation
of some and the damnation of others.

The fact that salvation was desired by all, and the necessity of it was
preached to all, but had been in some previous time allotted only to a few,
would in itself not have been as unnerving to those who were among the
elect if there had been a clear method of determining who was among the
elect. But as there was not a person could not truly know that she or he
had been allocated salvation. There were signs of regeneration, but none of
them sure or completely trustworthy.   A person's righteous behavior,
sorrow for sin, and desire for God and his word, were the signals that

Calvin and later Puritans understood as signs that the erstwhile sinner had been regenerated and given God's aid in living an ever more perfect life, but those behaviors could not be depended upon as evidence of salvation. Calvin had taught that, "he who thinks he has his own righteousness misunderstands the severity of the law..."[20] Indeed, one had to be careful not to be misled into false assurance by the devil, who worked diligently to try to implant false assurance. Some theologians went so far as to insist that the very assurance of election proved that the one so assured was being deceived. Anxious parishioners could never be completely certain that they were among the elect (or not).

Many of the Puritan clergy who were eventually to settle in the Massachusetts Bay Colony had studied under such men as William Ames and William Perkins, and had been taught that the process leading to salvation involved several distinct steps. It was this process, originally intended only to spell out the steps performed entirely by God upon the believer, that came to be seen by new England divines as a preparation for salvation: some parts of which could be performed by the seeker after salvation. Indeed, all who heard Puritan sermons were exhorted to undertake the first steps of the process, in hope (but with no assurance) that God would perform the transformation in the seeker, making her over into a believer, one of the elect.

In contrast to Cotton, who preached the terrible logic of Calvin, Thomas Hooker, Thomas Shepard, Peter Bulkeley, and many other of the ministers who came to the Bay Colony had begun to increase emphasis upon the preparation process. They began to expect those who were to receive God's grace to go through a rigorous conversion process that was psychologically exhausting—although they kept always in mind that having gone through the process did not guarantee salvation. They began to include in their understanding of the "morphology of conversion," as Edmund. S. Morgan christened it, steps of preparation for (at least the possibility of) conversion. The steps in the conversion process vary according to the compiler, and the differences are not theologically insignificant, but they follow a similar pattern in which the basics were always the same.[21] Morgan cites the writings of John Winthrop as including: "knowledge, conviction, faith, combat, and true, imperfect assurance."[22]

The issue of preparation was the one on which Thomas Hooker and Thomas Shepard, leading preparationist of the Bay Colony, and the other men who agreed with him, were to find themselves in major disagreement with John Cotton's theology, and with his pupil, Anne Hutchinson. Preparation became the issue which distanced those theologians in New England from the thinking of Calvin, and which incorporated the tension in their doctrine between the individual and the community. That tension was to play itself out in the trials of Anne Hutchinson and was to demonstrate its inherent centrifugal force. The centrality of the individual was an energy within the Calvinist doctrine of predestination that constantly exerted pressure against the communitarian cohesion necessary for the nurturance of the congregation. Because the force of predestination was so strong within the tenets of the theology, it would always render unstable the countervailing force for communitarian cohesion. This tension was containable in England, where the necessary emphasis was upon individual strength against the institutional church. Once in New England however the need changed radically. The new community was no longer subject to the Church of England, and was free to define itself. Thus, the need was no longer for staunch individualists; indeed such types worked against the need for cohesion within the new community. New circumstances rendered the dynamic unstable, as the old world thinking pressed its case against the new. Anne Hutchinson's trials were the test case for that unstable dynamic and thus were pivotal in pinpointing the crux of the problem at which Puritan New England was to begin its spin into the recognition that the individual would always be the ultimate determiner of doctrine within the Puritan congregation.

The ministers who were to figure so prominently in Anne Hutchinson's trials, were proponents of the theology that stressed preparation for conversion. Finally this emphasis upon preparation pointed to the instability between the individual and the community which was to cause the disintegration (or evolution, depending upon one's viewpoint) of Puritan theology. John Cotton and Anne Hutchinson being conservative stressed predestination in Calvin's terms. It was Cotton's—and Hutchinson's—essential conservatism, and the radical change in doctrine by the rest of the New England clergy that were the fundamental doctrinal disagreements at issue in the Hutchinson trials. However, Cotton never understood that this was the crux of the case. He did not believe that he held a radically different conception of the conversion process from his clergymen friends, and was perfectly content to allow them to differ from him—as long as he was allowed to continue to preach a strictly Calvinistic Covenant of Grace. He only changes his thinking on the subject when forced to do so by the recognition that he, like Hutchinson, would be cast out of the church if he did completely reverse his thinking and his preaching.

As it came to be preached by Hooker, Shepard, and the rest of the clergy in and around Boston, the first step in the process of conversion was the very necessary one of making the person realize that she stood in a precarious position *vis-à-vis* God. That is, the person must be brought to the realization that her situation was bleak and that God's help was needed. Perkins referred to this step as one which would "break and subdue the stubbornness of our nature."[23]   Given humankind's sinful nature, this was the critical first step. All of the Puritan clergy were as zealous as Calvin had been to stress that humankind was utterly evil and in desperate need of God's regeneration as the only way to achieve salvation. The first and foremost reason for preaching to the congregation was to demonstrate to them their vulnerability, their utter depravity, and their urgent need of God.

Once the hearer understood her own situation, God showed the sinner the rightness of the law so that she or he would have an understanding of good and evil and the logic thereof. Learning about good and evil in general would lead to an awareness of personal sin, which of course led to "conviction" of sin or "humiliation." These preparatory steps were practically, if not theoretically, needed. While, in theory, texts from the Bible indicated that God had foreordained who would receive grace, and that grace simply happened to the person, in practice, it became obvious (admittedly, to some more than to others) that the sinner must be in a proper frame of mind and understanding to receive grace. All of the Puritans agreed with these steps to bringing the hearer of sermons into a proper frame of mind. Indeed John Cotton had no quarrel with these beginning steps; he agreed that all must be brought to an understanding of their need for salvation. The next step in the process was the critical juncture.

At this level in the conversion process a person would have completed the initial phase and might well be forever stopped at this point. If God had not decided to extend grace to the sinner, then nothing more would happen, and the person would forever be stalled at this stage, feeling the need of grace, but not receiving it. If however the person was to complete the conversion process, more steps were involved. The sinner would now be ready to move to "a serious consideration of the promise of salvation, propounded and published in the Gospel." Then came the following step, the beginning of faith, "a will and a desire to believe."[24]

When this stage was reached the real problems began for the neophyte believer; perhaps Satan felt that this was the point at which he was likely to suffer real losses to his kingdom. In any case, this was the juncture at which worries and concerns would assail the soul, causing anguish to the believer. For the rest of her life wrestling with doubts would never cease, as Satan would try to delude the believer into not only incredulity, but also into false assurance. For, if one had indeed been chosen to be one of the elect, a sense of assurance and "persuasion of merry" was to follow.   One must always remain on the alert, however, because, as Morgan put it, "in order to be sure one must be unsure."25   "Even after he reached the stage of assurance, the doubts would continue. If they ceased, that could be a sign that he had never had faith to begin with, but had merely deluded himself and had not really entered into the covenant of grace."26   The last two steps of the process consisted of "a grief for sin, because it is sin" (not to be confused with the apparently oft-felt grief for sin because it leads to punishment), followed by a "new obedience" or, sanctification, given by God to the believer. Furthermore, in John Cotton's writing, not only were all those good works ineffective in leading in any way to salvation, they did not even signify election. God performed all the action of granting grace to the sinner. So, even though one might be acting as a model Christian in every regard, nothing was proved by those actions. After all, if one could prove one's election by good works, anyone could claim election by manifesting those works. That situation would merely be the same "works-righteousness" in which Puritans understood "Papists" to be trusting. Such a situation would eliminate the need for God's determination of election. One English Puritan who wrote of the steps he followed in order to come to knowledge of his salvation was Jeremy Heyward. His steps are included in a volume of John Rogers, printed in 1653. Heyward's steps in the process include: recognition of sin; knowledge of the inability of the self to do anything; trying to "make out my own righteousness" for a year; listening ever more closely to the word of scripture; coming to the realization that "nothing but Christ would serve;" much prayer; the voice of the Lord telling him, "Lo! My grace is sufficient for thee;" happiness to be one of the elect; a changed life.27

While Calvin and others made the strong argument that nothing one could do would have the slightest efficacy in leading toward salvation, Shepard and Hooker and others felt that if one took all initiative away from humankind, people would be understandably less likely to crave righteousness. If God would give grace no matter how unprepared the heart, why strive toward Him? Why search the heart at all? Obviously, Hooker and many other ministers in the colony claimed, God did not intend for people to lead lives of wickedness and unconcern regarding the states of their souls. He expected them to do something, which was to behave properly, searching their souls and be contrite for their sins. Hooker entreated in a sermon, "I exhort you above all things not to defer the time and say, we will gather the flower while it is green...and on our death beds then will we repent."28   It was not appropriate for people to delay repentance, much less ignore it. The problem of the two understandings of preparation, Cotton's: that one could and should be in a receptive frame of mind and behavior, and Shepard and Hooker's: that preparation was necessary in order to receive grace is summed up best in Edward J Gallagher's introduction to a facsimile of John Norton's life of John Cotton. He says, "One of the crucial problems in early New England theology was balancing God's sovereignty and man's initiative in the conversion process. Preparatory activity was a barrier to 'enthusiastic' excess, but inordinate belief in the efficacy of preparatory activity was a dangerous degradation of God's sovereignty."[29]

Norman Petit discussed this process of preparation in his seminal work, *The Heart Prepared: Grace and Conversion in Puritan Spiritual Life*.[30] He reminded the reader that the fact of a rigorous process of conversion was even more "extraordinary" when one considers that Puritan theology grew out of "the strict dogmatics of Reformed theology." He was of course referring to the fact that the long, carefully laid-out process that was expected of those to whom Hooker, Bulkeley, and the others preached was radically different from the Calvinist theology they accepted as orthodox. Cotton, unlike the others, did stress the orthodox line, and provided the pull backward, toward the doctrine that had been most persuasive while in England. Perry Miller traced the change in understanding by Puritans of the conversion process from the strictly Calvinistic one to a reevaluation of the emphasis upon the covenant God had made with humankind. This reappraisal of the doctrine was done by sixteenth- and seventeenth-century English theologians who were wrestling with their understanding of the metaphor of a covenant offered by God to his people. These divines argued that anyone who offers a covenant—in this case, God—must explain to the offeree the terms of the covenant. What logically follows from that is the notion that having understood God's terms of offer, a person could then place herself in an attitude of "inclination to accept faith, should faith ever come."[31] This idea that one could do something preparatory to the "holy rape of the surprised will" of conversion so shockingly described by Calvin, opened the way for human effort to ready oneself for the hoped-for state of election by God.[32] Preparation, once having been conceived, thus became for Hooker and other Puritan theologians an integral and necessary part of the process of conversion. William Perkins, and William Preston, two of the leading theologians shaping Puritan thought in the seventeenth century, wrestled with the paradox involved in preparation for an event for which one cannot have any part. Preston stated that while a sick man may be healed without any realization of illness, "if he be not sick, and have a sense of it, he will not come to the Physician."[33]

It was an added step in the process that took the logic one step further which really changed the emphasis altogether, and which completely changed the thrust of the arguments. That step posited that righteous

behavior in and of itself was an indication of election. If it was not improp-
er for people to ready their hearts for the possibility of the bestowal of
grace, it might also be possible to decide from their behavior if they were
indeed the recipients of grace. A believer would naturally have unimpeach-
able behavior, since she or he must always be examining the heart to be as
sure as possible of salvation. (Such examination could hardly be done in
any but the most sinless frame of mind). Therefore, many ministers
believed with Hooker that one's behavior was a signal to oneself and the
state of one's regeneration, or lack of it.

For if one's righteous behavior could prepare one for salvation,
perhaps even in some sense lead one to be properly receptive to God's
election, then it was also the case that it could be seen as an aid to the
effecting of salvation, and lastly, could be taken as evidence of salvation.
When a decision had to be made as to which of those seeking membership
in a church should be accepted—only the elect could properly make up a
church—evidence of a godly life was taken into account, along with a
description from the petitioner of her or his reasonable assurance of
salvation, and the process followed in attaining such assurance. Clearly,
the most obvious way for one person to judge another was by behavior,
since assurance of conversion could only be judged by the individual
herself. For that reason, sanctification, or righteous behavior, came to be a
significant factor in for many of the New England clergy.

For Calvinists like Hutchinson or Cotton, such evidence was not to be
the prime requisite for church membership. They placed the emphasis
upon the conversion experience and the prospective church member's
recitation of it. It was the person's understanding of her conversion that
indicated that she stood in proper relationship to God, having been regenerated by God. Cotton was concerned that such willingness to judge according to proper behavior was the road to a "covenant of works." Because it
was God who gave grace to the sinner, no human could determine the state
of another's heart. More importantly, to trust in one's righteous behavior
as a sign that God had granted grace, or as a step in the conversion process,
was nothing more than putting one's own efforts forth as a means—however small—to salvation. That of course was to trust in that old covenant of
works. However, while Cotton was careful to preach the covenant of
grace, he did not fault the other ministers for their theology, apparently
being quite comfortable with their understanding of sanctification. He did
not claim that they were preaching or practicing "works righteousness."
The problem for any Puritan seeker after salvation was to tread carefully
between the two extremes of Arminianism: assuming that human effort

could effect salvation, and Antinomianism: believing that once among the elect a person could do no wrong, so no effort toward good behavior was needed. Cotton taught a Calvinism that came to be suspected of Antinomianism; the other ministers of the Bay Colony preached a message that came to be seen by Anne Hutchinson as Arminianism. John Cotton held Calvin in the highest regard, often reading his works and studying them. Hutchinson had listened to Cotton's sermons for many years in England before she followed him to Massachusetts Bay, and was in full accord with his steadfast and logical Calvinism, regarding any deviation therefrom as evidence of the dreaded, covenant of works. By the time of her migration to New England she was ready and willing to leave her home rather than accept a lesser product from some other nearby clergy. Clearly Cotton's teachings were a critical factor in her apprehension of the doctrines, and were to remain so.

In addition, there is another factor that influenced Hutchinson, and which may have served to bolster her staunch Calvinism. Cotton and Hutchinson both studied the Geneva translation of the Bible. Printed in a small quarto edition in 1560, the first printing of the whole Bible of a size small enough to be used in the home, the Geneva translation came to be called the Bible of the Puritans. This translation was the first to include notes and commentary upon the scriptures: and this commentary was strictly—even rabidly—Calvinistic. Its marginal notes were useful for Bible study, and contained cross–references, explanation, and comments. The explanations and comments no doubt influenced many lay readers, most of whom would have few or no other reference materials. As an example of Calvinistic commentary, a note upon Matthew 11: 26-27 sternly reminds the reader that, "Faith cometh not of man's will or power, but by the secret illumination of God."[34] As another example of the decisive, Calvinistic, character of the notes, two more are useful: "As the only will and purpose of God is the chief cause of election and reprobation, so his free mercy in Christ is an inferior cause of salvation and the hardening of the heart, an inferior cause of damnation."[35] (Romans chapter 9) The next is a gloss on Revelation 9:3: "Locusts [discussed in the text] are false teachers, heretics, and worldly subtle Prelates, with Monks, Freres, Cardinals, Patriarchs, Archbishops, Bishops, Doctors, Bachelors & Masters which forsake Christ to maintain false doctrine."

Cotton, although a renowned Greek scholar who translated the scriptures for himself, owned a Geneva Bible.[36] Hutchinson quoted from the Geneva Bible at her trials and was remarkably conversant with that translation. John Winthrop, on the other hand, brought over the first known copy of the King James Bible, which was a later translation undertaken by order of James I of England and completed in 1611. He had a copy of the 1614 edition.37 This translation did not contain notes and commentary, and did not give its readers the strongly Calvinistic slant that the Geneva gave. The King James version was later to overtake the Geneva Bible in popularity in America during the seventeenth century. The very plausible case has been made that this difference in choice of Bible translations between Cotton and Hutchinson and Winthrop is significant in understanding their doctrinal differences as well. That assertion has some validity, more especially in the case of Hutchinson, who had no theological training. She would have been influenced to a greater degree than someone trained in theology by the commentary notes in her Bible, as she would have had no other authority against which to test the notes. Amy Schrager Lang and Harry S. Stout have written that the Geneva translation used by Cotton and Hutchinson was highly influential in shaping their thinking, just as the newer King James version was used by Winthrop, rendering him less susceptible to the Calvinistic arguments of the Geneva translation.38

Stout underscores that as the Geneva translation was intended to aid the common person in understanding the scriptures, it explained difficult passages, and drew heavily on Calvin's own notes to do so.39 He notes however that by the time covenant theology came to the forefront of Puritan thinking the commentary in the Geneva translation represented Calvin's older and more rigid interpretations of predestination.40 His argument is that as Calvin had taught individual scrutiny of the state of one's soul was constantly required. For this purpose, the Geneva translation was aimed at turning the individual reader inward to delve for assurance of the salvation that God may have implanted within. The new King James version [KJV], on the other hand, as it was devoid of admonitions to the reader to look inward, allowed for more control by the clergy. Because social control by the clergy was precisely what the magistrates and clergy felt was needed in the new land, this version would have been much more appealing to them as they sought to mold the new community. He states:

> The new version of the Bible [KJV] coincided with a period of new beginnings for the Puritan clergy. Now that the people had been indoctrinated in the truths of Holy Writ, it was possible to begin moving to the second, and more ambitious phase of building an entire social order according to scriptural blueprint. Where the Geneva Bible and its marginalia served well the purpose of an embattled religious minority with thoughts fixed firmly on martyrdom and the world to come, it was less useful in fashioning binding principles of social organization and order in this world. It is not coincidental that the Puritan leaders' preference for the Authorized Version [KJV] grew in direct proportion to their growth in numbers and influence.41

Stout goes so far as to state that once Hutchinson and her followers had been removed from the colony, and "the issue of who spoke for God was settled finally irrevocably," it was possible for the leaders of the colony to interpret scripture to their own taste rather than that of Calvin, and the use of the King James version grew.[42]   Stout's argument is compelling, but must be viewed carefully, as Thomas Shepard, one of the primary antagonists of Hutchinson during her trials, and the man who was most suspicious of Cotton's theology, also used the Geneva translation.[43]   Far more to the point in studying the outcome of Hutchinson's trials, however, is the conjecture that Hutchinson was apparently so steeped in the commentaries and notes of the Geneva translation that she was probably influenced by them.[44]

Another factor in the reformation that deserves more emphasis and relates to the translation of the Bible into the vernacular was to have ramifications for New England Puritans, as well. This factor was the way in which the invention of movable type led to a demand for more sermons. The creation of movable type in the fourteenth century had allowed the printing of books including the Bible to be done much more easily, quickly, and cheaply. The relative inexpensiveness of purchasing Bibles stimulated a very natural desire on the part of the public who could not read Latin or Greek to have the Bible in their own language. With the pressure for translations of the Bible into the vernacular, the technological advance of printing changed the social context of the religious scene as well as the theological conditions. There was an enormous increase in the average person's theological capabilities, once the Bible was available to all who desired to have it.[45]   The church was then forced by the availability of printed Bibles to change its proscription against Bible reading for lay people and lay public began to take an increasing interest in things doctrinal.

With increased interest in reading the Bible came a need to have scriptural intricacies explained to the people. This was the thrust that had led to the addition of marginal notes to the Geneva translation. However, reading was not felt to be enough, especially when there were trained clergy available. For this reason the public began to hunger for sermons that explicated the scriptures they could now read, rather than the usual Anglican homilies that dealt primarily with issues of proper living. The desire for sermons led to changes within the Anglican churches. Some of them began to allow "prophesying" or lay preaching and questioning during services, although this was not encouraged in England. In addition, lecturers were paid for by congregations with Puritan leanings, so that they could have more sermons, and sermons that dealt with the subjects becoming of ever greater interest to them. Eventually, as the sermon took on more and more importance in the theology of the Puritans, those ministers who preached in the ways desired by the people came more and more to the forefront of the movement, with increasing moral power over the people. This was to prove significant in Massachusetts Bay.

Beyond the fact that the public loved to hear sermons that clarified and "opened" the scriptures for them, sermons became the primary vehicle for teaching the means of salvation. Calvin taught, and the Puritans continued to believe that it was through the hearing of the Word that the sinner learned of her sinful nature and of her great need for God's grace. As this was the first, and vital, step in coming to a realization of election, a step that all were expected to take, it was of central importance to the Puritan church service. Their importance in the service had as well grown out of change from the Reformation. When the local church had consisted of everyone within a geographic area, and a congregation could count as members everyone who lived nearby and therefore was able to attend it, the sermon—or homily—had functioned as a less important part of the mass. The primary vehicle of salvation was the sacraments, so that the homily was not crucial to the service. The Reformation had changed the character and necessity of the sermon: what had been little more than a perfunctory exhortation to live properly became a central part of the worship service—both in duration and importance.

In the Puritan church the sacraments were no longer considered the primary vehicle through which God's grace could reach the hearts and minds of the people; the sermon now took on that function. Puritans assumed that God worked regeneration in the unbeliever by means of the word as read or preached by the minister. While a person could read the Bible for herself, the function of the minister was to "open" the scripture. That is that the minister carefully organized logical arguments based on the topic chosen from scripture for the sermon. Petrus Ramus, sixteenth-century logician, had laid down the principles of organization for sermons, and his works were exhaustively studied by Puritans during their college years. Their sermons were structured very painstakingly according to Ramus' precepts—although of course each man utilized Ramus in his own style as well.

By the time of the seventeenth century the sermon had grown until it took up one or two hours at a time, on Sundays, with another dose on Thursdays. Preachers of Puritan sermons themselves believed wholeheartedly in the efficacy of the sermon: most of them could trace a significant turning point in their own conversion to a particularly powerful sermon, leading them to expect the same for their hearers. John Cotton, Thomas Shepard, and others cited the particular sermon that had led them to begin to examine the state of their souls, or had led them to feel assurance of their election. Other ministers had in turn come to a crucial stage in their understanding of salvation through Cotton and other of the better-known ministers' preaching. Their personal experience underscored and made them completely convinced of the effectiveness of preaching and the sermon. The sermon rather than Bible reading became for these clergy their method of offering God's grace to the listener. The ability to preach the sermon thus gave the minister unusual power in the community—both godly and secular. For, as conversion was necessarily the focal point of life, any minister who could contribute to the likelihood that others would correctly understand and become more receptive to election held a position of great influence over the others in the society.

The power of the sermon in the religious lives of the people also meant that the clergy had an enormous responsibility to shepherd their flock properly. If the sermon, properly preached, had within it such possibilities for furthering God's kingdom, the preparer and deliverer of the sermon had a tremendous responsibility to prepare and deliver those sermons well. Cotton was well known for his long hours of study for each of his sermons. Hooker and the others must have studied equally as much. A story is told of Hooker, being asked to give a sermon, stuttering, and finally halting. He stated that he had need of time to prepare himself, so the congregation waited for half an hour, at which point he delivered a wonderful sermon. Cotton Mather, who repeats the story in his life of Hooker found in the *Magnalia Christi Americana*, cites it as proof of the depth of Hooker's scholarship that he could then preach for hours under such conditions.[46]

Ministers were expected to take great pains with troubled souls under their care, "striving" with them to aid in their conversion. Although each individual was responsible for the state of her own soul, the clergy had the obligation to preach in such a way that each person would necessarily be convicted of sin and led to turn to God. This point should be kept in mind in reference to Anne Hutchinson's trials where she claimed that all her ideas had come from her minister, John Cotton. That is exactly where Puritans would have expected a church member's ideas to have come from, and Cotton himself was expected by them to have accepted far more responsibility for her beliefs than he did. He claimed later that he had not been aware that her beliefs differed from his own, yet he also claimed that he had questioned her closely and found no fault with her beliefs. As her pastor, he was naturally held by others to be responsible for her thinking, as indeed it seems he was.

There was another reason why sermons and influence over the popu-

lace were important to the ministers. This was that the preparation/sanctifi-
cation question was of importance to the Bay Colony for another reason
besides that of salvation: it drew together the notions of salvation and of a
Christian commonwealth. It was covenant theology that led the Puritans,
both ministers and leaders such as John Winthrop, to posit a necessary
correlation between the individual and the godly society. Covenant theology cited an agreement between God and a society, as well as the agreement He had with individuals. The nature of this covenant was that pure
behavior on the part of the society would lead to God's treating the community in a benign fashion. This made the behavior of each individual important to the welfare of the whole and led to scrutiny of each person's conduct, as it affected the group.

John Winthrop had exulted in the idea that the new society would be
able to form such a pure commonwealth that the people of Old England
would look to them as a "City on a Hill," which would be a shining example for all others. This was to be the case, even though most of the people
of the Bay Colony were clearly not among the elect. The covenant that they
believed governed the society posited that God would protect and sustain
them as long as they remained a godly society. Apparently trusting in the
same thinking as Abraham when he asked God to save Sodom and Gomor-
rah if some few righteous men could be found, they felt that a "saving
remnant" of believers would be able to save their group from ills and
travails on earth as well. Needless to say, the more of the elect who could
be found within a community, and the purer the behavior of everyone, the
better treatment they could expect from God. For this reason, days of
humiliation, fasting and prayer were called in response to any calamity or
perceived imperfections of orthodoxy in the Colony.

It was fervently believed by the clergy that sermons could and should
be used to exhort all listeners to ever more decorous behavior, not only for
their own good, but for that of the whole colony. The connection that the
federal covenant, as it was called, had to the sermon was just as close a one
as the connection between preaching and the creation of belief in the
believer. As such, all the magistrates had a vested interest in orthodoxy of
doctrine, sermons preached to the community, and the resultant behavior
of the recipients of the sermons. It is perhaps not surprising then that the
doctrines preached by Hooker, Shepard, and the others, which exhorted
their hearers to good behavior were much to be preferred by the leaders of
the community, who were responsible for the cohesiveness of the commonwealth. The leaders saw the need for, and so would naturally be drawn to,
dogmas that stressed good behavior, and would be frightened of those that
appeared to give license to the regenerated, rather than keeping them

closely in line. For these reasons, being pragmatic and logical in their thinking, the majority of the ministers in the Bay Colony stood firm on sanctification, and were quite suspicious of those who were not. Anne Hutchinson and her insistence on strict Calvinism came to be a threat not only to orthodoxy, but to the civil order. Everett Emerson, biographer of John Cotton, refers to the change in theological emphasis that was brought about because of the Hutchinson trials. He says, "The doctrines preached by Thomas Shepard became dominant: in place of a warm pietism, preachers increasingly emphasized rigid morality, and they made more of man's moral capacities...they emphasized that the conversion process required action from man." Interestingly, he goes on to note that this shift in emphasis led to fewer conversions than in the past, as the new emphasis upon morality led away from heartfelt convictions.[47]

Perry Miller also emphasized that it was the differences in preparation doctrine espoused by Hooker and Cotton and the influence of those doctrines upon social cohesion that lay at the bottom of the trials of Anne Hutchinson. Miller states flatly, "John Cotton generally figures as the chief 'theocrat' of Massachusetts and is popularly remembered as the dictator of its intellect, yet in fact he differed widely from his colleagues, and his dissent came near to causing his ruin. On this fundamental point Hooker's influence eclipsed Cotton's..."[48] Miller noted that Cotton "sweetened his mouth every night with a morsel of *The Institutes*," and quoted several of Cotton's works where Cotton stated unequivocally such things as that, "for our first union, there are no steps unto the Altar," and, "there is no promise of life made to those that wait and seek in their own strength, who being driven to it, have taken it up be their own *resolutions*."[49] Miller stated that, "Cotton was the better Calvinist, and he knew it: not only would he plead the authority of federalists like Pemble in rejecting preparation, he would also cry out, 'Let Calvin answer for me'."[50] Miller also pointed out the connection between Hooker's theology and his strong social control of his community: "We should not be surprised that Thomas Hooker, the virtual dictator of Connecticut and one of the most socially minded among the early ministers, should be also the greatest analyst of souls, the most exquisite diagnostician of the phases of regeneration, and above all the most explicit exponent of the doctrine of preparation. Thomas Shepard and Peter Bulkeley followed his lead.[51] Miller notes further that the difficulty was not only between Hooker and Cotton, it was between Cotton and all the rest of the ministers: all of the clergy of the Bay Colony had come to accept the doctrine of preparation, with its emphasis upon sanctification.

Paradoxically, there was another result of the increase in reading of scripture that caused increased emphasis upon individual thinking. When average men and women could interpret as well as read the Bible for themselves, rather than relying solely on their clergy to interpret it for them (especially if they were reading the Geneva translation) many came to believe ever more strongly that the rituals of the Anglican church must be "purified" according to the readers' understanding of the early Christian Church. This freedom for individual interpretation of the Bible led of course to great differences of opinion. There was no longer a dependence upon the church hierarchy to provide the correct explication of the Bible and the doctrine. Each reader could not only form her or his own opinion, but do so in accordance with whatever degree of hair–splitting she or he might have the time and the theologically subtle mind to do. All the exuberant speculation that resulted from the change from earlier passive absorption to analysis of sermons, reading and interpreting the Word also led to individual thinking and the exercise of the individual conscience. As individuals, lay and clerical, became more and more expert at exercising their own judgment concerning the explanation of the scriptures and the proper structure of the church, an ever increasing tension developed between the individual and the social group. In this way individual decision–making, in tension with social cohesion, provided some of the impetus toward emigration to the new world. For the state, sensing the threat posed by those who pressured for their own interpretation to be accepted as the correct one in the English church, refused to relinquish control of the church. It began to exert more and more pressure to conform, holding inquiries and harassing those it believed desired to "purify" the church. Finally, by the 1620s, emigration had become one of the ways in which Puritans of various stripes could avoid the many pressures to conform.

Later, however, after emigrating to the new world the pressures were reversed. The very pressure to conform to the thinking of the church which had driven them from England would then be used by the authorities to force all deviant thinkers in the new colony to conform to the behavioral demands of their society or be banished from the community. It should perhaps not be surprising that a lay person like Anne Hutchinson would be unwilling to comply with the expectations of the community for her correct behavior, given the history of Puritans' belief that they must not conform to the expectations of their home church. Hutchinson had come from a home where her father had been jailed and forced to curtail his preaching because of beliefs that were only mildly Puritan. Therefore, she, like most of those who left their homeland, had grown up with the idea that one must be willing to exercise individual judgment in religious matters. She, however, could never become a member of the ruling authorities, so she was never forced to weigh the needs of the community against those of the individual in the way that they were forced to do. The leaders of the colony were convinced of the need for social cohesion; Hutchinson on the other hand continued her belief in the preeminence of individual interpretation. Her trials pinpointed the weak spots in the assumptions of the leaders of the Bay Colony that they could direct the community through its doctrine.

Notes

1. For a fuller discussion of the roots of Puritanism, the reader is invited to consult the classic writing of Perry Miller, *The Puritan Mind: The Seventeenth Century* (New York: The MacMillan Company, 1939).

2. John Calvin, *Calvin: Institutes of the Christian Religion in Two Volumes*, ed. John T. McNeill, trans. Ford Lewis Battles, (Philadelphia: Westminster Press, 1950), p. 773.

3. John Calvin, *The Best of John Calvin*, ed.Samuel Dunn, (Grand Rapids, MI: Baker Book House, 1981), p. 164.

4. John Calvin, *Calvin: Theological Treatises*, The Library of Christian Classics, vol. XXII, trans. J.K.S. Reid (Philadelphia: Westminster Press, 1954), p. 179.

5. John Calvin, *The Epistles of Paul The Apostle to the Romans and to the Thessalonians*, ed. David W. Torrance and Thomas F. Torrance, trans. Ross Mackenzie, (Grand Rapids, MI: Wm. B. Eerdmans Publishing Company, 1960), p. 180. In this volume Calvin lays out his understanding of predestination, and distinguishes his thinking from that of others, who did not hold such an inflexibly logical understanding.

6. John Cotton, *John Cotton on the Churches of New England*, ed. Larzer Ziff (Cambridge, MA: The Belknap Press of Harvard University Press, 1968) pp. 215, 216.

7. Quoted in Darrett B. Rutman, *American Puritanism: Faith and Practice*, (Philadelphia: J.B. Lipincott Co., 1970), p. 11.

8. Sargent Bush, Jr., "John Wheelwright's Forgotten Apology: The Last Word in the Antinomian Controversy" *New England Quarterly*, vol LXIV no. 1, March, 1991, pp. 22–45.

9. Perry Miller, "The Marrow of Puritan Divinity," in *Puritan New England: Essays on Religion, Society, and Culture,* ed. Alden T. Vaughan, and Francis J. Bremer, (New York: St. Martin's Press, 1977), p. 44.

10. John Calvin, *Calvin: Institutes of the Christian Religion in Two Volumes*, vol. 1, ed. by John T. McNeill, trans. Ford Lewis Battles, (Philadelphia: Westminster Press, 1950), p. 766.

11. Ibid., p. 776.

12. Ibid., p. 770.

13. William Ames, *The Marrow of Theology*, trans. John D. Eusden, (Durham, NC: The Labyrinth Press, 1983) pp. 3–5.

14. Ibid., p. 161.

15. Ibid., pp. 167–169.

16. Calvin, *Institutes*, pp. 560 and 564.

17. Ibid., p. 569.

18. Babbette Levy, *Preaching in the First Half Century of New England History*

(Hartford: The American Society of Church History, 1945), p. 37

19. Levy, *Preaching*, p. 38.

20. Calvin, *Institutes*, p. 777.

21. Edmund S. Morgan, *Visible Saints: The History of a Puritan Idea* (New York : New York University Press, 1963).

22. Morgan,*Visible Saints*, p. 72 ff.

23. Darrett B. Rutman, *American Puritanism: Faith and Practice* (Philadelphia: J. B. Lippincott, 1970), pp. 100-103.

24. Morgan, *Visible Saints*, p. 69.

25. Ibid., p. 70.

26. Ibid., pp. 69 ff.

27. Quoted in Owen C. Watkins, *The Puritan Experience: Studies in Spiritual Autobiography* (New York: Shocken Books, 1972), p. 38.

28. Thomas Hooker, *The Application of Redemption*, London: Cole, 1657, reprint (New York: Arno Press, 1972), p. 124.

29. John Norton, *Able Being Dead Yet Speaketh*, facsimile of 1658 edition with introduction by Edward J. Gallagher (Delmar, N.Y.: Scholar's Facsimiles and Reprints, 1978), p. xii.

30. Norman Petit, *The Heart Prepared: Grace and Conversion in Puritan Spiritual Life* (New Haven and London : Yale University Press, 1966), p. 2.

31. Miller, "'Preparation for Salvation' In New England," *The Journal of the History of Ideas*, vol. 4, June, 1943, p. 261.

32. Ibid., p. 261.

33. Ibid., p. 260.

34. *The New Testament of our Lord and Saviour Jesus Christ*, facsimile reprint of the 1557 edition of the Genevan New Testament, (London: Samuel Bagster and Sons, nd).

35. Brooke Foss Wescott, *A General View of the History of the English Bible*, edited and revised by William Aldis Wright, (London: Macmillan and Co., 1905), p. 230.

36. This fact is noted in *The Bible in America: Versions that have Played Their Part in the Making of the Republic*, ed. Marion Simms, (New York: Wilson-Crickson), 1936, p. 90.

37. Simms, *Bible in America*, p. 93.

38. These ideas are discussed in both: Harry S. Stout, "Word and Order in Colonial New England," in *The Bible in America: Essays in Cultural History*, edited by Nathan O. Hatch and Mark A. Noll (New York and Oxford: Oxford University Press, 1982), and Amy Schrager Lang, *Prophetic Woman: Anne Hutchinson and the Problem of Dissent in the Literature of New England* (Berkeley: University of California Press, 1987).

39. Stout, "Word and Order," p. 21.

40. Ibid., p. 23.

41. Ibid., pp. 25, 26.

42. Ibid., p. 33.

43. Thomas Shepard, *God's Plot, The Paradoxes of Puritan Piety: Being the Autobiography & Journal of Thomas Shepard*, ed. Michael Mc Giffert, (Amherst, MA: University of Massachusetts Press, 1972), p. 32.

44. A suggested bibliography for study of Puritan biblical translations and doctrines is given in Charles Lloyd Cohen, *God's Caress: The Psychology of Puritan Religious Experience* (New York: Oxford University Press, 1986), pp. 277–278.

45. Margaret Deanesly, *The Lollard Bible and other Medieval Biblical Versions* (Cambridge: Cambridge University Press, 1920).

46. Cotton Mather, *Magnalia Christi Americana: Or the Ecclesiastical History of New England; from its first planting, in the year 1620, unto the year of our Lord 1698, in seven books*, First American edition from the London edition of 1702, (Hartford: Silas Andrus, 1820), p. 342.

47. Everett Emerson, *Puritanism in America: 1620-1750* (Boston: Twayne Publishers, 1977), p. 79.

48. Miller, "Preparation," p. 266.

49. Ibid., p. 267.

50. Ibid., p. 268.

51. Ibid., p. 263.

Chapter Three

"What Sayest Thou Unto It, England?"

The Early Years

As the Puritan cause was boiling to a head during the early years of the seventeenth century in England, many men and women who were caught up in its energy found themselves far from comfortable with conditions in their homeland. Much of this energy was to be released in the English civil war, but then a large portion of it was to find its way, still simmering, across the ocean to New England. The energy was expended there in conceptualizing and administering the society of New England, and in dealing with the inherent tensions. Those tensions were exacerbated by dissenters from the acceptable norms, the decisions for acceptability having been based upon the conditions found in New England. The organization of authority in the new society was based upon that of the Massachusetts Bay Company, which sent out the settlers, but it was quickly reorganized according to the conditions at hand and the desires of the leaders of the colony for a perfect Christian commonwealth.

One of the principal developers of the New England society, both in terms of formulating its organizational principles and in the subsequent actual guidance of its administration was John Winthrop. Winthrop was to figure heavily in the trials of Anne Hutchinson, just as he was to do in all events of significance in the early years of Massachusetts. Born in 1588, he was brought up on Groton Manor, his father's estate. His father, Adam Winthrop, had been a lawyer before inheriting the estate, and he saw to it that his son was given a good education. John was sent to Trinity College, Cambridge at the age of fifteen, and he may have found his religious calling as a Puritan during those years at college. However, though the theological milieu was congenial, he was homesick there, and so he returned home after only two years to work at advancing the fortunes of the already prospering estate. His father arranged a marriage for him at seventeen, to Mary Forth, and in less than a year he was a father.[1] While she lived, Mary bore him six children. His second wife lived only a year after he married her; it is his third wife, Margaret Tyndal, whose letters to and from Winthrop have survived, leaving a picture of both of them that includes great affection and charm. It is obvious from his journal writings and his letters that he was a tender and loving husband.

In the years following his first marriage, he worked industriously at improving himself as a man and a Puritan as well as laboring on his estate. Winthrop was highly intelligent, industrious, self-deprecating, and possessed of a sense of humor—about some things. He wrote of his love of God using passionate, even erotic language and worked extremely hard on whatever project was at hand. During these young years he managed the estate, and studied law at Gray's Inn so that he could adjudicate cases brought to his manorial court, and was eventually named a justice of the peace.[2] He was to use his legal training to great effect in New England, formulating the underpinnings of a society that would be so pleasing to God and man that it would shine forth in all its glory for all to see.

Times were hard in England at this point, however. In addition to the upheavals presented by the fomentation of new religious ideas, an economic depression wreaked havoc during the period of the late 1500s that extended well into the 1600s across England and continental Europe.[3] There are estimates that the segment of population of England affected by the depression either in terms of unemployment or underemployment was nearly one quarter of the laboring persons, many of whom were brought close to starvation.[4]

Seventeenth-century observers understood their economies only in relation to labor, not production. They did not consider the overall condition of the economy as the primary indicator of depression but only the high unemployment. This being so, those attempting to overcome problems saw as the only indicators of depression factors which had had the effect of causing unemployment. Influences, such as enclosure of the fields, carried out earlier during the reformation were identified as having led to unemployment, which indicated to them a serious depression. Because they were concerned only with alleviating that situation they tended to look for more lands where workers could establish themselves. Since there was not enough land in England, emigration was seen as the answer. These new spaces would enable laboring people to create new wealth for themselves and their families. In addition, workers believed that in a new land, "every man may be master and owner of his own labour and land..."[5] In this way freedom from any sort of serfdom was touted as a possibility for those willing to begin again in a new land.

The economic depression had as well caused many losses in production and shipping in the wool trade in England. As woolen cloth–making had been a mainstay of the English economy for hundreds of years, the depression created and exacerbated other social upheavals. Edmund Morgan describes the effects of the depression in this way, noting the changes the depression caused in theological thinking: "clothworkers were unemployed, hungry but unable to pay for country produce; clothiers could not market their fabrics; farmers could not pay their rents. The cost of caring for the poor and unemployed rose steadily. Was this not a hint of God's displeasure, a warning of worse to come?"6 The economy of England and its relationship to the resulting   social disruption were interpreted by the religious folk of the time as a measure of God's unhappiness with their misbehaviors, of whatever sort. So, the economy itself caused social disruption, and the interpretation of that disruption caused more social chaos as people attempted to stave off God's displeasure by leaving their homes and country for other places.

The depression intensified the need for many Puritans, who might have remained quietly at home under better economic circumstances, to leave the country in search of a more congenial situation elsewhere. When the cloth trade went into serious decline during the late 1620s in the area of Suffolk county where Winthrop lived he saw his fortunes declining and felt he would have to move in order to support his family. He deliberated how best to deal with the situation and considered for a while moving to Ireland. By then he was traveling often to London to gain some income by acting as a legal consultant, and finally took a position as an attorney in His Majesty's Court of Wards and Liveries, but found it did not provide enough income. Further, his Puritan soul was troubled by working for the King's court.

By 1629, Winthrop had decided, after much soul-searching, that he could no longer live in England, nor could he continue as a member of the English Church. He was not willing to separate from the Anglican Church, and not being comfortable either financially or doctrinally, he felt he had to make a move. Two of his sons had by this time emigrated or traveled widely, attempting to help him decide where it would be best to settle the family. At last Winthrop was persuaded to invest in the Massachusetts Bay Company that was in process of being founded. Though he had not felt quite comfortable about the company he decided to become a member. Winthrop concluded that if he must move he should go where he could not only better his economic status and find freedom for his conscience, but also where he could best serve his God. He wrote, "and so if he [Winthrop] should refuse this opportunity, that talent, which God hath bestowed upon him for public service, were like to be buried."7 He recognized that the move would give him a chance to use his God–given talents for building and later governing the new colony.

The Massachusetts Bay Company had been organized similarly to other joint-stock companies that had sent folks to the new world. The colony's charter, given by royal patent on March 4, 1629, was set up to bring in capital for its investors, on the usual trading company model: with a governor, a deputy governor, and eighteen assistants, as managers of the company. The hope was that those who settled in the new world would be able to exploit the natural resources of the area, such as cod and furs, and recoup the investors' investments, and of course more. Normally such a company would have sent out "planters," or colonists, and would have been managed from England.[8] John Endecott had been sent out by the company before the patent, or charter, had been secured. He had gone with a small group of settlers and some animals, and had set up camp at Salem during 1629. That group had been told to export fish and other commodities to the extent that they could find them, and also to evangelize the natives.[9] The original intent of the company changed during 1629, however, as several prominent Puritans became interested in the venture. John Humfry, who was the son-in-law of the Earl of Lincoln, held discussions in his home as to the feasibility of setting up a Puritan state in the New World. Others who took part in the discussions included prominent Puritan laymen like Thomas Dudley and John Cotton, and they pressed John Winthrop to join them. These deliberations led to the decision in the summer of 1629 to make significant changes in the intent and therefore the organization of the company. So, the company was reorganized in 1629 as this organization of "'undertakers' asserted control of the original capital stock." They changed its purpose and "divided the trading and governmental aspects of the venture" so that it was no longer a joint stock body. Its "purpose now was the governing of a plantation in the New World."[10] It was decided to implement a "corporate colony" whose management would not remain in London, but would be transferred to New England along with the charter. There the oversight of the company would "be merged with the government of the colony."[11] Not only was this structure new, but the men who founded the colony also differed from those who had traveled as part of previous companies; like Winthrop, the rest were well-to-do and were not being harassed in England. They did not need to leave England in order to make their fortune, or to escape persecutors. Rather, they wished to separate themselves physically from England, and from the English church, in order to establish a Puritan commonwealth and become a bastion of Puritanism in the new world. Because of this change in the intent of the company, trade was to be handled privately upon reaching the new country, rather than for the enrichment of the company.[12] The administrative positions of governor and assistants were to function similarly to those of a mayor and burgesses in town government, and the charter specified that the officers, assistants, and other stockholders, called freemen, were to meet annually in what was to be called a General Court. The General Court would function as the management of the colony, and would elect officers, allow new freemen to be admitted, and enact laws for both the company and the colony.[13] The assistants were to meet each month with the officers in an executive session called the Court of Assistants to conduct other business.[14] As it was to turn out, almost all of the freemen who went to the new colony were to become assistants, which meant that in practice the Court of Assistants and the General Court were to be almost the same body of men.[15]

The other investors in the company were eager to have Winthrop to function as their point man because they recognized his outstanding leadership capabilities. He was stable, well-to-do, even-tempered, well educated, and calm. Of course the fact that he would be willing to go in a leadership capacity lent great credibility to the venture and enabled the company to attract wealthy and reliable men. Winthrop was aware that those who had persuaded him to lead the company wished to use his reputation for godliness and godly affluence to encourage other wealthy men to join the company. Hard–headed business man that he was, he realized that if those who were "known to be godly and live in wealth and prosperity here, shall forsake all this" in order to go to New England, other such well–to–do folk would be more likely to join, and the company would need them.[16] He spent the summer provisioning the ship and making the other needed arrangements for the trip and subsequent settlement. At the same time, the stockholders who had been given the office of assistant but who would not be traveling to the new world resigned from the office, so that all those who would have the office of assistant would be in the colony.[17]

Winthrop's first choice for settlers were those who had capital to invest in the Massachusetts Bay Company, who could provide provisions to support themselves for a time until the country brought forth the fish and furs to be caught and traded for the support of the company, and for repayment to the shareholders. Winthrop would have preferred to have a preponderance of wealthy burgers in his group of settlers, and expended a great deal of energy in trying to convince many such burgers to join him; his practical nature saw the need for the well–to–do to be the leaders of stable communities. However, as the time to leave neared, he needed men and women to join the group, so he did not discourage poorer folk. The decision to allow poorer people who were looking more toward economic rather than religious betterment, was later to prove to be a burden for the community, as those who had brought little with them had to be supported by the others when it proved longer (and harder) than expected to become self–supporting. A number came as indentured servants, and did not bring enough provisions to sustain themselves once in New England, and Winthrop himself had brought at least four poorer families with him, to swell the ranks. As a result, he and other of the wealthier members of the group would have to support the poorer folk during the difficult winter of 1630–1631, just after the arrival of the first wave of the Massachusetts Bay settlers in the spring of 1630. Because of this experience, Winthrop would advise those looking to come to Massachusetts Bay at a later date to be sure to bring supplies for more than a year.

In addition to those like Winthrop who were well off but feared what the depressed economy would do to their own situation, many who were not especially religious, let alone Puritan, decided to emigrate. They were leaving England not primarily in order to have freedom to worship as they pleased but to find a place where they could make a living. Closest to Winthrop's heart, however, was the religious motivation for emigrating. Thus, when Winthrop had taken on the task of finding enough colonists to sail with him he had hoped to people the colony not only with comfortable burgers, but with staunch Puritans like himself. He and the other men who had set up the venture had wanted believers who shared their ardent desire for purity of religious practice, though they recognized that it would not be possible to ensure that all were as ardent as themselves.

Winthrop's willingness to become the governor of the company allowed the project to go forward, and his impact on the viability of the venture was enormous; Winthrop recognized his effect on the endeavor, and he took his responsibilities in that regard most seriously. He concluded his family business, and leaving Margaret—who was pregnant—and John Jr. behind, embarked on the Arabella on April 7, 1630. With him were a deputy governor, ten assistants, and about seven hundred others. Of the group, only about twenty to twenty-five percent were church members.[18]

At the same time that John Winthrop was pondering how to handle his economic and religious troubles, another Puritan was beginning to face similar religious difficulties. John Cotton was coming to the close of his long pastorate of the church in Boston, England. Many years later, when Cotton Mather wrote his short biography of his grandfather, John Cotton, he lamented that he had not the eloquency of Palladius as he "embalmed" Chrysostom, Posidonious, as he "eternized" Austin, and other well-known greats, in order to do proper justice to Cotton.[19]   It is arguable whether Cotton deserved quite so much acclaim, but it is quite true that he was revered by his friends and parishioners in Old, and later New England.

Cotton was born on December 4, 1585 in Derby, England. Son of a lawyer, he attended grammar school in Derby, studying under one Mr. Johnson, readying himself for Trinity College, Cambridge, which he entered at thirteen. Cotton received his A.B. in 1603, and though he intended to continue his education, he found that there was no funding available at Trinity for scholarships. This lack of funding may well have changed the course of his life, as it caused him to apply for a scholarship that was available at the hotbed of Puritanism, Emmanuel College, Cambridge. In order to receive the fellowship it was necessary for him to undergo a rigorous examination the crucial part of which was a Hebrew examination based on an Old Testament passage. The passage was extremely difficult to translate, but Cotton was able to pass with ease and qualified for the fellowship.[20] He remained at Emmanuel for nine years, and took his M.A. in 1606 gaining a reputation for great scholarship during his time there, at one point defending his thesis against a "famous disputant William Chappell."[21]

A history of Cambridge states that theology had been "almost the sole professional aim of either Oxford or Cambridge" for three centuries, beginning in 1550, and the study of Greek and Hebrew was the backbone of the curriculum for that reason.[22] A detailed list of the curriculum taken by students at Cambridge gives insight into the coursework of the time. Master Holdsworth, who had been a student of Emmanuel College, Cambridge at the same time as Cotton, and who wrote a treatise dealing with the course of study there, outlined the studies undertaken by an undergraduate at Emmanuel College, Cambridge, in the early seventeenth century. The list included most of the work of Aristotle, in addition to the *Testamentum Graecum*, and *De Idiotismis Praecipuis Linguae Graecae*.[23]

More specifically as regards Cotton's studies and their relationship to his later dealings with Anne Hutchinson, in his fourth year as an undergraduate he would have studied Aristotle's *Peri Psyches,* or *On the Soul*, which discusses the attributes of the soul.[24] This subject of study is pertinent to the question of the translation of the words *pneuma* and *psyche*, the meaning of which were questioned by Hutchinson at her ecclesiastical trial. Hutchinson read the two words, which are translated, "spirit" and "soul," and clearly refer to different things, and raised questions that Cotton and the other ministers felt were threatening to the faith. Yet, Cotton had studied *On the Soul,* which deals at some length with the dissimilarities and commonalities in souls possessed by all living beings from plants to humankind, as Aristotle discussed the "souls," or animating life forces, of all living beings. The soul is clearly differentiated from the spirit, which is what Christians translate as the immortal soul. No one who studied this work would have misunderstood the differences in the meaning of the words. And of course, the study of the Greek New Testament would also have made abundantly clear to all of them that both words are used in the Bible, and that they are used to mean different things.

Cotton came to be known throughout his life as a scholar. His reputation began when he was at Emmanuel College, and grew during his life, as, apparently, did his scholarship. Cotton's biographer, John Norton, a friend who knew him well, said of him, "He was a good *Hebrician*, in Greek a Critic, and could with great facility both speak and write Latin in a pure and elegant Ciceronian Style, a good Historian, no stranger to the Fathers, Councils or Schoolmen, abundantly exercised in Commentators of all sorts."[25] Other ministers considered Cotton to be extremely scholarly, as well. Everett Emerson says, "In 1636 Hugh Peter preached a sermon before Cotton's congregation in which he asked that Cotton be spared for a time 'that he might go through the bible and raise marginal notes upon all the knotty places of Scripture'"; the purpose being his legacy of scriptural notes that would be left them.[26] Interestingly, some time before 1640—whether before or after the Anne Hutchinson trials we do not know—Cotton delivered a series of sermons on Ecclesiastes, the source of Hutchinson's discomfort about the differences between "soul" and "spirit," and they were later published.

In addition to the life of application to scholarly pursuits that was begun during his college years, Cotton's conversion came also during his years at Emmanuel. After wrestling for many years with the worry that if he became too religious he would not be able to become as learned as he wished, he was "effectually awakened by a sermon of Dr. Sibbes, wherein was discoursed the misery of those who had only a *negative righteousness*, or a civil, sober, honest *blamelessness* before men."[27]

During this time at Emmanuel he gave sermons that were noted for their flowery eloquence, full of quotations from classical authors, in Latin and Greek. Mather declares that at the funeral oration he presented for Dr. Some, "he approved himself such a master of Periclean or Ciceronian oratory, that the auditors were even ready to have acclaimed, *Non vox homimem sonat!*"[28] However, that voice that seemed so expressive as not to be human soon changed its style: after his conversion Cotton became convinced that such a florid style did not comport with his beliefs, and he adopted the more theologically correct, "plain style."

In 1612 he left Emmanuel for a post in Boston, Lincolnshire as the Vicar of St. Botolph's church. The story is told that unlike the usual case, where the "living" of a parish was held by a wealthy individual, the city of Boston held the living of St. Botolph's, and so was responsible for filling the vacancy of the vicarage. When the vote was taken whether to ask Cotton to become their vicar, the result was a tie. The mayor, however, inadvertently voted twice, breaking the tie and giving Cotton the post. This appointment was considered by the bishop to be too prominent for the young Cotton, but he was convinced to authorize the post by some of the parishioners, who were especially eager to have Cotton as their pastor. Cotton moved to Boston with his wife Elizabeth Horrocks, but after some years Cotton and his wife were both stricken with the tertiary ague, and he was seriously laid up for two years. His wife was not able to withstand the disease, and she died.[29] In 1632 he was married again,to Sarah Hankridge, a widow member of his parish, who outlived Cotton, and later married Richard Mather.[30]

Cotton was to remain at St. Botolph's for twenty-one years, resolving several vexing political problems within the parish during that time. A number of his old mentors at college sent him students, and his Sunday and Thursday sermons gained him a wide reputation, as he kept up his studies—usually studying twelve hours each day—while he labored as pastor of St. Botolph's.[31] He also preached Wednesday, Friday, and Saturday sermons during that time, these being less formal than those on Sunday and Thursday.

Within his congregation at St. Botolph's there grew up a special group of folks who "entered into a Covenant with the Lord, and one with another to follow after the Lord in the Purity of his worship."[32] It is likely that Anne Hutchinson was one of that group, as she makes reference to such a group during her trials. Cotton himself evidently felt that by encouraging such a group he was gathering a real church within the parish system where all those within a geographical area constituted a parish. He was using what would become the method for determining church membership in New England. Although a staunch foe of separation, Cotton saw a great number of his friends leave the country for New England, and he was the one to preach the sermon to Winthrop and the rest of the folks on the eve of their sailing from Southampton. After 1630, while Winthrop and his group settled in New England, Cotton continued for two more years his struggle with his conscience and with the fear that he might be arrested or forced to flee England.

Cotton's most celebrated parishioner was Anne Hutchinson. A number of biographies have been written about Anne Hutchinson; she has been fascinating to biographers and historians since the 1630s. After her trials she was to be reviled by John Winthrop, Governor of Massachusetts Bay Colony as, "a woman of haughty and fierce carriage, of a nimble wit and active spirit, and a very voluble tongue", thus giving credit for her high intelligence, but scorning her for her strong character and unwillingness to knuckle under to him and the other leaders of the Bay.[33] In recent times

Hutchinson has been lauded as the first feminist in American history by Winifred King Rugg, derided as menopausal with "neurotic manifestations" by Emery Battis, and several other designations in-between.[34] No one seems to have been able to form an objective picture of her. Each of her biographers presents the same fairly meager information known about her from her or his own strongly stated point of view. None of the biographies is presented in anything resembling an objective manner; clearly this woman still elicits intense reactions.

Born in 1591, Hutchinson came from a family with strong opinions. Her father, Francis Marbury, a member of the Anglican clergy, had been tried in 1578 for stating that the bishops were "ordaining ministers unfit for their calling," which is an interesting description, as it foreshadows the claims his daughter would later make about the clergy in Massachusetts. At the time of his imprisonment Bishop Aylmer of London had called him 'an overthwart proud puritan knave'."[35]   He had gone to prison for his high principles, and even though he had later been allowed to have the living of Alford parish for some years, by the time Anne was born in 1591, he was no longer allowed to preach. It was not until Anne was fourteen that he was again allowed a parish, this time in London.   Anne's mother, Bridget Dryden, had come from a Puritan family, and it may be that it was from her that Anne's Puritan beliefs came, as her father did not support the Puritan cause, however much he regretted the state of the Anglican clergy (Aylmer was incorrect in his calumny).   We do not know if her mother influenced either her behavior or her beliefs, but whether or not her mother was outspoken in her Puritanism, or whether it was her father who was her role–model, Anne grew up to trust her own instincts and rely on her own mind to seek truth for herself.

On August 9, 1612, Anne married William Hutchinson, who was a well-to-do mercer from Alford in Lincoln County. William was twenty-six at the time, and while his family's social standing was not as high as Anne's, his male forebears had been propertied burgers in several areas of the wool trade.   (One of William's brothers, also in the cloth trade, became so wealthy as to be able to sustain a loss of sixty thousand pounds in the London fire "without being ruined," indicating a large fortune.)   Anne and William were to have fifteen children during the next twenty–two years, the first nine months after their marriage; obviously Anne was physically quite strong, and she had great stamina.   Only three of those children died in childhood, which would indicate that equally clearly, she must have cared for her children skillfully, using the herbal remedies she would later use in New England as well.

Little is known about William Hutchinson other than that he was a quiet, well-to-do merchant, apparently circumspect in his religious behavior, and remained a devoted husband to Anne Hutchinson throughout his life. Having come from a family of merchants, he continued in that line, and was himself a sheep farmer and a wool merchant.[36] Anne and William were for many years members of the church of St. Botolph in Boston, where John Cotton was the vicar. The years of 1616–1617 were mentioned by her as critical years, and may have been the time during which she experienced a conversion, as a baby born during that time was named Faith. Anne came to be convinced that those who did not teach "the new covenant...and not ordinances, forms, and ceremonies imposed by man" were of the anti–christ.[37] She wrestled with the state of her soul and the need to hear the Word from a truly regenerate pastor during this time, finally deciding that while she did not have to become a separatist, still it was the case that only some few preachers within the church preached the true Word. Later, at her trial for sedition she stated that God had given her discernment at this time so that she could tell with certainty who were those who preached the new covenant and who did not. Her pastor at St. Botolph's church, John Cotton was, she believed, one of the best. Anne, and no doubt William, were among those who formed the small group that comprised the special inner circle of believers who constituted the true church within Cotton's parish, and they were particularly concerned about pure worship. During the early 1630s the harassment of Puritan clergy intensified, and many of them left England to avoid losing their benefices or receiving prison sentences. Cotton was aware that his preaching and practices set him apart as a man to watch, and undoubtedly the Hutchinsons, members of the special inner circle of worshippers in the parish, must have been aware of the situation as well.

Meanwhile, Winthrop's group landed in New England and made their way to what is now Boston, in July of 1630, three months after they had set sail. The trip had been difficult, as all such ocean crossings were at the time, and on shipboard Winthrop had worked assiduously on the political theory that would guide the new venture, as well as on the theological assumptions that would direct them. He preached his famous sermon on shipboard, where he exhorted those embarked on the new venture to remember that they would be scrutinized as a "City on a Hill." They would be an example, whether a success or not, at which the world would point. Winthrop had been the cornerstone and chief arranger of the trip, its primary apologist for the rest of the group, and he remained so after reaching New England. Once in New England he worked energetically for months, too busy to write to his wife or in his journal. He shouldered the fundamental moral responsibility for the company, and he aided with practical arrangements as well. The first task was to build homes and secure food for those who had brought little with them. Winthrop was responsible for assaying the land, and deciding where to make permanent settlement: his decision was that the area around Boston would provide the best physical surroundings and security for the group.38 Massachusetts Bay Company had been granted land ranging from the Atlantic to the Pacific Oceans, but only from an area just north of the Merrimac River to just south of the Charles river. In this area they were to set up their colony, with the company governor, assistant governor, and eighteen assistants to administer it.

They had brought their charter with them to New England, although charters normally stayed in England. But they had been able to do so because no place of residence for meetings had been specified in the charter.39 Taking the charter gave them far more authority in the governance of the colony than would have been the case had it been governed from England. Had the charter remained in England, the Crown could, and undoubtedly would, have sent a governor to the company who was entirely to the taste of Archbishop Laud. In 1629 Archbishop Laud, a strong Arminian, had come to power. In fact his access to power had been a factor in Winthrop's decision to emigrate to New England. Laud was busily extending his authority, so that by 1636 he had been given broad enough powers to review all such charters, and revoke them if he felt they allowed liberties that should not be allowed for the health of England.40 The threat that this might come to pass at any time hung over the colony from its beginning, but it was hoped that as long as the colony did nothing to outrage folks at home, things would be left as they were. The colony's charter "empowered the freemen or stockholders to legislate for the company...as long as its laws were not repugnant to those of England."41 This meant that the leaders of the colony had always to be watchful of how well things were going within the community, so as not to raise too invitingly the interest of England.

There was a political problem that developed in this regard very quickly upon beginning the governance of the new colony. Winthrop and the other leaders of the colony had changed the governing method, shortly after arrival, in such a way that they were able to consolidate their power by controlling the government. The charter stated that the General Court required the governor and six assistants to make up a quorum for purposes of holding sessions and accomplishing the tasks of running the colony, but seven assistants would constitute a quorum in the Court of Assistants, and only a majority of them were necessary in order to enact business, which meant that once in the new world, it would prove preferable to have the

Court of Assistants conduct most of the colony functions.[42] In October of
1630 the General Court gave the assistants, who had earlier been made the
equivalent of a Justice of the Peace in England, and were now called Magistrates, the power to select the governor and deputy governor from among
themselves. In addition, they gave them the authority to make laws and to
"select officers for carrying them out." This put all of the executive, legislative, and judicial functions together in one controlling group. The charter
had not specified that the assistants could levy taxes nor the General Court
draft laws.[43] At this time it was recognized that there would be many new
freemen drawn from among the settlers in the near future, so the assistants
desired to keep control of the colony among themselves. Consequently, the
General Court ruled in 1631 that in order to become a freeman, a man must
be a member of a church. This was in "flagrant violation of the charter,"
which had made no such stipulation and meant that the colony government
was now in the hands of no more than seven or eight per cent of the men of
the colony.[44]

By 1632 there was a revolt in the town of Watertown over this state of
affairs, when the Court of Assistants attempted to impose taxes on the town.
Their minister warned them not to pay the taxes, because they had not
"consented" to the tax. Having refused to pay, they were called before
Winthrop, who told them that the Assistants had the power to levy taxes.
However he saw that he must give in to their concerns, so he proposed that
from that time forward, two representatives from each town should confer
with the Governor and Assistants. As a result of this compromise, two
deputies, elected by the freemen of each town, were sent to decide what
would be brought to the General Court. Then, in 1634, the deputies demanded to see the charter, and having done so found that according to the charter,
all of the laws were to be drawn up by the General Court, rather than the
Court of Assistants. Going again to Winthrop, they were told that this was
true, but once again he was able to convince them to accept a compromise.
He pointed out that there were too many freemen to draft laws, and suggested that they should choose some who would be their representatives and
undertake the legislation. The next May two men from each town met and
voted that only the General Court could now admit freemen and make laws,
or decisions about the dispersal of land.[45] All of this pressure that was
brought to bear on Winthrop as governor brought about the result that the
political conditions had now been restored to those stipulated in the charter.
However, the freemen were still not able to elect the Governor, and it was
always likely that they might push to do so at some time in the future. This
of course was not desirable from the leaders of the colony's point of view.
Furthermore, having made such deviations from the charter's stipulations,

Winthrop and the others in authority were understandably nervous about possible revocation of the charter, should things in the colony not go well.[46]

The result of a revocation of the charter would likely be a governor imposed upon them by England, who would of course be an Arminian of Laud's choice. That possibility caused them much anguish, and increased their fear that if they appeared to be abusing power and not respecting their charter such a consequence might well come about. Conversely, it also made them aware that keeping the King's peace and maintaining proper order in the colony was absolutely necessary.[47] It was imperative to have a well-run colony so that they would be left alone.

There were other worries for the new colony, too. Winthrop had given the little colony a definition of itself that was dramatic and powerful. In addition to his challenge to them that they must be a "City on a Hill," the colonists pictured themselves as following in the footsteps of Moses and Jesus into the wilderness.[48] This depiction of themselves as wanderers in the spiritual and physical wilderness of course had enormous theological significance to these deeply devout folk. It also, however, held no small social meaning for them. They have been described as envisioning themselves as having been planted in a garden within a wilderness, with Christ serving as a hedge surrounding them and protecting them from theological and physical harm.[49] John Cotton was to use this metaphor later in a sermon where he described the entire church to folk wandering in the wilderness. He said, "all the world out of the Church is as a wilderness, or at best a wild field."[50] God had led them to the new country just as He had led the Israelites to wander in the wilderness, and God would provide for them and protect them in the same way. However, this protection and provision would only happen if the Puritans, like the Israelites, behaved in approved ways. If they strayed from the behavior expected of them, God would withdraw His help from them, as he had the biblical wanderers. This, too, encouraged them to keep close watch upon the governance of the colony, and the behavior of the colonists as well.

There were severe trials and tests to be faced by the group, and from the moment of arrival the settlers found themselves having great difficulty adapting to the physical surroundings and demands of the new country. They had been told of differences between the new country and England, but many of the descriptions of the country had painted it in glowing and unreal colors. The expectation that the new land would abound with healing "air and water, fruits and fish," as the writings of William Morrell, Sir William Alexander, and Christopher Levett, writing from 1623 to 1630 had described it in their tracts about the new world, was not entirely fulfilled. Most of those who came over did in fact find that the air seemed to be healthful, but other conditions were less to their liking. The weather was difficult to adjust to, both hotter in summer and colder in winter than English folk had experienced at home, and the days were of different lengths, as well. Furthermore, a large number of those who had come to the colony were tradesmen, not farmers; many were weavers who had been put out of work in England.[51] These men had to learn the new trade of farming, and with it new farming methods, and they had to learn to build homes and towns from the ground up.

Learning how to farm the land was a haphazard experience, with the men initially reluctant to use the methods taught them by the Native Americans because they did not feel comfortable with methods so different from what they had known in England.[52] Nor did they want to innovate in any case, and so they continued using the preferred agricultural techniques of England until forced by the meager harvests to change their practices.[53] Furthermore, there were no staple commercial crops of the kind that they were used to growing that were at home in the harsh New England climate. The settlers had brought with them seeds of wheat, rye, oats, buckwheat, and field peas, and had expected to raise those English products on the land. However, there was the problem that "the fields of New England produced grain and stones, the latter more easily and abundantly than the former."[54] The staple that the Indians taught them to raise was maize. Maize grew in the new country, but even maize "will not grow there except the ground be manured with fish...," as John Winslow had noted. Winthrop felt that only if cattle were brought in "to till the ground" would the land yield much.[55] Once they became accustomed to growing it, however, this maize, or corn, very quickly became the staple food of the settlers, with bread and corn dishes such as johnny–cakes and corn pudding "all washed down with beer" becoming predominant in their diet.[56]

It was of course the case that this new life, besides being confusing with its strange weather, crops and diet, was physically extremely hard for the settlers, with little but backbreaking work and church–going making up their entire lives. The men had to build houses, the first ones being dugouts, then wattle and daub houses similar to those in England. These houses were framed with hewn logs, using two–man saws and adzes. While men worked together in gangs to erect the framing for the houses, the work was extremely strenuous, and was work that few of the immigrants had been accustomed to performing in England.[57] Naturally the women, too, had to learn new work and new ways. They had to learn the new methods of cooking required to make maize into palatable dishes, and they had to learn to catch some of their food. Potable water was at first difficult to locate, and there was a great deal of illness during the first winter in New England.[58]

The life was cruel and there were some who were unable to maintain their stability. The stresses of the physical demands coupled with a constantly preached insistence that the heart be incessantly evaluated for signs of regeneration—or the lack of it—caused mental instability in some. Even as late as 1637 and 1638 incidents are recorded of women becoming so depressed ("distracted" or "falling into a melancholy" as they were described at the time) that they killed one of their children.[59]   Life in the wilderness into which God had led them demanded discipline and stamina, both physical and mental.

The leaders of the colony knew that it was 'necessity' that had led many of their folks to come rather than religious piety, but they did not recognize that the conditions of want that would be theirs during the first winter in the new land would also cause emotional and social difficulties for the settlers.[60]   The pressure from those who had not brought much with them now proved to be a serious drain on the rest of the community in more than an economic sense, as in the new world economic hardships led to social dissension. Poorer people, who had not been as fervent to begin with, but had come because of economic necessity, began to complain of what they considered to be the high–handed way in which Winthrop and others held the reigns of authority. These folk discovered that the reality of the new place was in "all things so contrary to the high reports given out" with the result that they felt quite disillusioned and unsympathetic to the orthodox of the community. Worse, Winthrop noted that Satan was causing the settlers to be more wicked in America than they had ever been in England.[61]

Wicked or not, it had been economic upheavals that were responsible at least in part for the decision to take the drastic step of leaving their homes to come to the new world, and this meant to most of them that a stable social order in New England was vital, so that they would have the energy to learn new trades and do well in the new world. Although some were unable to adjust to the new world and so returned to England, most recognized that their futures were in the new country. Those who saw the possibilities in the new country were quite aware that they needed a quiet and stable social community in order to thrive. Men like Winthrop were under a great deal of pressure to keep the local situation on an even keel so that the fledgling colony would offer social equilibrium for those who were struggling to make a new life and community for themselves.

Into this matrix of social concerns one must add the variable of religious unanimity. For, while independent thinking and a personal approach to God may have been the crux of English Puritanism, and a driving force for the emigration to Massachusetts, what was needed after the voyage was unquestionably something different. Now it was the cohesiveness of the community that would protect them from the dangers that their enterprise presented to them. Winthrop stated, "We are entered into covenant with God for this work."[62]   Order and harmony were of crucial importance to the growing communities in the new world. Any heterodoxy, any differences in belief threatened the cohesiveness needed by the colony to survive and thus accomplish its mission. The brawn of the rugged individualist might be needed for the physical establishment and building of the colony, but unique religious interpretations were not called for. Docile agreement with the ministers' preachments coupled with hard work were demanded, and any sign of heterodoxy was a more than ordinary threat. Furthermore, dissent from the orthodox line of thinking was taken to be equal to dissent from obedience to the laws of the colony, and Winthrop and the magistrates had their charter to back them that dissent would not be tolerated. The charter had given the power to the government of the colony to banish those who seemed to offer any danger to the establishment of the colony.[63]

When the first signs of potential problems from Anne Hutchinson and those who agreed with her reading of the scriptures appeared, the community had begun to enlarge, and the settlers were beginning to see endeavor as a success. While the colony never made money for its investors, it was at the point where it could be expected to be self–supporting (and more) if governed carefully so as to avoid the disruptions that would be caused by social dissension. Kai Erickson relates, "In 1636, when the [Antinomian] dispute first came to public attention, Massachusetts was in the midst of a vast building program. The flow of immigrants from England had reached a high peak, and settlements were spreading across the hinterlands of Boston Bay and reaching far out into the wilderness."[64]

Thus, any internal threat to the colony was a threat to both the civil and church order because they were considered interrelated. These builders felt that social unity was necessary for the ecclesiastical unity of their hilltop city, and in fact was a condition for it. Winthrop wrote in his journal that all of the settlers had been "sealed with the same seal," referring both to their theological unity and to their social cohesion.[65] Winthrop also extolled social unity as being like that of an ideal family. Winthrop himself was a strong family man who expressed his love for his wife easily and often in his letters to her, so his metaphor relating, "a family is a little commonwealth, and a commonwealth is a great family," demonstrates how basic social unity was to his thinking.[66]

The social order was not seen as separate from church order. It is clear from the writings of John Cotton and John Winthrop that social unity had theological significance in their way of thinking, as well as practical significance. They stressed social cohesion and unity for both reasons. All the men who were among the first to leave England wrestled with the charge leveled at them that they were "separatists." They took such a charge seriously, as they did not believe it was right to separate themselves from the body of believers in England. Winthrop argued with himself that he was not attempting to separate himself from the Church of England, but only to establish a better place for that church to thrive. He wanted the colony to be a shining example for the rest of those left behind in England, so that they would be eager to emigrate also, in order to join the superior example of a model church and a model social order. Winthrop in fact gained a reputation for being a conciliator in the colony who "walked the extra mile" to avoid disunity and dissension. He worked hard to heal rifts that developed in the community, both religious and social in nature. Morgan describes Winthrop as "patient, conscientious, firm but not arbitrary."[67] However, he was felt by some of the community to be too lenient, and he was rebuked at one point for being too easy on some peace–breakers, which he did out of a concern to keep peace in the community rather than enforce strict laws. He wrote in his journal that he believed "that in the infancy of plantations, justice should be administered with more leniency than in a settled state, because people were then more apt to transgress, partly of ignorance of new laws and orders, partly through oppression of business and other straits."[68] Thus, Winthrop found himself in the position as governor of the burgeoning colony, of having to analyze and reanalyze the proper weight to give to enforcing social unity and allowing individual differences.

While this expanding new society was establishing itself in the new country, John Cotton found himself in increasing difficulties with the authorities in England. Although himself a staunch foe of separation from the church of England, John Cotton had been among the group that had discussed with John Winthrop the need to migrate, and he had watched while a great number of his friends left the country for New England. As he grew more and more concerned with the religious condition of England, he recognized that it was becoming more and more unhealthy for him to remain there. More importantly for Cotton, however, was his belief that God's judgment was coming shortly upon England to chastise the country for her sins. Cotton's farewell sermon for Winthrop's group when they left England in 1630, in which he warned of God's displeasure with England, was important enough to become his first sermon to be printed.

By 1632, Cotton was under attack by Archbishop Laud, and in that year proceedings were brought against him to appear before the High Commission Court. This forced him to flee to London, and eventually to New England, rather than abandon Puritan ideals. He was aided in his flight to London by one of the other well-known ministers of New England Puritanism, Thomas Hooker. In 1633 Cotton and his wife left for New England on the *Griffin*. Hooker and a number of others who would figure in the trials of Anne Hutchinson sailed on the *Griffin* with him.

On September 4, 1633, Cotton, his friends, his wife, and his newborn son, named Seaborn, landed and began life in New England. Within four days Cotton and his wife were admitted to membership in the Boston church, and on October 10 he was elected to be teacher of that congregation. As the congregation already had a pastor, John Wilson, Cotton was given the role of teacher, with the expectation that he would be responsible for doctrinal education of the flock. He was able to continue living his life much as he had in England, working and studying long hours each day, concentrating upon his scholarship in order to preach heavily doctrinal sermons to the Boston congregation. His preaching style continued to be logical and plain, "emphasized by occasional gestures of his right hand." Cotton was considered to be an excellent preacher, but his charisma must have been in his personality, as it is not evident in most of his written sermons. His sermons are flat, and have none of the charm of those of other ministers, such as his friend Thomas Hooker, nor the passion of another of the ministers who would figure in Anne Hutchinson's trials, Thomas Shepard. Hooker made extensive use of homely metaphors, often extending the metaphor for some paragraphs. Cotton, however, must have left all his capacity for lively writing behind him when he renounced the flourishes of classic quotations early in his career. His sermons explain, they do not exhort. They rationalize, but they do little to illustrate. Clearly, the small, rotund, cheery man must have had a passionate delivery style that made his congregations, as well as other clergy, so vitally absorbed in his sermons. Although he concentrated on themes having to do with salvation, at times he included references to local social and political problems, such as in 1634 when he defended the veto power for the magistrates, or a discussion of the ethics of trade when a Boston merchant had been accused of price-gouging.

John Cotton was able to involve himself in the life of the colony in other ways as well. Although as a minister he was not eligible to become one of the magistrates, he was to exercise his gifts in the colony in ways other than his preaching. By 1634 John Winthrop was finding himself under increased pressure from the freemen to have a set of written laws. Having become more involved in the legislative process, the freemen were concerned that the magistrates were creating laws judicially rather than legislatively. They expressed their desire to Winthrop for a carefully drafted set of laws. Winthrop resisted this pressure for as long as he could, as he did not wish to draw attention to the colony's differences from English law, and he and the rest of the magistrates believed that laws for the new colony should develop independently, and as a result of response to local conditions[69] And in any case he did not wish to take away the overarching power of the magistrates by allowing the average person to point to written laws in arguing their cases.[70] But the freemen demanded to see the charter, and finally forced Winthrop to agree that a systematic set of laws should be drafted.

After several abortive attempts to find a good working committee, Winthrop asked Cotton to head a group that would draw up such laws. He worked on those laws with a few other men, but, "Mr. Bellingham, of the magistrates, and Mr. Cotton, of the clergy, had the greatest share in this work."[71] The laws Cotton and the others drafted covered the governance of the colony, "taxation, military affairs, inheritance, trade and commerce, crime, wrongdoing, and the administration of justice." The laws required that there be two witnesses to convict in both civil and criminal trials.[72] When finished, however, Winthrop apparently did not feel that Cotton's laws were acceptable for the colony as they were so harsh, and he let them die quietly on a shelf. It is ironic that the resulting laws, patterned after the Mosaic law, were adopted in revised form later by several of the other colonies. The laws finally adopted by Winthrop and the rest of the colony were far less severe than those drafted by Cotton. A footnote in Thomas Hutchinson's history of the colony states, "In the first draught of the laws by Mr. Cotton, which I have seen corrected with Mr. Winthrop's hand, divers other offenses were made capital, viz... Reviling the magistrates in highest rank, viz. the governor and council. Exod. xxii. 18. I Kings xxii. 8,9,44."[73] This particular offense underscores Cotton's basic philosophy, which was that "reviling the magistrates" was a crime worthy of death. Anne Hutchinson later was charged with sedition, and the charge was based upon allegations that she had slandered the ministers, a charge remarkably similar to that of "reviling the magistrates."

Although Cotton's laws were not accepted by Massachusetts Bay, the fact that Cotton was asked to draft the laws reemphasizes the fact of his high standing with the leaders of the community. It also underscores his knowledge of the law. George Lee Haskins, writing of Cotton's draft of laws in his landmark study of seventeenth-century law, states, "what is remarkable is that Cotton, who had no legal training and who was not an officer of the colony, should have had as complete a grasp as he did of the fundamentals of its government, of the laws already in existence, and of the need in certain directions for guarantees of due process and civil rights."[74]

As he became a highly regarded member of the clergy in the colony, he too became greatly concerned with the need for social unity and conformity. Cotton, in his first sermon of the series, "God's Mercie Mixed with his

Justice," stated that "we are all one mystical body; and I cannot tell how better to compare it, than to a musical instrument, wherein though there be many pipes, yet one blast of the bellows puts breath into them all, so that all of them at once break forth into a kind of melody, and give a pleasant sound to the ears of those that stand by; all of them do make but one Instrument, and one sound and yet variety of music."[75] This delightful (and for him, unusual) metaphor indicates the depth of his belief that all of the brethren and sisters must be in perfect harmony in all their efforts, both civil and ecclesiastical.

Cotton was becoming more and more one of the right-hand men of John Winthrop, as he accustomed himself to his new life. But while Cotton was settling in to his new parish, and garnering the love and admiration of his flock, the magistrates and his fellow clergy, the blemishes that he was never quite able to remove from his happy life were readying themselves for him in the persons of Roger Williams and Anne Hutchinson.

Notes

1. Edmund S. Morgan, *The Puritan Dilemma* (Boston: Little Brown and Co., 1958), pp. 3-7.

2. Ibid., pp. 7-16.

3. Geoffrey Parker and Leslie M. Smith, eds., *The General Crisis of the Seventeenth Century* (London: Routledge & Kegan Paul, 1978).

4. A study of the effects of the economic crisis is found in a chapter by Stephen Innes: "Fulfilling John Smith's Vision: Work and Labor in Early America," in *Work and Labor in Early America*, ed. Stephen Innes (Chapel Hill: University of North Carolina Press, 1988), pp. 4–5.

5. Smith, quoted in Innes, p. 3.

6. Ibid., p. 21.

7. Ibid., p. 43.

8. George Lee Haskins, *Law and Authority in Early Massachusetts: A Study in Tradition and Design* (Lanham, MD: University Press of America, 1960), p. 10.

9. Haskins, *Law and Authority*, p. 10.

10. David Thomas Konig, *Law and Society in Puritan Massachusetts: Essex County, 1629-1692* (Chapel Hill: University of North Carolina Press, 1979), p. 23.

11. Haskins, *Law and Authority*, p. 11.

12. Ibid., p. 25.

13. Ibid., p. 26.

14. George L. Haskins, "Lay Judges: Magistrates and Justices in Early Massachusetts," pp. 39–56, in *Law in Colonial Massachusetts: 1630-1800*, vol. 62 (Boston: The Colonial Society of Massachusetts, 1981), p. 43.

15. Haskins, *Law and Authority*, p. 26.

16. Morgan, *Dilemma*, p. 46.

17. Haskins, *Law and Authority*, p. 23.

18. Ibid.

19. Mather, *Magnalia Christi Americana*, p. 252.

20. Williston Walker, *Ten New England Leaders* (New York: Silver, Burdett and Co., 1901), p. 56.

21. Cotton, *Cotton on the Churches*, p. 7.

22. J. Bass Mullinger, *A History of the University of Cambridge* (New York: Anson D. F. Randolph and Co., nd), p. 118.

23. Eugene E White, 'Master Holdsworth and 'A Knowledge Very Useful and Necessary'," *The Quarterly Journal of Speech*, vol. LIII, Feb., 1967, pp. 1–16.

24. White, p. 4.

25. Norton, p. 24.

26. quoted in Everett Emerson, *John Cotton* (New York: Twayne Publishing, 1965, p. 103), from Winthrop's *Journal*, p. 179.

27. Mather, p. 255.

28. Ibid.

29. Selma Williams, *Divine Rebel: The Life of Anne Marbury Hutchinson*, (New York : Holt Rinehart and Winston, 1981), pp. 65–67.

30. Walker, p. 60.

31. John Cotton, quoted in Emerson, *John Cotton*, p. 35.

32. Walker, p. 64.

33. John Winthrop, "A Short Story of the Rise, Reign, and Ruin of Antinomians, Familists and Libertines, that Infected the Churches of New England," London, 1644, in *Antinomianism in the Colony of Massachusetts Bay, 1636–38*, ed. Charles Francis Adams (Boston: Publications of the Prince Society, 1894), p. 138.

34. Rugg, p. ix; Battis, p. 346–7.

35. Helen Augur, *An American Jezebel: The Life of Anne Hutchinson* (New York: Brentanno's, 1930), p. 10.

36. Williams, pp. 39–41.

37. Rugg, pp. 39–43.

38. Morgan, *Dilemma*, pp. 55–61.

39. Lee Schweniger, *John Winthrop* (Boston: Twayne Publishers, 1990), p. 31.

40. George F. Willison, *Saints and Strangers: being the Lives of the Pilgrim Fathers & Their Families, With Their Friends & Foes; & an Account of Their Posthumous Wanderings in Limbo, Their Final Resurrection & Rise to Glory, & the Strange Pilgrimages of Plymouth Rock* (New York: Reynal and Hitchcock, 1945), p. 298.

41. Solberg, p. 124.

42. Haskins, *Law and Authority*, p. 26.

43. Ibid., pp. 26, 27.

44. Ibid., pp. 29, 30.

45. Ibid., pp. 30, 31.

46. Winton U. Solberg, *Redeem the Time: The Puritan Sabbath in Early America* (Cambridge, MA: Harvard University Press, 1977), p. 135.

47. Rugg, p. 117.

48. A thorough discussion of this concept is found in the work of Peter Carroll, *Puritanism and the Wilderness: The Intellectual Significance of the New England Frontier, 1629–1700* (New York: Columbia University Press, 1969).

49. Carroll, pp. 109–126.

50. Ibid., p. 111.

51. David Cressy, " 'Reasons moving this people to transplant themselves' Migrant Motives and Decisions" in *Coming Over: Migration and Communication Between England and New England in the Seventeenth Century* (Cambridge: Cambridge University Press,1987), pp. 74–106; and "Migrants and Motives: Religion and the Settlement of New England, 1630–1640," *New England Quarterly*, vol. 58, 1985, Virginia DeJohn Anderson, p. 365.

52. Masefield, *Chronicles*, p. 354.

53. David M Scobey, "Revising the Errand: New England's Ways and the Puritan Sense of the Past," in *William and Mary Quarterly* vol. 41, 1984, p. 13.

54. John J. McCusker and Russell R. Menard, eds., *The Economy of British America, 1607–1789* (Chapel Hill: University of North Carolina Press for the Institute of Early American History and Culture, 1985) check quote

55. Information about farming problems and techniques is found in the following articles: Glenn T. Treworthan, "Types of Rural Settlement in Colonial America" in *Geographical Review*, vol. 36, 1946, p. 575; Sarah F. Mc Mahon, "A Comfortable Subsistence: The Changing Diet in Rural New England, 1620–1840," in *William and Mary Quarterly*, vol. 42, 1985, p. 34; Masefield, *Chronicles*, p. 354.

56. Mc Mahon, p. 44.

57. Treworthan, p. 569; Anderson, "Migrants," p. 365.

58. Edward Johnson, "Wonder-working Providence", in Perry Miller and Thomas H. Johnson, eds., *The Puritans*, vol. 1, revised edition (New York: Harper Torchbooks, Harper and Row, 1938), p. 150.

59. Winifred King Rugg, *Unafraid: A Life of Anne Hutchinson* (Boston and New York: Houghton Mifflin Company, 1930), p. 93.

60. Philip Gura discusses their emotional and social problems in, *Glimpses of Sion's Glory* (Middletown, CN: Wesleyan University Press, 1984).

61. Gura, pp. 26, 27.

62. Winton U. Solberg, *Redeem the Time: The Puritan Sabbath in Early America,* (Cambridge, MA: Harvard University Press, 1977), p. 126.

63. Haskins, *Law and Authority*, p. 51.

64. Kai T. Erickson, *Wayward Puritans: A Study of Deviance* (New York: John Wiley and Sons, 1966), p. 71.

65. Winthrop, Journal, p. 137, quoted in Darrett B. Rutman, *American Puritanism: Faith and Practice* (Philadelphia: J.B. Lippincott Co., 1970), p. 93.

66. Rutman, *American*, p. 72.

67. Morgan, *Dilemma*, p. 102.

68. Ibid., pp. 105–6.

69. Haskins, *Law and Authority*, p. 120.

70. Ibid., p. 121.

71. Thomas Hutchinson, *History of the Colony and Province of Massachusetts Bay,* ed. Lawrence Shaw Mayo (Cambridge MA : Harvard University Press, 1936), p. 369.

72. Haskins, *Law and Authority*, p. 125.

73. Thomas Hutchinson, *History of Massachusetts Bay*, pp. 373.

74. Haskins, *Law and Authority*, p. 126.

75. David D. Hall, *Worlds of Wonder, Days of Judgment; Popular Religious Belief in Early New England* (New York: Alfred A Knopf, 1989), p. 124.

Chapter Four

A Woman of Great Industry:
Anne Hutchinson in New England

The year 1633 brought a time of serious study and decision-making for Anne Hutchinson. She found herself in the position of many Puritans who had no access to a pastor who preached the untainted Word: the minister upon whom she relied to preach the pure gospel had left England, and she was distraught at the thought of living without hearing the Word correctly preached. More and more she became convinced that this need was too critical to her spiritual well-being to be ignored, and she had to find a way to continue to hear John Cotton preach. She pored over her Bible, and a verse presented itself to her; she read: "Though the Lord give you the bread of adversity, and the water of affliction, yet shall not thy teachers be removed into a corner any more, but thine eyes shall see thy teachers."[1] Here she found reassurance that she would see her beloved mentor and teacher again. Studying further, another passage directed her to follow her teacher from the old Boston to the new: "He delivereth and rescueth, and he worketh signs and wonders in heaven and in earth, who hath delivered Daniel from the power of the lions."[2] She interpreted this to mean that God would guide and protect her if she were to follow Cotton across the ocean. She had found her answer from God, and she believed she had to go, and so she convinced her husband and family, and made plans to leave for New England. There is no way of knowing whether William had been as eager as she to leave England. What little is known about him suggests that it was Anne's powers of persuasion that directed the move, rather than a burning desire on his part. He seems to have been a quiet, respected, well-to-do merchant, apparently circumspect in his religious behavior, and a devoted husband to Anne Hutchinson.

Anne's reading of the scriptures apparently having carried the day, in the summer of 1634 the Hutchinson family, consisting of Anne, William, and six of their daughters and five of their sons sailed on the *Griffin* for the new Boston in Massachusetts Bay. While still in London and during the trip Anne spoke to a number of people of her firm belief that God would continue to reveal to her beforehand all important happenings just as He had directed her to come to New England. Assuming she meant that God would direct her through the scriptures, as He had already done, this claim was of course not unorthodox for a Puritan to make. However, The Reverend Mr. Simmes [or Symms] was on board ship with her, and later stated that he was shocked to hear her claim such beliefs. He noticed that a number of people gathered to hear her hold forth on biblical matters, and he was concerned. In September, after reaching Boston, William applied for and was admitted to membership in the Boston church without any fuss, but Mr. Simmes had relayed his hesitations about Anne, so she was forced to undergo additional questioning for a week.

During this time it must be assumed that her "revelations" from God were discussed among the clergy and laity in order to decide upon their orthodoxy, and were found to be acceptable, as after her questioning she too was accepted into the church at Boston in November. The matter of her claims to God's guidance and its discussion by the church at Boston should be kept in mind, as it was precisely the claim of divine guidance, made later at her civil trial, that was to cost her her case. At the civil trial Mr. Simmes was to rehearse once again his doubts as to Hutchinson's orthodoxy, and at that time the decision was to be that her claims bore witness to heresy. But, because the matter had already been aired at her request for church membership, where doctrinal orthodoxy would loom especially large, and discussed by the clergy and laity who undertook to analyze questions of doctrine raised by prospective members, the fact that it was later seized upon as evidence of heretical beliefs becomes much more obviously a last grasp at an available straw.

Once having been accepted into church membership, however, Anne Hutchinson seems to have fit into the community quite well, and she began working with the women of the town immediately. She used her knowledge of herbals to heal diseases and her skills at midwifery to come to the aid of women in childbed. John Cotton wrote of his favorable impression of her conduct at this time long after her trials, when his part in the trials was under assail, that she, "did much good in our Town, in woman's meeting at Childbirth-Travails, wherein she was not only skillful and helpful, but readily fell into good discourse with the women about their spiritual estates. And therein cleared it unto them, That the soul lying under a Spirit of Bondage, might see and sensibly feel the heinous guilt, and deep desert of sin ..." Cotton wrote in detail of her spiritual guidance to the women of the community, stressing that she taught a veritable catechism of instructions, exhortations to do good, and doctrinal clarification to the goodwives of the town. She was evidently quite thorough in her teaching of the finer points of doctrine, explaining to the women that, "the Soul might find some tastes and flashes of spiritual comfort in this estate, and yet never see or feel the need of Christ, much less attain any saving Union, or Communion with him, being no more but Legal work ...," as Cotton put it.[3] He stated approvingly that many women were enabled to come to an understanding of their sadly lacking spiritual condition through such explanations, and "were convinced, that they had gone on in a Covenant of Works, and were much shaken and humbled thereby, and brought to enquire more seriously after the Lord Jesus Christ ..." He was quite happy with this ministry of hers, and felt that her counsels agreed with what was taught from the pulpits of the area, so that, "these private conferences did well tend to water the seeds publicly sown." Furthermore, not only was he delighted to observe her capabilities, he claimed, but everyone else was equally pleased, and "blessed God for her fruitful discourses."[4] It seems that there had been a revival of sorts in the community shortly after the arrival of the renowned preacher, John Cotton in 1633. John Winthrop himself had been reawakened from a lethargic spiritual estate during that period, and was profusely thankful to the ministry of Cotton during that time. Cotton's ministry, he avowed, had awakened him from his, "drowsy state," and reenergized him.[5] However, a time of religious questioning and disinterest had been the aftermath of that exuberant time, and folks had begun to feel indifferent once again. The work of Anne Hutchinson was so well received by the ministers, then, as an antidote to the general lethargy and the dull assurance felt by many of the faithful by now. She awakened them to the need for further diligent soul-searching as to their spiritual estates, and this was—at first blush—welcomed by the clergy. However, as the time of aridity in spiritual matters wore on, some folks became embittered with their ministers. As Thomas Shepard was to report the problem, folks "care not for...that food which they find nourisheth them not."[6] It is probable that people who felt unhappy with their ministers' lack of spiritual guidance were drawn to hear Hutchinson.

Even with all her healing and spiritual community activities, however, she was criticized for remaining aloof from some of the social/religious gatherings in the community. She was admonished by Cotton for being unsociable and not attending meetings held in other women's homes for the purpose of discussing Sunday sermons. The result of this remonstrance was that shortly afterward she began to organize similar meetings in her home for women to discuss the sermons they had heard in church. Her reputation as an interesting speaker quickly grew, and soon she was compelled to add a meeting for men in addition to the one for women. Large numbers of both men and women attended the meetings, often sixty to eighty at a time, on Tuesdays and Thursdays. At the meetings Hutchinson would expound upon the sermons she had heard, and "prophesy," or give extemporaneous sermons of her own. In time a large portion of the membership of the Boston church came to listen to her and felt that her doctrinal teachings were compelling and persuasive. The central purpose of the meetings, to discuss the Sunday sermons, was not only considered acceptable of course but laudable and more and more people continued to come. At this point appears that no one criticized her for holding the meetings, and Cotton claimed that at this time not only was she his parishioner, but she was his "dear friend."[7]

It is apparent that Hutchinson was strong-willed, as well as enormously intelligent, with a quick mind and a retentive one, and unmistakably a charismatic speaker. She memorized scripture passages, and could quote the relevant ones for any occasion or to buttress any argument. Later at her trials she was able to refute the ministers' quotations with those of her own with amazing skill. In the records of the trials one reads of the ministers asking what verse she is quoting, but there is no instance where she does not recognize their quotes, whether or not citations are given. Even John Winthrop, who acted as chief judge and questioner at her civil trial, mentions her intelligence and her strength of purpose. Having grown up in a household where her father allowed himself to be silenced from preaching rather than preach something he did not believe, she too spoke her piece.

While Anne was doing good works in her home and in the wider community, William seems to have been quietly tending to business. He was very prosperous in his business as a mercer and was soon able to purchase a six-hundred acre farm as well. Because of his standing as one of the pillars of the community, he was designated by the title, Mr., and their son, Francis, was made a freeman at the age of fifteen. The general consensus about William persistently indicated that it was not he who had the strong opinions, expressed without reserve, but rather his wife, while William quietly stood by her. He does not seem ever to have engendered any harsh feelings. In fact, probably the only critical words spoken about him were those of Winthrop's when he declared that William was a man of "weak parts" who was "wholly led by his wife," and were no doubt uttered out of frustration at his inability to force Anne Hutchinson into proper womanly behavior.[8] This characterization of him as having "weak parts," however, is not as cutting a criticism as it sounds; Thomas Shepard was also described as having this disability. Edward Johnson's history of the colony states of Shepard that, "his natural parts were weak, but spent to the full."[9] Presumably it meant only that while he was not especially gifted, yet Shepard was able to overcome his deficiencies and become a well-respected preacher. It may also have meant that someone so described was not especially intellectual, or it may simply have meant that the person was quiet and rather meek in bearing. In any case, it was not the disparagement it sounds upon first hearing. William must have been highly respected in the colony, for he was elected deputy to the General Court, selectman, and appraiser. He would hardly have been elected to all of these different, influential offices unless the men of the community had been convinced of his judgment and good sense, so it is likely that it was his demeanor rather than his intelligence that was "weak."

With a husband well-respected in the community, a court deputy and a district court judge, Anne was parlaying her own considerable gifts into a position of more and more influence in the community. Her charisma and forcefulness of intellect, as well as her works of ministration and midwifery, were bolstered by her husband's wealth and social standing. In addition, during 1635 Anne Hutchinson's influence in the community was given a signal boost, as Boston was honored with a newcomer who was a rising star in England, the son of a powerful politician, and a man favored by the King as well, Henry Vane. Vane was the son of Sir Henry Vane and Darcy, Lady Vane. He had served in governmental capacities in London and Vienna before coming to Boston, as his father's standing had afforded him the opportunity to exercise his intellectual and administrative gifts. Born in 1613, Vane had become a Puritan in 1628 while at Oxford and like Winthrop he looked to the New World as a place where he could further demonstrate his capacities for administration in a setting that would be congenial to his beliefs. He was dashing, young and emotional, and probably for all these reasons he became quite a favorite with the people and was elected to serve a term in the governorship in 1636. He had also become interested in the meetings held at the home of Anne Hutchinson, and was so persuaded of her correctness in doctrinal matters that he added his political strength to her cause.

At some point, as her meetings were swelling with interested churchgoers, Hutchinson's prophesying began to take on a less happy tone. She began to criticize the clergy of the area for preaching doctrine that was not as completely Calvinistic as she wished. Their shortcomings, it would seem, had to do with their teaching that sanctification could be used as evidence of justification. As was noted earlier, the ministers were part of the leadership of the colony, and had begun to stress that proper behavior, good works and upright carriage, could be used by seekers for signs of regeneration as evidence that they were among the chosen few. They taught that good works, while not completely reliable signals of God's regenerating work in the soul, were strong indications. This had not been acceptable to Calvin, and it was not to John Cotton, nor was it tolerable to Anne Hutchinson. In her analyses of the local sermons she began to express disapproval of those whose Calvinism was found wanting.

An internal danger added to the growing tension in the community. Roger Williams, a minister at Salem, had been making more and more radical statements concerning church polity. Finally, he was considered such a menace to the public peace that he was banished from the colony. Williams's case paved the way in the community for Hutchinson's trials. His case had a bearing on her trials not only because he preceded her in his punishment for a similar crime, but also because he kept alive the claim that he had been punished for his beliefs or for "conscience sake." His claim that John Cotton and others had not dealt with him properly was echoed once again after Hutchinson's trials, and Cotton later became very defensive about his treatment of both of them. Further, Williams's and Hutchinson's doctrinal stances were similar to that of Cotton, and that was perceived by Cotton as particularly troublesome.

Williams was born in London sometime between 1599 and 1603, and was the son of a merchant tailor. He was a bright boy, and sometime before he went off to college, he was hired by Sir Edward Coke to take shorthand notes for Coke in the Star Chamber. Coke was one of the most celebrated jurists of his time, and his writings on civil law are some of the most important that have been written. The experience of working with him and studying his legal methods was invaluable to Williams later in his life, as it gave him a great deal of valuable training in the practical aspects of the law; it was to serve him well as he formulated his political theories after he was forced to move to Rhode Island. Some time after he had spent time taking notes for Coke and learning the ins and outs of various aspects of the law he was matriculated into Pembroke College, graduating in 1627. He was ordained in the Church of England, but later became a Puritan. A history of Rhode Island describes him as a, "warm-hearted, generous, earnest man of considerable charm, despite his perfectionist temperament. Modest, yet frank, he was unafraid of hardship, danger, or authority."[10] It would seem that he was personally attractive to others in spite of his propensity to follow any argument to its logical conclusion, and then insist that the conclusion must be validated by those who would claim to be logical. This insistence upon logical conclusions was another irritating personal characteristic he shared with Anne Hutchinson.

Williams came to Boston in 1631 and immediately sought to demonstrate to the leaders there that they ought to separate from the English church. When he arrived in Boston he was offered the position of minister in the church, but he rejected the offer. He did not feel he could accept it because he was not willing to remain in a church that would not separate itself completely from the church of England. Like Anne Hutchinson and John Cotton, Williams was in his doctrine essentially Augustinian, but unlike Cotton, he was able to brook no differences of opinion. Because he did not agree with Winthrop, Cotton, and the others, that it was enough to "purify" the church, he held that each congregation had to consist only of carefully certified believers, and be completely separate from and untainted by any unregenerates. He lived for two years in new Plymouth with the separatists there after he came to the new country but returned to Boston in 1633, and continued to cause difficulties for the magistracy with his ideas. He wrote disparaging comments about the king, and becoming pastor of the Salem church, he began to insist that such matters as swearing oaths were against God's commands. Such ideas were insupportable in Boston, as the colony could hardly afford to alienate the King, and preferred to keep a low profile in any case. Eventually he made efforts to have his church members write letters criticizing the other churches, and he expressed "opinions against the authority of magistrates."[11] For those opinions, he was banished in 1636.

Like Hutchinson after him, Williams seemed to be advocating a religious position unthinkable for those in charge of the religious stability of the colony. Although quite strident in his claims that the colony's churches must separate from the churches in England, Williams was able to retain friendships with several of the leaders of the Bay colony even after he had been banished and had left to found what was to become Rhode Island; this must be credited to his charismatic personality. Indeed, on some occasions he was to be useful to the colonies, a having become friendly with many of the Indian tribes including the Pequots he interceded for the colony from time to time.

Winthrop, Cotton, and other leaders of the colony believed themselves in a position to describe, structure, and set in place the intertwined ideal civil and ecclesiastical order that they had debated and envisioned for years. No doubt those discussions that had taken place in London in 1629 included many hopes for the possibility of an ideal commonwealth, and it is clear that the leaders of the colony continued to refine their ideas as they experienced the reality of their imaginings. One result of the religious revival that took place shortly after Cotton's coming to Boston was an opportunity for the new congregations to increase membership.

Further, for the ministers there were opportunities to gather and discuss model church arrangements as well as civil ones. They could now meet freely in regular discussion groups, and they could visit one another's churches, as they had not been able to do in England. Some of these men had been members of what was called "spiritual brotherhood," where they encouraged one another and insisted upon doctrinal teaching and behavior that conformed to their precepts.[12] This brotherhood, begun shortly after the turn of the century in England, gave them a method of supporting one another in their difficulties there, and also knit them together in doctrinal thinking. John Cotton had come to a knowledge of his sin through the preaching of William Perkins, and his influence had been responsible for the conversion of John Preston, one of the premier Puritans in England. Preston had later been instrumental in showing Thomas Shepard his need for conversion.[13] In other words, the Puritan ministers of New England had learned long since the value of interdependence in all things, both spiritual and secular. Now, their egos, their most dearly held beliefs, and their practical sense of proper order were given expression in this experimental hilltop city, not only in regard to a proper church order, indeed, but a proper civil order as well.

Not only their egos and religious beliefs were involved in defining the ideal state of course; influential Puritans had been involved in dialogue leading to definition of the ideal state in England before they had come to the New World. Assumptions made regarding the appropriate combination of the intrusion of secular authority into the religious realm and the genesis of secular authority had been central to their dialogue with the Kings of England. Many well-known and well-read Puritans concerned themselves with parliamentary discussions of the limits of secular power and its derivation during the decades shortly before large numbers of them migrated to Massachusetts Bay. Such discussions necessarily included consideration of questions of the relationship of church and state, as well as the derivation of the authority of law, and the limits of the obligation of citizens to obey the law. These discussions had shaped their understanding of how a commonwealth is imbued with proper authority, but it also molded their sense of to what lengths a citizen is compelled to go in obedience to the law. Williams, having worked for Sir Edward Coke, who was the great champion of common law in Parliament, was well aware of the understanding that had driven Puritans within Parliament to state that the citizen must be allowed to obey a higher law when necessary.[14]

All of them were aware that they were creating a new type of commonwealth, in that they recognized that their laws and customs must be tempered to fit the new environment in which they found themselves. Yet, although they knew that circumstances must to some extent dictate their responses, and although they had accepted in England that each person must obey a higher law than that of the land or the King, they insisted upon conformity among the colony community from fear of disorder and even annihilation. Thus, in some ways Williams posed a greater threat to the establishment than Hutchinson was to do: he was educated, in law as well as theology, and could argue law and political theory as well as doctrine with the best of them. Hutchinson of course was not formally educated nor could she have hoped to become a member of the clergy or serve in any other capacity of leadership other than the one she chose, as a lay leader in her church. She could not and did not argue political theory; she might have fared better if she had. Williams's education was unusual, because he had had the opportunity to work with Coke at the time the place of the common law was under discussion, and had begun to formulate ideas of proper polity that he would later expand in Rhode Island. Williams's ideas seemed horrifying to the leaders of Boston at the time, and some, such as the suggestion that Christians should not swear an oath, do not seem convincing now. Nevertheless, he was articulate and persuasive, and had the ear of men of power back in England.

Further, Williams had standing in the community, and because of his charismatic personality, he had a certain cachet among the people. Thomas Hooker stated that Williams was banished because of his "divers new and dangerous opinions against the authority of magistrates" and for defaming both the magistrates and the churches.[15] He could however have presented a much stronger challenge to the little community, had he wished: he might have tried to stay in the colony and build an opposition church using as a nucleus those members of his church that agreed with him. He did not try to muster his own church because of his strong beliefs that a church must only be assembled from among the true saints, which made for difficulty in gathering together such a church. (Eventually the logic of his position was to lead him to believe that he could be sure of the spiritual purity of no larger congregation than himself and his wife. Even then, while he noted the problems therein, he did not stray from his logic.) That Williams did not attempt to gather his own new church must have been a great relief to Winthrop, Cotton, and the others in leadership of the colony.

The threat that Williams held for the community undoubtedly increased the perception of a colony under siege from within, and therefore set the stage for the harsh reaction to Anne Hutchinson. Having felt forced to deal with Williams, the community was all the more skittish when it came time to deal with Hutchinson. John Cotton was especially threatened by Williams, and then by Hutchinson in her turn. Cotton had perceived Williams as a danger to the public peace just as Winthrop did, and corresponded with Williams before his banishment and for seventeen years afterward about the issues. Cotton was none too kind to Williams in his actions or in the letters he wrote him, and the letters back and forth were later published with Williams's help, showing Cotton in a poor light. When Williams complained, for instance, of having been sent out into the wilderness during a particularly hard winter, Cotton replied shortly that he had been given plenty of time to ready himself for removal. Later when Williams defended freedom of conscience from the interference of the state, Cotton spelled out his belief that the state was an arm of God, and had the right to persecute beliefs if a person had been dealt with by the church and refused to accept their understanding of doctrine.[16]

Williams and Cotton exchanged diatribes for some years, beginning with letters from Cotton to Williams, since lost, leading into books published by Williams. The books are gnarled and labyrinthine dialogues with a personification of Cotton's position arguing with a personification of Williams's position. The feelings must have run deep, for John Cotton, Jr., a minister like his father, wrote a bitter letter to Williams long after the death of John Cotton Sr. The animosity of the senior Cotton and Williams, cloaked in loving terms of Christian endearment, seems to stem from the fact that each recognized the other as a foe worth fighting. For while ministers such as Hooker and Shepard were able to win the battle of correct theology during the Antinomian Crisis, and to shape Cotton to their system of conversion process, Williams fought Cotton on his own side, and was far more of a personal thorn to Cotton.

Williams like Anne Hutchinson was a threat to Cotton because he argued from the same side of the theological battle as Cotton. He was a threat because his arguments like those of Hutchinson demonstrated where the logic of Cotton's dogma led. Perry Miller, in his biography of Williams, claims: "Like Mrs. Hutchinson, Williams expected Cotton to live up to the vision he imparted to his followers. Cotton failed Williams, as the next year he also failed Anne Hutchinson; hence forth the very existence of these two was for him a standing rebuke."[17]

Williams like Cotton (and of course like Hutchinson) believed in humankind's utter depravity. It was the fact of Williams's willingness to follow the logic of his theology that pointed most starkly to John Cotton's inability to do so. Williams, in other words, made Cotton appear to be not only a hypocrite but a coward. That is why he was such a thorn in Cotton's side.[18] The differences and likenesses of the theology of Williams in respect to their treatment of Christ's kingdom demonstrate the core of their differences, as the particular typology followed by each man was the pivotal point of his doctrine.[19]

Cotton saw the history of the salvation story as unchanged from the Old Testament, when the Covenant of Works had been established, to the New Testament, when the prophesies had been fulfilled through Christ and his redeeming work. Williams, however, saw Christ's act of redemption as having completely refocussed the picture, and changed it fundamentally.[20] Thus Williams was arguing with Cotton that the typology of the Old Testament was inapplicable in the present, as it had nothing to do with the new dispensation under which humankind was now living. He was impatient with Cotton because he believed that the logic of Cotton's own doctrine should have led him to the same conclusion. Cotton's debate with Williams was an attempt to convince Williams, and possibly himself, that he had not abandoned his Augustinian underpinnings, to insist that his convictions had not really changed. Williams, recognizing the size of the chasm between the two doctrinal systems, was frustrated and disgusted with Cotton's attempts. Hence the rancor of the two men; and, hence the anxiety that Williams caused Cotton by his continuance of the debate.

Williams also argued with Cotton on another matter rather close to Cotton's heart: the rights of the ministry. Williams argued that ministers should not give evangelical sermons. Following Calvin's logic that those who will be saved have been predestined from the beginnings of time, it was wholly unnecessary to preach that anyone should do anything at all, even put him or herself into an attitude of submission or acceptance. The person who will be saved will be no matter what the attitude of heart, and there is nothing an individual can do, nor could or should the clergy.[21] Further, since any church was supposed to be made up of believers, it made no sense at all to preach of the necessity of salvation to those who were already saved. This was literally "preaching to the converted." Williams wrote later of his disagreement with Cotton, stating that,

> Now then that man that professeth to feed a Flock or Church, with the Ordinances of Word and Prayer, he must needs acknowledge that his proper work is not to preach for conversion, which is most preposterous among a converted Christian people...the Pastor's work is to feed his Flock, Acts. 20. and prophecy [preaching] is not for unbe{li}evers, but for them that believe, to edify, exhort and comfort the Church, I Cor. 14.3. 22.[22]

This proposition made perfect sense if one followed Calvin's strict doctrine of predestination to its logical end, but it is not difficult to see why it presented a problem to Cotton. Before John Cotton adopted the "plain style" he had been ambivalent about doing so, because he valued the plaudits he received for his quotation-studded preaching. For the rest of his life he was considered one of the masters of preaching. For Williams to claim that Cotton's special providence, that of sermonizing, was for the most part unnecessary, even worse, illogical, must have been extraordinarily galling to Cotton.

Anne Hutchinson was not a trained theologian, although it is clear from the subtle arguments she made at her two trials that she could easily have been. Williams of course was, and years after both he and Hutchinson had been banished from the Bay Colony he was able to find publishers to make public his debate with Cotton. From the time in 1635 when Williams was banished, however, Williams argued with Cotton over a particular point which especially rankled with Cotton, and which was addressed again and again by Cotton, Winthrop and others who saw its importance both to the banishment of Williams and of Hutchinson: what was called, "persecution for conscience." Because Williams understood the importance and the arguments concerning the question, he was particularly dangerous to Cotton: and Cotton knew it. Williams was not only a fellow believer who had followed the reasoning of the doctrine to its logical conclusion, he was also able to describe the particular weaknesses in Cotton's position.

Williams argued that it was unlawful for Christians to be yoked with unbelievers in any way, especially in the churches. That is why he passionately contended that the Boston church should separate itself from the Church of England. If the Boston church was not constituted as a parish church, but was made up only of those who could describe their conviction of having had a conversion experience, then it should not be yoked in any way with a church that was made up of any who lived in a particular geographical area. That position cost him the pulpit of the Boston church, and it rankled with Cotton, because it touched upon an inconsistency in Cotton's theology. Neither Cotton nor the other ministers of the Colony were separatists, but for the other ministers, the reasons for not separating were more logical. The other ministers did not argue as strongly as Cotton that people were totally unable to effect any part of their own salvation. So, for them the issue of separation from churches that were not as pure as his was not such a burning one. In a parish church, it could be argued, each seeker after eternal salvation could attempt to work out her or his own salvation. In a church composed entirely of those to whom God had granted grace, though, there was reason to keep apart from parish churches, and remain wholly pure. For Cotton, who preached so clearly that men and women were utterly unable to participate in their sanctification before their conversion, the matter was of great importance. There could be no middle ground, and no ground on which to argue that true churches ostensibly made up of believers could be linked with parish churches.

Moreover, Williams asserted further that no one could be banished for conscience sake, because to do so would be to arrogate unto human understanding the right of God alone to search the heart of the believer.23 The question of persecution for conscience was a real one, for Lord Saye and Sele was to raise it when he heard of the banishments of Williams and Hutchinson. Hutchinson too raised it during her trial, in answering a question from Winthrop, claiming that she could not be penalized for, "conscience sake," and Winthrop agreed with her that a belief which was a matter of conscience was not to be a matter for punishment.24

Cotton like John Calvin before him had a creative answer to the question of persecution for the sake of conscience. He believed that only conscience "rightly informed" is protected. When the conscience of the seeker does not rightly understand the true religion, it must be coerced to do so.25 Hutchinson was unable to win her trial, but Williams made the point for himself and for all time since. He is held to be the father of the tenet that no one should be persecuted for conscience sake, as he was indeed able to set up the state of Rhode Island on that basis and to argue the point successfully in England. He posed a serious threat to Cotton, then, even before he published his arguments against Cotton's position in 1644.

Quite clearly Williams had posed a major problem for the colony in 1636 when he was banished and that difficulty had been recognized by the clergy and magistrates in the colony at the time. The fear of a serious split in the community strengthened the concern over the hazard of schism when Anne Hutchinson came along. Cotton and the others were more than ready to destroy, root and branch, any new such situations, more especially if they resembled Williams's vexatious thinking in any way.

As Hutchinson's popularity and her differences with the majority of the clergy came to be recognized by the leadership of the colony, then, they were already inoculated with fear of social disruption or possibly disintegration, and they reacted extremely strongly to the threat. Williams had been banished from the colony and had gone to Rhode Island fairly easily, preferring to leave rather than to contaminate himself with their insufficiently pure thinking. It is likely that Hutchinson had not thought the logic of her position through to the extent of wishing to separate herself from them. She desired to stay in the colony and purge the churches of their inadequately consistent Calvinistic doctrines. Winthrop, Cotton, and the others had already seen that the dissenter who was not rooted out could be extremely dangerous to the civil peace. It did not occur to them of course that they might simply allow another, different church to be a part of the colony. They did not see any reason for separating the powers of the state from the doings of the church: they considered it to be perfectly logical to have a trial for sedition in which the charge was libel against the clergy or magistracy. They had no intention of letting what to them was heresy or threat of schism go unpunished.

In addition, they saw the banishment of Williams as having had good results. Williams went quietly to found Rhode Island, and while he was to cause them embarrassment in subsequent years, they did not yet know that. So, they felt quiet confident that the best possible course of action when dealing with a heretic or schismatic was to expel her or him from the colony. The experience that they had recently had with Williams's effects in the colony, which had been quite negative, had lent itself to a feeling that they had to be as severe and quick as possible in amputating the offending member of the church and cauterizing the wound.

For these reasons Hutchinson walked into a much more combustible situation than she realized when she began to criticize the ministers and their doctrine. Cotton, too, was rather uncomfortable with the situation. Williams had singled out some possibly illogical theological thinking on Cotton's part, and he had also acted as a personal demonstration that any Christian who did not conform to the educated, thoughtful decision of the majority as to correct doctrine posed a serious threat to the community. Thus, when Hutchinson began to be viewed by the leaders of the colony as a menace to the stability of the status quo, Cotton was: a. primed to act severely; b. annoyed that his logic had been assailed; and c. aware of the necessity for agreement among all the clergy as to what was acceptable orthodoxy. Williams had created a hazard for her that she could not have expected, and he caused Cotton to act in ways that she could not have foreseen.

Indeed, all of the leaders of the community were becoming more and more nervous about dissent. It must be remembered that these folk had only had experience with governments that demanded behavioral conformity. To their way of thinking and experience it was expected that any government would seek to enforce its will on anyone perceived as a trouble-maker. They felt that they were not unreasonable in expecting some conformity of those God had placed under them; that is what governments were for. They all expected the government to do so, and felt it good that the government should uphold the right. Cotton would later write, "Though the peace of the country or commonwealth be civil and human, yet it is distracted and cut off by disturbing the spiritual purity and peace of the church."26 The situation in which they found themselves only exacerbated this expectation; the colony was in its infancy, and in precari-ous straits economically—if not in dire straits any longer, a poor harvest could change things quickly—so those who had been put in place to govern did not hesitate to demand conformity. Further, in this fledgling colony the clergy with their status in the community were of necessity a force for cohesion: in fact the clergy were of paramount importance to the colony. They were highly educated, with libraries of books, and could read the Greek and Hebrew needed to fully understand the Bible. They were the ones who could expound the all-important way of salvation to the rest. For this reason they were held in high respect by the rest of the settlers.27

Because of their ecclesiastical influence, which derived from their ability to study and rightly interpret the scriptures, and also from the importance of their preaching to the community as it disseminated the way of salvation to the masses, the clergy held great power in the community, and were expected to use this power for the public good. Clergy were well paid at the time, and had exceptionally high social standing, as befitted men of such special gifts to the community. The ministers of the colony met in weekly "consociations" to discuss both civil and theological matters, and these meetings promoted both unity among the clergy and a perception of them as special, an "order of society separate from the laity and united to one another through their shared vocation."28

Although the colony's ministers were not allowed to hold public office, they were called upon to interpret the theological significance of the decisions made by the magistrates, and thus in a sense had a kind of veto power over such decisions. For, if a judicial decision were declared to be unbiblical in that situation, it simply could not stand. It was absolutely necessary for the clergy and the civil powers to work together. "It became their job to keep order among the various congregations, to instruct men in their duty toward the state as well as toward God, and perhaps most importantly, to lead the congregation in deciding what persons were eligible for membership in the larger corporation," notes Kai Erickson in his sociological study of the Antinomian Controversy. Erickson holds three men to be the most influential in Boston at that time: John Winthrop, John Cotton, and John Wilson.29 Winthrop had been governor, although he was not at the time that Hutchinson's claims that some of the ministers were not preaching the pure covenant of grace began to be a concern to the ministers. Wilson "ruled the congregation with a loyal eye toward the needs of the magistracy," while Cotton taught doctrine.30

To further complicate this need for orthodoxy to help sustain social stability, a political threat from England arose at this time, in the form of attempts to "reduce the colony's independence" by changing their charter and the political liberties they had.31 A man considered unacceptable to the leaders of the nearby colony at Plymouth had attempted to settle there, which resulted in a feud in which the intruder was killed. In spite of discipline meted out to those who had killed the man, Winthrop and others feared that Lord Saye and Sele, who had employed the deceased man might take action against their charter. Clearly, it was a time of disquiet, in which Anne Hutchinson was to find herself enmeshed. For shortly after Roger Williams was banished from the colony, Hutchinson herself was to be the subject of inquiries.

Notes

1. Hall, *Antinomian,* p. 337.

2. Ibid., p. 338.

3. Ibid., p. 412.

4. Ibid., pp. 412–13.

5. Morgan, *Dilemma*, p. 137.

6. Quoted in Hall, *Antinomian*, p. 15.

7. Ibid., p. 413.

8. Quoted in Battis, p. 12.

9. Quoted in Edmund S. Morgan, *Builders of the Bay Colony* (Boston and New York: Houghton Mifflin Co., 1930), p. 112.

10. William G. McLoughlin, *Rhode Island: A Bicentennial History* (New York: W.W. Norton, 1978), p. 6.

11. Ibid., p. 8.

12. David D. Hall discusses the brotherhood and its impact on the cohesiveness of the Puritan ministry in, *The Faithful Shepherd: A History of the New England Ministry in the Seventeenth Century* (Chapel Hill: University of North Carolina Press), pp. 49-51.

13. Ibid., p. 50.

14. Ralph Barton Perry, *Puritanism and Democracy* (New York: The Vanguard Press, 1944), p. 182.

15. Quoted in Leon Howard, "The Puritans in Old and New England" in *Essays of Puritans and Puritanism, by Leon Howard*, ed. James Barbour and Thomas Quirk (Albuquerque: University of New Mexico Press, 1986), p. 101.

16. Cotton claimed in a letter to Williams, "the civil magistrate, whether Christian or pagan, may, and ought to ... be able to judge, though not of all questions, yet of capital offenses against religion ..." Irwin H. Polishook, *Roger Williams, John Cotton and Religious Freedom: A Controversy in New and Old England* (Englewood Cliffs, NJ: Prentice-Hall, Inc., 1967), p. 80.

17. Miller, *Williams*, p. 76.

18. I call upon Jesper Rosenmeier's useful insights into the theology of the two men, and the reasons for their strong feelings about one another, in, "The Teacher and the Witness: John Cotton and Roger Williams" in *William and Mary Quarterly*, 3rd ser., 25, (1968), pp. 412–431.

19. Ibid., pp. 413 f.

20. Ibid.

21. Edmund S. Morgan, *Roger Williams: The Church and the State* (New York: Harcourt Brace and World, 1967), pp. 40–42.

22. Ibid, p. 41.

23. The tortuous arguments of Williams on this point and that of the separation of true churches are found in Rosenmeier, "Witness," pp. 112–156.

24. Hall, *Antinomian*, pp. 312, 313.

25. Polishook, p. 72.

26. Ibid., p. 99.

27. Stout, p. 27.

28. Stephen Foster, "English Puritanism and the Progress of New England Institutions, 1630–1660," in *Saints and Revolutionaries: Essays on Early American History,* ed. David D. Hall, John Murrin, Thad W. Tate (New York: W. W. Norton and Co., 1984), p. 11.

29. Erickson, p. 75.

30. Ibid.

31. Ronald Cohen, "Church and State in Seventeenth Century Massachusetts: Another Look at the Antinomian Controversy," in *Puritan New England: Essays on Religion, Society, and Culture,* ed. Alden T. Vaughan, and Francis J. Bremer (New York: St. Martin's Press, 1977), pp. 177–78.

Chapter Five

"Outrageous Opinions":
Events Leading To The Trials

In the fall of 1636, shortly after Roger Williams was sent away, Anne Hutchinson's brother-in-law, John Wheelwright, came to town, and she used her growing popularity and influence on his behalf. Wheelwright had the distinction of being the only minister other than John Cotton that she felt preached a clear gospel of grace. Not even John Wilson, although minister of the church at Boston, was found acceptable by her, and she made known to those who gathered at her house her opinion of the deficiencies of the clergy in the area. Wheelwright though, married to her sister Mary, had passed her scrutiny and been found to preach the pure gospel. He had been the minister at Bilby, near Alford, where Anne and William had lived in England. When John Cotton had not been available, Anne and William had gone on occasion to hear him preach. It is not clear why they did not join his church, but rather traveled to Boston to hear John Cotton, but perhaps Wheelwright was not quite up to Cotton's caliber of sermonizing. It may be, though, that Wheelwright was one source of ideas that inspired Anne and caused her to become so sure of the correctness of her own views. As soon as he arrived in Boston, Wheelwright's proximity became a source of problems, however. Hutchinson began to suggest to those who came to hear her hold forth upon the ministers' sermons that John Wilson was not especially able, nor did he preach the gospel of grace sufficiently clearly, certainly not as well as Cotton or Wheelwright.

Her weekly meetings had by now swelled to the point at which large numbers of the members of the Boston church sided with her in calling the rest of the clergy of the colony teachers of the covenant of works. Hutchinson agreed completely with Cotton's assertion that "the indwelling not only of the Gifts of the Holy Ghost, but of his Person also in the Regenerate" was "an holy Truth of God."[1] From this followed the claim that ministers who did not clearly preach this distinction were teaching, and in fact were living in the old Adamic covenant of works, and not teaching or living in the all-important covenant of grace, thus essentially consigning them and theirs to hell. Followers of Hutchinson then began to spread their general dissatisfaction with the clergy by visiting other churches in the area, and making "much disturbance by public questions and objections to their doctrines..."[2] Winthrop had strong objections to women's asserting themselves in what he felt was a man's world, and John Cotton had written in his work having to do with church discipline (1634) that any man could ask questions during the church service, after the sermon, but women were not to do so. They were to be quiet. Undoubtedly, the fact that it was a woman, not a man, who raised the hue and cry about the covenant of "works" must have made it more difficult for the men in charge to deal with.

However, the problem was larger than annoyance about the sex of the leader of the group of dissidents. For it was not simply the overheated imaginations of Hutchinson's followers that led to the perception that John Cotton's teachings were indeed different from those of the pastor of the church, John Wilson, a much less gifted man. Cotton had been asked to become the teacher of the church on the basis of his substantial talents as a preacher, and Wilson was neither the scholar nor the preacher that Cotton was. Larzer Ziff points out that the congregation noted differences between Cotton and Wilson quite early on, with Wilson faring poorly by comparison. He writes, "there was no discrete point at which the congregation rejected Wilson's ministry, but gradually signs emerged that Mr. Wilson was in far less favor because of the content as well as the manner of his preaching."[3] Wilson was a bit younger than Cotton, having been born in 1588, and like Cotton attended Cambridge for his education. His disposition was rather choleric, and he did not suffer slights easily. However, he had his engaging side, as when he was told upon one public occasion that all men loved him, and he replied that he loved each and every one of them, too. Yet he does seem to have been quite inflexible and unable to comprehend even slightly what motivated Anne Hutchinson.

One incident that sheds light on some of his problems took place during his early years in the colony. He had come to the New World by himself, as did many of the men, with the intention of returning to England to bring his wife over if things worked out well. His wife, however, refused to be persuaded to leave England for several years. John Winthrop's wife, Margaret, was amazed at her behavior. She wrote to Winthrop, Jr. "Mr. Wilson cannot yet persuade his wife to go, for all that he hath taken pains to come and fetch her. I marvel what mettle she is made of. Sure she will yield at last."[4] Wilson did not have much luck dealing with women, and his limitations in doing so may well have hindered his ability to deal with Anne

Hutchinson when she became a member of his church. He seems always to have reacted rather than acted, and he did not react well to Anne Hutchinson. Hutchinson had now become so determined that she had to point out the shortcomings of the ministers that she encouraged her followers to chide any and all of the ministers they found deficient. Not only did they criticize, but at one point she even led a group of women out of the church service in protest against what she perceived as Wilson's inadequacies. Such treatment would have been irritating for any minister, and it pointed the attention of the clergy to Anne Hutchinson.

Another minister, Thomas Shepard, whose reputation has lived on after him almost as grandly as that of John Cotton, had become disturbed about the situation in the Boston church; he deduced that it was Cotton's teachings that were at the root of the problem. He had heard John Cotton preach, and felt that his doctrines were not sufficiently clear to his congregation, causing them to draw unorthodox conclusions from him. He wrote to Cotton, asking for an explanation. Having learned of Anne Hutchinson's claims about the clergy, he saw the connection between Anne Hutchinson, troublemaker and John Cotton, teacher. Shepard was very worried about the effects of this woman who could convene a goodly number of the members of the church at Boston in her home, and exhort them to mistrust the wholesome teachings of the ministers of the colony.

Shepard was younger than Winthrop and Cotton, having been born on November 5, 1605, to the daughter of a grocer, and a grocer's apprentice. Evidently he must have been especially bright, as his schoolmaster saw to it that he had enough schooling to prepare him for studies at the university, and facilitated his admittance as an indigent scholar at Emmanuel College, Cambridge, in 1620. He received his degree in 1627, and served in the dioceses of London and York. Shepard came to the colony in 1635, and became the pastor of the New Town [Cambridge] church. The gathering of that church was of great importance for the colony, as it became the model for the founding of all subsequent congregations.

Shepard had become so convinced that Hutchinson was a serious threat to the clergy that he applied his initiative to stamp out what he believed were the unwholesome propensities of the Hutchinsonians. He preached against them with much vigor, persuading at least one man, Edward Johnson, of the serious consequences of agreement with Hutchinson. Johnson had originally come to Boston in 1630, and after ascertaining that the colony was the best place for a man of his beliefs to rear his family, he returned to England to bring them back with him. When he returned, however, he found that Boston was in a turmoil, with the two clear-cut factions behaving with great enmity and lack of Christian charity toward one another. His friends on each side of the controversy tried to convince him of the rightness of their side, but he could not see clearly that either side had the right. Praying fervently, he went to services, and heard Shepard preach passionately against the Hutchinsonians, which enabled him to make up his mind that Shepard and the rest of his group were correct. Johnson was an important man for Shepard and the rest to have on their side of the issue, as he was later to write a history of the times, which has become one of the prominent documents of the period.

Shepard has been called, "the young minister of the church in Cambridge, and next to Cotton, the finest theologian and most effective preacher in the Bay," and he was now very concerned about Cotton.[5] Winthrop had corresponded with him earlier about Cotton, sending him a draft of a letter to be sent to Cotton detailing Cotton's shortcomings in theology. Shepard however wrote to Winthrop that he had better look to his own theological discrepancies, for Cotton would make short work of them if he did not. Winthrop did not send the letter.[6] Shepard himself then corresponded with Cotton, however, asking him to reply to questions about his doctrine. His questions make it clear that he harbored doubts about Cotton's orthodoxy, as they include the statement, "for I do willingly consent thus far with you," implying that he could not go further than that particular point to which he referred, and insisted Cotton clarify the rest of his claims.[7] The questions Shepard raised with Cotton dealt with the ability of a person to delude himself as to his spiritual condition, that is, to misunderstand the voice of the Holy Spirit assuring them of their salvation should they believe they had heard it. He also warned him that some of this congregation, "may do your people and ministry hurt, before you know it..."[8] Cotton answered the request with thanks for Shepard's concern for his well-being, but his answers reflect the assurance and confidence of the older divine to the younger. "I do not conceive, that any man can truly lay hold of a saving Promise, till he lay hold of Christ, and so the promise never faileth him, nor his taking hold of it."[9]   Peter Bulkely, minister at Concord, also wrote to Cotton during the middle of 1636 with his concerns, claiming that "union with Christ" takes place after the believer has been given faith by God. Cotton replied to this, "The Spirit of God sent into the Soul worketh Faith, That is the Union."[10] Once again his unequivocal answers give evidence of his confidence in his own reasoning, and not incidentally, his complete agreement with answers Anne Hutchinson was to make in her trials.

As a first step in the process of determining what connections could be found between Hutchinson, Wheelwright, and Cotton, a meeting was called in October, with Anne Hutchinson, Cotton, John Wheelwright, and the ministers. At this meeting Cotton was surprised to hear that there was any dissatisfaction with either his preaching or the members of his church, which indicates how isolated Cotton had allowed himself to become, spending his life studying as he did. The result of the meeting, though, was that Cotton apparently used his ability to see both sides of any question. In any case, the ministers went away satisfied that Cotton had shown his agreement that sanctification was indeed useful in indicating justification.[11]

But the result of the meeting for Hutchinson was to strengthen her belief that she could continue to direct some of the town's events. By now she had such a numerous and influential following that she decided to move on behalf of her brother-in-law. She was able to convince her followers that Wheelwright should be named an assistant teacher to the Boston congregation. Thus John Wilson, pastor of the church, having not long before had to accept the acclaimed John Cotton to be the teacher of the church, was now to be embarrassed by the suggestion that yet another minister of the Word was needed. John Winthrop, realizing the danger, mounted an effort to thwart the new appointment, tactfully arguing only that Wheelwright was not needed at the Boston church, as the congregation was already provided with two good ministers. Cotton was not much help, as he managed to argue on both sides of the question at one time or another, but Winthrop's judicious intervention carried the day, and Wheelwright was sent to a congregation at Mount Wollaston, ten miles from Boston. One of the primary methods used in New England at the time to settle differences was discussion at meetings. Whether from theological conviction that consensus enabled them to arrive at truth, or from a realization that cooperation encouraged fewer hard feelings, this method for dealing with difficulties was to serve them well on many occasions. And so they attempted to use this means to deal with the situation, with the result that all the ministers of the area had come to town to discuss the matter, and they of course sided with Wilson, who had felt terribly threatened by the attempt to install Wheelwright at his church.

Although Wheelwright was thus forced to go to another congregation, the incident demonstrated Anne Hutchinson's political strength: she "could gather almost the entire congregation to her defense, while Wilson was left in a painfully insecure position."[12] Once again Boston was divided over the issue, with most of the membership of the Boston congregation on Hutchinson's side. Wheelwright was to continue to be vocal in the affairs at Boston, however, and his high profile did not help his sister-in-law.

Now the situation was intensifying for Anne Hutchinson. She and her followers had become so strident that some of them were disrupting services at churches where they felt the gospel was not clearly preached. Given that John Cotton was her teacher and the fount of her wisdom, a wise next step seemed to be to determine his position *vis-à-vis* Hutchinson. To that end,

Cotton was called to explain his theology, to discover whether his teachings were at the root of hers. In November of 1636, the ministers of the colony gave Cotton a list of questions to answer, to determine exactly where he stood on the issues. They gave him sixteen questions to answer in writing, in order to convince them whether or not his preaching was orthodox; Thomas Shepard drew up the list of questions. The questions were aimed at clarifying whether Hutchinson's teachings had, as she claimed, come from Cotton's, and in addition whether Cotton taught a gospel and system of conversion that was consonant with their teachings, or deviated from theirs in critical respects.

It was of course the case that each minister preached according to his understanding of doctrine, and each differed from the others in some respects. Hooker's sermons used figurative language that evoked images of home and family while stressing the need for repentance. Shepard's laid emphasis on sanctification and righteous behavior. Cotton's were strongly logical and emphasized justification, and the need to be wary of having a false sense of security based on seeming sanctification. Cotton's earlier change in delivery of sermons to the plain style was a result of his belief that the logic of the theology was the heart of the matter that must be emphasized in his sermons, rather than the style of articulation. He was convinced that it was logic rather than emotional appeals or erudite presentations that would turn the heart and mind of the sinner toward thoughts of God. Indeed, it was his rigorous Calvinistic logic that had attracted and held the respect of Anne Hutchinson for so many years.

The great question that was being forced on Puritan clergy in New England, and one that was never definitively answered, was to what extent differences in theology must be allowed, and how to define the point at which the line of heterodoxy had been crossed. This process was a frustrating struggle whenever it was undertaken because the problem originated in the doctrine. Purity was felt to be necessary by definition, and thus its parameters must be clearly delineated. Yet, since each soul was individually responsible to God, and each minister was expected to struggle toward his greater understanding of the scriptures without a written platform of beliefs to guide him, each would as a matter of course arrive at varying interpretations of dogmas. How much variation was within acceptable limits was thus a question that constantly lay under the surface of all ministerial discussions of the faith. One advantage that the clergy in New England had available to them was their consociation meetings. As they met often to discuss their common trials and efforts, and to exchange views of doctrine, they were enabled to keep their differences within bounds while they simultaneously built feelings of fraternity. It was also a vehicle for the clergy to use in solidifying their political influence in the colony, as the more they agreed to work together and acted in unison, the more strongly would their weight in the community be felt. For these reasons it was imperative that Cotton's teachings be scrutinized, and if necessary, brought into line with the teachings of the other ministers.

Cotton had always felt that individual differences in teaching were to be weighed according to their centrality of doctrine, and where they were peripheral, to be allowed. He was not overly worried about minor disparities, and in fact prided himself on his tolerance for other clergy. It appears that he did not have as strong a sense as the others did of the ways in which theological purity was tied to community cohesiveness; his tolerant attitude, had it been shared by the rest of the leaders of the community, or had he had the fortitude to stand up to the rest of them when they insisted on his and Hutchinson's agreement with their understanding of orthodoxy, would undoubtedly have prevented the rather pathetic and tragic outcomes of the Hutchinson trials.

In addition to his willingness to tolerate variations in doctrine, moreover, he was also willing to listen to the viewpoints of others, and where indicated, be persuaded that he should change his thinking. His flexibility in this regard was as useful to him, yet it led the other ministers to suspect him as time went by. He believed that each should be guided by the collective wisdom of all, which added to his impatience with Hutchinson during her church trial, when she refused to declare herself persuaded until she was shown irrefutable logic of a position differing from her own. Cotton, however, was to prove so flexible that he was to reverse his positions completely after being persuaded by the other clergy that it would be wise to do so. By November, 1636, however, he merely wished to tolerate differences of others and have his views be conceded as well. So his answers to the questions clearly laid out his beliefs, which were much more insistent on the logically Calvinist position that a person could not trust in his own righteous behavior as evidence of justification.

The list of questions answered by Cotton at this time is of interest, as it mirrors some of the questions asked of Anne Hutchinson at her church trial. The questions revolved around the justification/sanctification issue. The first eight questions dealt with the "seal of the spirit," its meaning and function. The next six raised issues of definitions of and functions of sanctification, and the last two were miscellaneous questions about the use of reason and spiritual mercies. As Hutchinson was questioned about the seal and sanctification, Cotton's answers reflect the extent to which she drew upon and agreed with his teachings. Cotton declared that, although some of the ministers might think he had stated otherwise, there is only one seal of the spirit, which is "the Witness of the Spirit itself." He recognized that some meant by the term, the "seal of the spirit," sanctification, others meant the witnessing of the spirit to the soul that the soul was regenerated. He acknowleged that both functions were undertaken by the spirit, but the meaning of the term was only the speaking of the Holy Spirit to the soul. This witness both "regenerateth and reneweth our spirits; and ... comforteth us with evident assurance of our Adoption, Rom. 8. 16."[13]

The question of his belief on the subject of the seal was no doubt raised relative to three concerns. The first has to do with the spirit speaking immediately, or without mediation, to the soul; the second has to do with the chronolgy of sanctification with respect to justification, the third has to do with what the "seal" means, and how many seals there are. Cotton addressed all those questions in his answer that there is only one seal, and it is the witness of the Holy Spirit to the believer that she or he is among the regenerate, and that this happens first, before any sanctification is possible. He went so far as to state unequivocally, "full settled comfort he [the believer] cannot take, nor rest in, till it be witnessed to him by the spirit." Indeed, "the Testimony of the Spirit is so clear, as that it may witness immediately, though not without some work of Christ in a man."[14] The seal of the spirit, then, is the word of the spirit bearing witness to the believer's soul that she or he is among the elect; and this is done without intermediary, directly to the soul, before any sanctification is possible, a position to be echoed by Hutchinson later.

In regard to questions about sanctification, he said that it is only the fruit of the spirit in the regenerate, as described by St. Paul. Temporally, therefore, it must follow from, not lead to, justification. He argued with Calvinistic logic that sanctification cannot be used as evidence of justification, as "I cannot prove myself in a state of Grace by my Sanctification: For whilst I cannot believe that my person is accepted in justification, I cannot believe that my Works are accepted of God, as any true Sanctification." To do that that would be "to build my Justification upon my Sanctification, and to go on in a Covenant of Works."[15] And as far as the issue of sanctification was concerned, he believed that sanctification was in fact "the Image of God renewed in us."[16] He went on to say that the Holy Spirit dwelt in the believer. This kind of statement was exactly the kind for which Anne Hutchinson would be called a heretic a few months hence, and it is noteworthy that Cotton felt comfortable making such a statement. Obviously, Cotton meant the statement to be taken metaphorically, just as Shepard did when he made similar statements. And, of course, his statements were taken in this way by the ministers. However, in a few months, these same men would insist that Hutchinson meant such statements literally, even though she vociferously denied it.

Shepard was disconcerted about these views. He had preached and written that it was not a complete renewal of humankind that takes place when grace is conferred to the sinner, but that "when the saints are reborn they recover Adam's obedience to the natural law as well as his power of holy action."17 This meant that the believer was merely given power to become like prelapsarian Adam, capable of choosing to live without sinning, but required to follow the law; it most certainly did not mean that the Holy Spirit dwelt within the believer, to enable the person to act without reference to the law.

Shepard argued that the "creation of faith in the heart need not be experienced," and that if one sees the fruits of the spirit, or righteous behavior, the gift of grace can be inferred.18   Shepard was extremely wary of Cotton's interpretation of conversion as including the indwelling of the Spirit, and stated explicitly in his work, "The Parable of the Ten Virgins" that the "Joining the soul immediately to [Christ] and filling it with himself...we cannot enjoy yet."19

The ministers called upon Cotton to discuss further some of his answers to their first set of questions, and he did so at even greater length, explaining and arguing in detail why it was completely illogical to hold that sanctificaion could in any way lead to justification. He spoke quite sternly to them, and analyzed exactly why some of their arguments were not only false but dangerous. He claimed at one point, "for I know not how to excuse it from going in a way of the Covenant of Works, first to see a work before the seal and witness of the Spirit...the danger whereof is evident."20

Cotton however, did not believe himself to be in any danger for expressing differences in doctrine from those of his colleagues.   Even at this date Cotton still felt that he could state publicly such opinions. When the ministers were not satisfied with his answers, they asked him for clarification, and he stated his opinions even more forcefully. He would not let them call him on any statement he had made, even demanding, "you may not put me off..." with the kinds of distinctions they desired to make.21 He quoted Calvin at length in answer to their quibbles, and on the whole reacted to their questions in as confident a manner as one could possibly expect to find.

Yet, while Cotton's argument that sanctification could not be counted upon as evidence of salvation was logically Calvinistic, it was recognized as different from the teachings of the other ministers. "Such evidencing, recognized by all the ministers save Cotton and Wheelwright, equated the pious man with the proper man, the believer with the citizen...Cotton, therefore, insisted that such evidencing did betoken a covenant of works."22

The other ministers were holding to their more recent formulation of the order of salvation that most clearly tied behavior—both civil and religious—to justification. In the wilderness, where cohesion of community was so vital, such a view was understandable, but it was not as strictly a logical product of Calvinistic theology as was the view held by Cotton. They felt strongly that behavior that threatened the stability of the churches and the state, and which did so furthermore by calling into question their juxtaposition of righteous conduct and justification, was not to be tolerated in the colony. They were of course not interested in allowing doctrinal differences—no one but Roger Williams and finally Harry Vane saw that logic demanded freedom of religion—and they saw that Cotton's insistence on Calvinistic predestination with no possibility of human effort was undermining community cohesion. Therefore the ministers felt an urgency in bringing Cotton, Hutchinson, and the others into line.

Cotton however was convinced of the validity of his position, and as he was willing to tolerate the doctrines espoused by the others—he was not calling anyone unorthodox, after all, and he was quite pained to be told that Hutchinson did—he was surprised at their unwillingness to allow his position. The result of Cotton's reply to the sixteen questions was a number of letters back and forth on the nuances of the doctrines. Cotton's vigorous defense of his doctrines forced the others to realize that they could do nothing to him unless something changed. All of their arguments were useless, so they finally were constrained to take the stance that they must watch and wait: "although they could not dissuade him from his inexpedient doctrine, at least they could hold him to it. If his followers made one move beyond it, then they could act."23

Henry Vane, now governor and an ardent follower of Anne Hutchinson, had become quite upset about the questioning of Cotton and of the implications such questioning had for Hutchinson and for himself. In November Vane was questioned about the meaning of his thinking on, "the indwelling of the Holy Ghost," but Winthrop felt that agreement was reached on the subject. However, Vane became so unnerved by the dissensions that at one point the young man threatened to leave the country. In December a session of the court was held, during which he was persuaded to stay, but he made clear his concern about the discord. At this time the ministers again met and discussed the situation with Cotton, and Vane expressed his displeasure at this meeting as he should have been informed previous to it, due to his office as governor of the colony. Hugh Peter, one of the ministers, began to lecture Vane at the meeting of the court, telling him in no uncertain terms that things had been quiet before he had come to Boston. The court was also concerned that Mr. Wilson had been insulted by the followers of Hutchinson, and so attempted to placate Wilson by asking him to preach before it, but instead of attempting to calm the heated passions he exacerbated the situation by continuing the tirade against Vane, and even claimed that Cotton's doctrines were unorthodox.

Cotton turned to Winthrop, who was always ready to mediate and find a middle ground, but even Winthrop was unable to ease the situation, because the congregation at Boston then decided to ask for a censure of Wilson for his inflammatory speech. Cotton was able to oppose this action on the part of his church, and was aided by Winthrop who insisted on unanimity before Wilson could be censured. In spite of his questioning by the other clergy and the problems following, Cotton continued to remain unconcerned about Hutchinson's beliefs, and even publicly reprimanded John Wilson on the last day of 1636 for expressing his apprehensions about Hutchinson and her friends, as Cotton said he did not find anything radical or nontraditional in her teachings.

Winthrop and the leaders of the town saw that something had to be done to try to quiet the mightily troubled community. On January 18, 1637, the community held a day of fasting and prayer to ask God to guide them and put an end to their strife. Cotton gave the sermon in which he exhorted the people to put an end to their enmities. However, his sermon was not the last word on that day, and all his work to put together a persuasive, pacifying, and soothing sermon was to be for naught. Wheelwright, Hutchinson's brother-in-law, was asked to prophesy, or speak to the congregation in the afternoon, after Cotton's sermon had been heard in the morning, and he took the opportunity to take a very different line. Wheelwright proceeded to harangue the faithful with a diatribe that included references to fasting as having been a favorite passtime of the Pharisees, who had been berated for their hypocrisy by Christ, and stated that fasting should not be undertaken except as an admission that Christ was absent from his people. He made it quite clear that: "If he be present with his people then they have no cause to fast: therefore it must be his absence that is the true cause of fasting..."[24] Warming to his cause, he used martial metaphors throughout the sermon that were taken by the authorities to be a call to arms by Wheelwright to those faithful to him and Anne Hutchinson. This was not the way to heal the growing rift in the community. It was, in fact, the signal to the community leaders to take action.

Another factor that influenced the community leaders to take energetic measures to quell the disturbances in the community was the memory firmly planted in the minds of the governing bodies of the time, of the "Münster" episode that had taken place one hundred years earlier in Europe. At that time a group of Anabaptists had taken over the town of Münster, Germany, with execution, "a reign of terror," and finally the people allowing their old nemesis, the bishop-prince to exterminate the Anabaptists.25   The powers that existed in Boston greatly feared this sort of uprising, and so decided to move against those who were fomenting disquiet.

They proceeded against Wheelwright in March, bringing him to trial for the sedition displayed in his divisive sermon.   Winthrop stated that "when the minds of the people being assembled are kindled or made fierce upon so sudden occasion, so as they fall to take part one against another, this is sedition."26   Sedition, unlike the more serious charge of treason, thus was a stirring up of the people, whether with any resulting violence against the civil peace or not.   At his trial, Wheelwright was found guilty, but the vote was close, and it was decided to put off the sentencing until the threat of retaliation from Hutchinson's followers would not be so likely, as that party in the Boston church was strong enough that it was felt to be prudent to delay sentencing to give him a chance to change his mind.   He was to come back in May for sentencing.   But before that could happen the men of Boston became so incensed about the treatment of Wheelwright that they signed a petition declaring that the verdict should be overturned.

By the time of the next election of colony officers in May, Winthrop had been discussing the situation with all those he could to convince them that the state of things was perilous, by reminding them of the dire consequences of any serious rift in the community, and assuring them that he, rather than the inexperienced Henry Vane, could handle the difficult situation.   He was able to convince the court to move the election to New Town (now Cambridge), where opinions were not running so hot, and of course, where the Boston faction would not be heavily represented.   At the court, Vane opened the proceedings by attempting to read the petition demanding the overturn of the verdict against Wheelwright, which caused noisy dissension from Winthrop's camp.   John Wilson, surprisingly, saved the day for Winthrop, and convinced the voters to toe the line, by climbing a tree, and regaling the voters to remember their duty.   In this way, Winthrop was able to have the election held before the petition could be heard.   The result of his hard behind-the-scenes work was that Winthrop was elected governor; Thomas Dudley, a hard-liner who had earlier taken Winthrop to task for his laxity in attitude against law-breakers, was elected deputy governor, and Vane was not elected to any office.

Winthrop next persuaded the General Court to order that strangers could remain in the colony no longer than three weeks unless they had permission from one of the magistrates.   The purpose of this law was to circumvent the political effects of a large group of newcomers on their way to New England, who were friends and relatives of Hutchinson, and who would likely be sympathetic to Hutchinson and Wheelwright, and swell the ranks of her followers. This was also intended to forestall any attempt to bring in supporters of Vane from England, and he knew it. Vane was furious, but could do little about the situation, except to encourage some childish behavior on the part of his supporters, who refused to acknowledge Winthrop's governorship, and slighted him every time they could.

Vane was especially upset by the tone of the law of exclusion that had been passed by the court; shortly afterward he turned his efforts toward repudiating that law. He began to carry on a correspondence with Winthrop that some believe has earned him a place alongside of Roger Williams in the history of political thought. Vane's analysis of the repercussions of the law led him to see the seriousness of excluding from the civil order those with whom one disagreed. While these writings contained, "a tentative formulation of his ideas about the relation of liberty of conscience to the governance of a Christian commonwealth," it was not nearly as strong an argument as Williams would later make, as the ideas did not go as far in the direction of separation of church and state.[27] One of his arguments was that even heretics should not be excluded by the church as no one can rightly judge another's orthodoxy, and to attempt it poses the possibility that good Christians could in this way be excluded from church membership. Winthrop on the other hand argued in his side of the correspondence with Vane a pragmatic belief that the colonists had compacted to live harmoniously in their commonwealth, and that therefore any disturbance to the civil peace, doctrinal or otherwise, should be prosecuted by the civil authorities. Winthrop's thinking was driven by the practical question of civil peace; Vane had recognized the dilemma posed by trying to decide another's orthodoxy.

John Cotton now became so concerned by the direction things were taking that he considered moving with sixty members of his congregation to "Quinipyatk," which was later called New Haven, and settled by John Davenport. He may have discussed with Vane and Hutchinson the possibility of moving there with them. Vane visited Roger Williams, looking for a place for new colonists to settle, and wrote to Williams to ask for "asylum for the people on their way from England, and perhaps to the Hutchinsons, and himself, and Mr. Cotton."[28] However, when it was made clear to Cotton that the other ministers in the Colony would not agree to overlook his differences of theology no matter where he moved, he thought better of his idea of moving. Vane then made a decision that had substantial ramifications for Anne Hutchinson. Still angry about his loss at the polls, he decided to return to England, possibly with some idea of returning later with more supporters, to confront the colony leaders. Vane's political power in the community had lent strength to both Cotton and Hutchinson, and his leaving the colony withered much of that support, and left Hutchinson without a political friend to champion her cause. She had only Cotton for support after Vane left. It became a critical loss to her when Cotton finally abandoned her, as there was then no one of enough eminence in the community to argue her case at any point in the trials to make a difference for her case. Those few men who argued for her were unable to effect any change in the outcome, as an impassioned plea on her behalf by Cotton or Vane could have done.

During that summer the Pequots, an ever-present threat to the safety of the colonies, had become a serious concern to all of the colonies because they had been killing and torturing settlers, so it was agreed by all the colonies that something had to be done to stop them. Shepard writes about the Pequots as being one of two threats to the community that needed "crushing and curing" by the Lord. The other threat was Anne Hutchinson.[29] The menace that the community felt from the Indians had "added to the atmosphere of crisis in which the Hutchinsonian faction would emerge and be judged."[30] So, in July, a large group of men drawn from all the colonies was able to wipe out the rest of the tribe, after the Narragansetts, a friendly tribe, had killed many of the braves. Although this alleviated some of the serious worries about the Native Americans, it served to exacerbate the frictions between Winthrop and the others, because many of the men of Boston refused to take part in the effort. They were angry about how Vane had been treated at the election, and claimed that they had the right to refuse to serve with men whose doctrinal purity they did not find acceptable.

The doctrines of Cotton and Hutchinson were still at this time intertwined in the minds of clergy and laity alike. The only way for Cotton to extricate himself from this linkage was to clear Hutchinson or dissociate himself from her. Cotton continued to discuss his theology with Shepard, who had serious doubts about Cotton's readiness to accept the positions of the other ministers. Yet Shepard's doubts could not have been too strong, as he preached a mollifying sermon reassuring the people that he and Cotton had only minor differences in doctrine. Finally, the authorities decided in late summer of 1637 that a synod of all the colony's churches would help to solidify their rapidly improving position, as it could bring pressure on Cotton to signal his acceptance of their insistence that sanctification could be used as evidence of justification, and that the Holy Spirit does not dwell within the believer. It was agreed that the synod would be held in late August and early September. The seriousness of the situation in Boston must have made itself felt all through the colonies, as "all the ministers and learned men" of the community, including Cotton and Wheelwright came to the synod.[31] The synod continued for twenty-four days of deliberation and disputation during which time Winthrop noted happily that the minsters debated with "the opinionists" and "truth began to get ground."[32] At the end it was decided that eighty-two "errors," or opinions of questionable orthodoxy were to be found among Hutchinson's followers.

Shepard had gained an extremely strong position in the colony, having made himself the spokesperson for the leaders of the colony. Probably this resulted from his having earlier established himself as advisor to John Winthrop. Now he was to give the opening prayer at the synod. At his opening prayer Shepard took the opportunity to make his case quite vigorously that the problems in the colony had to do with "unscriptural enthusiasms and revelations." John Wilson jumped up at the end of the prayer and pleaded passionately that "you that are against these things, and that are for the Spirit and the word together, hold up your hands!"[33] It would have been difficult for Cotton to come out against those ideals, and he did not. By the end of the synod Cotton was to state that he repudiated each and every "error" found in the list of eighty-two "errors."

Thomas Hooker had been brought in from Connecticut to be the moderator of the synod, with Thomas Bulkeley as his assistant moderator. Frank Shuffleton notes in his biography of Hooker that Bulkeley was next after Shepard and Hooker in his strong insistence on preparationist theology.[34] Shuffleton, in his careful analysis of the antinomian controversy, states:

> The basic problem facing the ministers in the synod was not to dispose of particular religious dissenters, which they had no civil or religious power to do, but to restore a credible image of themselves as a spiritual brotherhood of godly preachers united in the one truth. This they did under the leadership of Hooker and Bulkeley, defining themselves and their truth by imagining and refuting the whole spectrum of errors which could be inferred from the antinomians' known tenets.[35]

Many of the eighty-two "errors" are refinements on the theme of the indwelling of Christ but touch upon questions of sanctification/justification, and "graces" possessed (or not) by the believer. The list of "errors" matches closely in content the kinds of allegations that were made against Anne Hutchinson at her trials, so it is probable that the "errors" were paraphrases of what her teachings were alleged to have been. Cotton's teachings must indeed have been at the heart of her thinking, for the doctrines expressed had not up until this point been considered to be suspect by Cotton. Although many of the errors are similar to doctrines expressed by Cotton in his sermons, he was at last persuaded that he must come out against them. It has been stated that the list of errors was long enough and serious enough that it finally induced Cotton to see that he must come out against them in order to save the commonwealth from destruction by the Hutchinsonians, seeing in the body of the errors the threat to community harmony. However, this does not seem possible, as the "errors" were too similar to what he himself had been teaching for him to have believed that they were dangerous to the community.[36] It must have been for some other reason than the safety of the commonwealth which persuaded him to repudiate Hutchinson and her followers, and eventually change his teaching.

Undoubtedly Cotton now decided to repudiate the "errors" and dissociate himself from the Hutchinsonians for his own good. Of course Cotton believed that a Christian should compromise, and should be led by the teachings of all of the learned men of the community, and it is clear that the synod was his turning point, at which he began to change his own doctrines. If he did so because he believed that the harmony of the community should be the foremost concern, he would have been doing violence to his understanding of correct doctrine, merely for the sake of peace within the community. It is difficult to believe that a man who had been as well-respected as Cotton in England and had given up his standing in the community there to come to New England to be able to practice the true faith would so easily change his most cherished theological positions for the harmony of the community without so much as stating in any place that that was his reason for doing so. However, in whatever manner he was persuaded to do so, he did change his thinking at this point, and declared that he saw that "some of the Opinions, to be blasphemous: some of them heretical: many of them, Erroneous: and almost all of them incommodiously expressed."[37]

In fact, however, there is little in the eighty-two errors that Cotton could have found more than "incommodiously expressed."   Almost all of the list can be understood as completely in harmony with Puritan theology, but baldly stated, and taken out of context, seem more extreme than might be the case with some of the long, heartfelt explanations Cotton gave earlier of his own beliefs. Further, the refutations to the errors, which were written by the ministers, take each of the errors to its extreme position. This acts to skew the thrust of the list to an unorthodox position that is not necessarily the one that should be concluded from them. Three examples will demonstrate the thrust of the list and refutation by the ministers. The first example is error no. 35: "The efficacy of Christ's death is to kill all activity of graces in his members, that he might act all in all." This appears to be a paraphrase of Colossians 3:11, which says that having put on the new man, "Christ is all and in all things," but the refutation makes the rather creative point that: "This is contrary to Rom. 6.4. Our old man is crucified with him, that the body of sin might be destroyed, that we should not serve sin: contrary also to Hebr. 4.14. that he might through death destroy him &c. and I John 3. 8. whence we infer, that if Christ came to destroy the body of sin, to destroy the Devil, to dissolve the works of the Devil, then not to kill his own graces, which are the works of his own Spirit."[38] The last of these verses states that Christ came to kill the works of the devil; the second says nothing at all that is to the point, and the first, interestingly, says that believers are buried with Christ through baptism, and are raised with Him, which would be interpreted as agreeing with the error, rather than refuting it.

Another "error" is no. 59. "A man may not be exhorted to any duty, because he hath no power to do it."[39] This undoubtedly meant that no human being has power in himself to do good, but rather his power is in Christ. It echoes John 15:5, "I am the vine: ye (are) the branches: he that abideth in me, and I in him, the same bringeth forth much fruit: for without me can ye do nothing"[40] The confutation given was, "This is contrary to Phil. 2.12, 13. Work out your salvation &c. for it is God that worketh in you both the will and the deed, Ephes. 5.14. Awake thou that sleepest, so I Cor. 15. ult."[41] The confutation here is again interesting, as it can be used to prove the point rather than disprove it, stating as it does that God provides the power, rather than the human person. Furthermore, this "error" clearly echoes John Cotton's answers to the earlier questions regarding the ability of the believer to do anything good on his own before regeneration, in which he argued strenuously and at length that sanctification cannot be used as evidence of justification, because the unregenerate person can do nothing on his own without the indwelling Holy Spirit.

"Error" no. 68 reads, "Faith justifies an unbeliever, that is, that faith that is in Christ, justifieth me that have no faith in my self." This may be a paraphrase of Ephesians 2:8, " For by grace are ye saved through faith, and that not of your selves: it (is) the gift of God." It is also in perfect agreement with Cotton's contention that justification comes without effort from the receiving person. The confutation to this "error" too does not seem to deal with the "error" well at all, reading, "This is contrary to Hab. 2.4. for if the just shall live by his faith, then that faith that justifies is not in Christ. So John 3. ult. He that believeth not, the wrath of God abideth on him: it is not another's faith will save me."[42] However, although the "errors" appear to be very similar to his own teachings, Cotton disavowed them all.

Now that Cotton had declared the opinions to be blasphemous, heretical, or at best incommodiously expressed, the community could take action against Hutchinson as being the fomenter of the opinions. Cotton was well-known as a formidable debater, and was therefore too strong to be attacked. The ministers were not willing to dispute publicly with him, nor did they want to split the community by doing so. At last he had publicly made it unequivocal that he was not on the side of the Hutchinsonians—that is, if they held the eighty-two opinions, as was alleged. He then did a complete turnabout in his actions as well as his declarations of belief: he began to discuss the alleged errors in doctrine with the Hutchinson faction. Unfortunately, he later stated, they would not make any erroneous statements in the presence of two witnesses, so no one could move against them.[43] He was therefore now ready not only to repudiate them, but to help the other side by endeavoring to expose to the magistrates the errors of his devoted friends. Frank Shuffleton makes the case that the synod was indeed the point at which the ministers forced Cotton to perform his theological volte-face. He says of the topics of agreement reached between Cotton and the other ministers:

> the important fact about them is that they indicate the extent of Cotton's concession to his opponents. Earlier Cotton had maintained that the soul's union with Christ was 'not without, nor before the habit (or gift) of faith, but before the act of faith'; in the synod 'the consent was that there was no marriage union with Christ before actual faith, which is more than habitual.[44]

Cotton had capitulated entirely to the other ministers, and was now ready to sell out his pupil for holding the very tenets he had preached.

The other ministers recognized that what they had sought had been achieved. It was now possible to proceed against Hutchinson, having separated her stance from that of Cotton. They had not been able to move against her in May, although some of them had undertaken to do so, but were persuaded not to do so by Cotton. Now, however, they could bring her and some of her followers to trial. In November, they held the first of the trials to be held, the civil trial. Those who had signed the petition alleging that Wheelwright had been improperly found guilty were tried for sedition first, and banished, fined, or disenfranchised. Those trials were apparently short, and swift. There is little in Winthrop's record of them to indicate that the men who were tried were able to argue their cause, or even that many of them tried to do so. One of them, William Baulston, did tell the court "that he knew that if such a petition had been made in any other place in the world, there would have been no fault found with it."[45] Hutchinson's son, Ed, informed the court that "if they took away his estate, they must keep his wife and children; for which he was presently committed to the Officer." The men of the court "reasoned a good while with them both..." but finally disenfranchised them both and fined Baulston twenty pounds and Hutchinson forty. By the next morning Ed Hutchinson had however thought better of his behavior, "and so was released of his imprisonment, but both were disabled from bearing any public office." Two of her followers, both former deputies to the General Court received heavy sentences: William Aspinwall was banished, and John Coggeshall was disenfranchised. After having dealt with the other offenders the court prepared to deal with Anne Hutchinson.[46]

Notes

1. Walker, quoting from John Cotton's *Way of the Congregational Churches Cleared*, p. 78.

2. John Winthrop, *Journal*, p. 219.

3. Larzer Ziff, *The Career of John Cotton: Puritanism and the American Experience*, (Princeton: Princeton University Press, 1962), p. 114.

4. Williams, pp. 107–8.

5. Jesper Rosenmeier, "New England's Perfection: The Image of Adam and the Image of Christ in the Antinomian Crisis, 1634 to 1638," *William and Mary Quarterly*, 3rd series, 27, (1970), pp. 435–459, p. 436.

6. Hall, *Antinomian*, p.

7. Ibid., p. 26.

8. Ibid., p. 28.

9. Ibid., p. 30.

10. Ibid., p. 37.

11. Ibid., p. 6.

12. Quoted in Erickson, p. 80.

13. Hall, *Antinomian*, pp. 48–9.

14. Ibid., p. 49.

15. Ibid., pp. 52–3.

16. Quoted in Jesper Rosenmeier, "New England's Perfection: The Image of Adam and the Image of Christ in the Antinomian Crisis, 1634 to 1638," *William and Mary Quarterly*, 3rd series, 27, (1970), p. 439.

17. Ibid., p. 441.

18. Ibid., p. 442.

19. Ibid., p. 443.

20. Hall, *Antinomian*, p. 85.

21. Ibid., p. 103.

22. Ziff, *Career*, p. 119.

23. Ibid., p. 120.

24. Hall, *Antinomian*, p. 154.

25. Rugg, pp. 113–4.

26. Ziff, *Career*, p. 124, quoting Winthrop, from "Short Story," p. 204.

27. J. H. Adamson and H. F. Folland, *Sir Harry Vane: His Life and Times (1623-1662)*, (Boston: Gambit, 1973), p. 104.

28. Augur, p. 162.

29. Shepard, *Plot*, p. 66.

30. Francis Bremer, *The Puritan Experiment: New England Society from Bradford to Edwards*, (New York: St. Martin's Press, 1976), p. 69.

31. John Winthrop, quoted in Hall, *Antinomian*, p. 212.

32. Hall, *Antinomian*, p. 213.

33. Both quotations found in Battis, p. 165, and are taken from Johnson's *Wonder-working Providence*, p. 252, and Mather's *Magnalia*, I, p. 282.

34. Frank Shuffleton, *Thomas Hooker: 1584–1647,* (Princeton: Princeton University Press, 1977), p. 249.

35. Shuffleton, *Hooker*, p. 250.

36. Ziff, *Career*, p. 33.

37. Ziff, *Career*, p. 134.

38. Hall, *Antinomian*, p. 228.

39. Ibid., p. 234.

40. *The New Testament Octapla: Eight English Versions of the New Testament, in the Tyndale/ King James Tradition*, ed. Luther A Weigle, (New York: Thomas Nelson & Sons, nd), Geneva translation, 1562.

41. Hall, *Antinomian,* p. 235.

42. Ibid., p. 237.

43. John Cotton, "The Way of the Congregational Churches Cleared," in *John Cotton on the Churches of New England*, ed. Larzer Ziff, (Cambridge, MA: Harvard University Press, 1968), p. 248.

44. Shuffleton, *Hooker*, p. 251.

45. Hall, *Antinomian*, p. 261.

46. Ibid., p. 262.

Chapter Six

"The Stamp of Authority":
The Foundation of the Law

The civil trial of Anne Hutchinson is pivotal in the history of the colony and the premises on which it stood. This trial provided the testing ground for the viability of the state, both in terms of whether it could withstand a challenge to its very being, as well as an examination of its authority and the logic of its structure. At her civil trial the sentence of banishment was given to Hutchinson. This fact underscores the importance of her challenge to them. Therefore the examination of the legal basis for the trial becomes an investigation of the premises for the colony itself.

John Winthrop recognized the importance of the trial, although he could hardly be expected to see it in an objective way; his viewpoint was governed by the desire to save his commonwealth from an irreparable rent in its fabric. He realized that if Hutchinson should continue to exert influence upon more than half of the membership of the Boston church, the colony would be split. It would have been ruined, because it would no longer have been able to function in the way it had begun. The colony would have had to reorganize itself and to question seriously its underlying premises if she and her followers had been allowed to lead the church in the direction it seemed to be headed. Winthrop could not let that happen, and he, Dudley, and others of the leadership of the colony strove mightily to forestall that eventuality by ridding themselves of her challenge. They did not recognize that there was in actuality no way for them to evade the ordeal. The trial itself provided the test of their design.

The authorities of Massachusetts Bay Colony quite openly intended to use the civil trial of Anne Hutchinson to rid themselves of a trouble-maker. Winthrop wrote in his journal, using language of the "healer," speaking of "cures" and the "incurable," that the group of followers of Anne Hutchinson had been given enough chances to improve their behavior and had not done so, which left the colony no option but to try them for disrupting the

civil peace. Although unspoken, his statement leaves the unmistakable
conclusion that the disturbers of the civic peace had to be excised, as an
incurable cancer on the body politic.

> Then after this mean was tried, and the Magistrates saw that neither our
> Preaching, Conference, nor yet our Assembly meeting did effect the cure,
> but that, still, after conference had together, the Leaders put such life into
> the rest, that they all went on in their former course, not only to disturb the
> Churches, but miserably interrupt the civil Peace, and that they threw
> contempt both upon Courts, and Churches, and began now to raise sedition
> amongst us, to the endangering the Common-wealth; Hereupon for these
> grounds named, and not for their opinions, (as themselves falsely reported,
> and as our Godly Magistrates have been much traduced here in England) for
> these reasons (I say) being civil disturbances, the Magistrate convents them,
> (as it plain appears...) and censures them; some were disfranchised, others
> fined, the incurable amongst them banished.[1]

So, in November the verdicts of the General Court led to banishment of
Wheelwright, disenfranchisement of eight others, and to disarming "seven-
ty–five persons in the country, including fifty–eight from Boston alone."[2]
This group of a number of Hutchinson's most prominent supporters had
been tried first because it was necessary to silence as many as possible of
her followers, in order to keep them from coming to her defense. But now
that Cotton had been persuaded to declare himself in opposition to the
repugnant doctrines, and Wheelwright and the others had been successfully
disposed of, it was time to raise the scalpel of the law against the nucleus of
the disease, Anne Hutchinson. A few of her followers did attempt to speak
up for her at her trials, but with little success, and those few were too law-
abiding to do anything more than speak in her behalf. Winthrop and the
other leaders of the colony assumed that she was the ringleader of dissension, and the trial was intended as surgery necessary to excise her noxious
presence from the colony.

The trial was conducted in such a confusing and seemingly disorga-
nized fashion that the modern reader is tempted to assume that there was no
structure or method to it other than the quite obvious desire to convict
Anne Hutchinson. Although Winthrop, as governor, was in charge of the
court, other members of the magistracy questioned her and argued with
her and with one another. In fact, the overall tone of the trial that comes
through quite clearly to the reader is that the haphazard method used in the
trial miscarried on the prosecution, as it allowed Hutchinson herself to
maneuver the direction of the questions much more ably than Winthrop. It
is not the case, however, that the trial was simply an illustration of a frontier justice attempt to secure a conviction using all means necessary, with
no regard for proper procedure or legal grounds. The General Court had

been trying cases since the beginning of the colony, and its authority and procedure were not unsimilar to some of the courts in England at the time. Nevertheless, the disorderly character of the trial does demand a closer investigation of the legal and political underpinnings of the judicial practices of the day.

The colony's charter vested in the officers of the colony authority to organize the governance structure of the colony; freemen were also to be involved in the drafting of laws and in the governance process. However, the charter had allowed a great deal of freedom in conceptualizing the legal structure of the colony, which left the framers of the governance and judicial system of Massachusetts Bay Colony with wide latitude in determining the needs and the resultant organization of the colony. All of the colonies had been given the same authority to organize themselves as they saw fit, and each of them took advantage of this prerogative to do so. The charter of the corporation of Massachusetts Bay stipulated that the General Court could "make, ordain, and establish all manner of wholesome and reasonable orders, laws, statutes, and ordinances, directions, and instructions not contrary to the laws of this our realm of England..." so long as English subjects "shall have and enjoy all liberties and immunities of free and natural subjects within any of the dominions..." of the crown.[3] Thus, within the parameters of English laws, guarantees, and freedoms the officers of the colony were allowed considerable latitude to erect a model of principles and procedures that would be suited to their particular circumstances.

The model they designed could have varied substantially from what they had known in England. They could, for instance, have set up a theocracy similar to that of Calvin's Geneva, or they could have organized themselves as a complete democracy, without straining the limits specified in the charter. They did not do either of these things. Nor did they organize themselves in a fashion that was patterned after either the system in England or any other model with which they were familiar. The system of government that Winthrop and the other leaders of the colony established was much more democratic than that of England, in that it gave ordinary freemen a much greater share in the governance process. This was chiefly because the charter itself, based upon the form normally used for the incorporation of a joint stock company, stipulated certain rights for the freemen. After the founding of the colony, when Winthrop and the other leaders of the colony attempted to remove those rights the freemen forced the issue within a very few years by insisting on being allowed to read the charter and then pointing out that their rights had been abrogated. However, reasons for the democratic nature of the society also include the fact that there were far fewer people to incorporate into the structure, and thus it was to allow much more political activity and responsibility for the average man.

Although the charter stipulated that laws drafted for the colony could not be antithetical to English law, nor could English citizens' rights be violated, the legal structure designed by the leaders of the colony was not entirely based upon English common law; nor was it based completely upon biblical strictures. Winthrop and the other founders of the colony did not feel themselves subject to the laws of England and thus required to conform all their laws to English common law. They read the charter's provisions as indicating that they had complete freedom to enact laws and to set up whatever kind of system would please them, so long as English laws were not violated, and the rights of the people as English citizens were not abrogated. Winthrop stated unequivocally in his "A Model of Christian Charity," drawn up on board the Arabella, that as they had compacted with God to begin the new commonwealth, "we have taken out a Commission, the Lord hath given us leave to draw our own Articles..."[4] In 1634 the colony was given a copy of a commission which they were told was intended to apply to Massachusetts Bay Colony, which "granted to the two archbishops and ten others of the council, to regulate all plantations, ...to call in all patents, to make laws, to raise tithes and portions for ministers, to remove and punish governors, and to hear and determine all causes, and inflict all punishments, even death itself, etc."[5] At this point the deputies and Magistrates took action to raise a large sum of money for fortifications, as they were not willing to allow a new governor to be forced upon them, or to allow anyone, even those commissioned by the Crown, to have a say in their system of laws and government.

The legal system that the leaders of the colony had established was not based upon a written constitution other than the charter, nor was a written code of laws enacted. Rather, the method used was to allow law to develop judicially. Although not all were satisfied with this system, Winthrop stressed the importance of the uniqueness of the colony and its individual circumstances, and therefore held out for flexibility for individual judgment on the part of the magistrates as they created laws and judged the petitioners. Given his emphasis upon maximum room to maneuver he did not want a system of written laws, because he believed that would unnecessarily tie the hands of the Magistrates, as they ruled on cases. He held that the magistrates of the colony must have the latitude to respond to the challenges of the new environment in which they found themselves, and so he resisted a written system of laws for this reason. Winthrop regarded the Magistrates as God's regents upon earth as they administered justice, and therefore he wanted them to have as much liberty as possible to do so.[6]

In 1634, after Winthrop was pressured to set up a commission to draft a model of laws, he asked John Cotton to chair the committee. However, he shelved the resulting systematic list of laws Cotton had drafted when they were presented, as he deemed the punishments contained in the list to be too strict and harsh for the new land. He resisted for as long as he could the importuning of the freemen for a code of laws, working to keep the highest degree of flexibility for the Magistrates. As Winthrop and Dudley and the other leaders of the colony regarded one of the greatest needs for the burgeoning colony to be peace and harmony in which to continue to grow, it might be assumed that this desire for leeway for the Magistrates was in order to enable them to eliminate any and all dissent or other threats to the civil peace without reference to a body of laws. That does not seem to have been the case however. Although Winthrop was at one point held to be too lenient by several of the other leaders, such as Dudley, those leaders were far more interested than Winthrop in having a code of laws drawn up and agreed upon by the colony. They apparently did not see the benefit of continuing without a code of laws which allowed for easier extinction of dissent. However, none of them advocated too closely following the common law of England. Thus it appears that, like Winthrop, the rest of the officers of the colony were comfortable with the idea that they should fashion a quite idiosyncratic legal system for the colony. Winthrop touted the positive advantages for the colony in having substantial freedom in organizing the government of the new commonwealth, rather than having to follow English laws and customs too closely. He argued later in his journal that it was proper to have the laws of the colony come into being judicially rather than legislatively, as that was the way "the laws of England and other states grew, and therefore the fundamental laws of England are called customs, *consuetudines*."[7]

In addition to the method for establishing law, Winthrop concerned himself with the necessity to make laws that would not "transgress the limits" of the charter by virtue of being "repugnant to the laws in England."[8] He was quite aware of the fact that the charter would be in jeopardy if they did so. For this reason, he recognized the need to delineate the relationship between English law and whatever basis there was for the laws of the colony; therefore the question whether the laws of England followed her subjects into a newly established colony and whether the King had ultimate authority figured in Winthrop's thinking. This issue had been debated in English courts in *Calvin's Case, the Case of the Post-Nati* in 1608, during the time period when the patent of the Virginia Colony was drafted. Sir Francis Bacon, counsel for the plaintiff, had argued what came to be called the "birthright theory," that a subject of England took

English law with him as a birthright.9 Had this idea been accepted in the colony it would have meant that the colonists were to be under English common law alone, and would have greatly complicated the issue, as all laws drafted would then have become mere additions to the body of the common law, rather than establishing precedent. Those appearing in court would have had the right to be judged according to the common law and could to appeal to the king.

In later years in Massachusetts Bay, various colonists were to make the claim that the colony was indeed intended to be governed by the laws of England. However, those claims were unsuccessful, and the leaders of Massachusetts Bay did not interpret their charter in this way; they fully intended to establish a colony according to their own ideas of how a commonwealth should be governed. Beginning shortly after the Hutchinson case there were repeated challenges to the idea that the colony was independent and its laws separate from English law. Winthrop answered each challenge by claiming that the colony was independent of England and could frame its own laws autonomously.10 Winthrop was careful to reiterate that the colonial leaders were aware that they could not draft laws repugnant to those of England, and that they would follow that dictum; however, he and the General Court later also staunchly defended the colony's right to develop its own system of laws so long as they were not "contrary to the law of God and of right reason, which the learned in those laws have anciently and still do hold forth as the fundamental basis of their laws..."11

The result was that the framers of the legal system in Massachusetts Bay Colony did not craft a system according to any carefully laid-out theory of government, law, or jurisprudence.12 As Winthrop was to declare on more than one occasion, flexibility for the Magistrates in order to respond to the special circumstances in which they found themselves deciding cases was more important to the colony than other considerations. Their decisions then would be based upon English law where necessary, and God's law and right reason in all cases. The outcome of this method of judicial, rather than legislative, growth of the law was that a systematic listing of the rules and regulations of the colony was not forthcoming until Winthrop finally felt forced to see that one was drafted. When the laws of the colony were codified in 1641 the result was a systematic, although not comprehensive, code of laws, and not merely a collection of the laws in effect at the time.13

Winthrop's insistence upon latitude for the magistrates demonstrates the way in which the political and legal development of the colony was dependent not only upon the authority that was imparted to any English corporation, but also upon the background and temperaments of the men who guided it, and the intersection of that prior training in law, politics, and theology with the realities of the new land. Several of the men who first determined to take the charter with them to New England and subsequently became leaders of the colony were trained in the law, and others like Cotton had a substantial understanding of theology and the law as well. The temperaments of Dudley, who was more rigid and choleric, and Winthrop, who was genial and eager to compromise for the sake of Christian harmony often clashed as they wrestled with issues of administrative and legal organization. Winthrop was to make attempts to curb excesses of prosecutorial zeal at Hutchinson's trial; Dudley would allow his temper to guide his tongue at times as his irritation with her insistence on proper procedure grew. Their personal styles also led to heated discussions as they searched for a legal model for their colony.

One of the most significant dimensions with which they had to deal and which was naturally very close to the heart of these devout Puritans was the proper interrelationship between church and state. This question is central to Hutchinson's civil trial. For although she was charged with sedition, the case against her was based upon the claim that she maligned not the magistrates of the colony, which could more easily be seen as undermining the properly constituted government of the colony, and therefore constituting sedition, but the ministers. Hutchinson's brother-in-law, John Wheelwright, had also been tried for sedition based upon his having stirred up the people against the ministers "with much bitterness and vehemency," and calling them "anti-christs," which would seem to be a more severe traducement of their status than the charges alleged against Hutchinson.[14] Both cases indicate that the ministry was considered a part of the governance structure, if only unofficially. Officially the colony was not governed by the church, but the relationship between the two institutions was indeed raised in Wheelwright's trial, and must figure in any examination of Hutchinson's trial.

Assumptions made regarding the appropriate combination of the intrusion of secular authority into the religious realm and the genesis of secular authority had been central to the ongoing dialogue of the Puritans in England in Parliament concerning common law and the rights of the people. Many well-known and well-read Puritans in England had concerned themselves with parliamentary discussions of the limits of secular power and its derivation during the decades shortly before large numbers of them migrated to Massachusetts Bay. Such discussions necessarily included consideration of questions of the affiliation between church and state, as well as the basis of the authority of law. These discussions had shaped their understanding of how a commonwealth is endowed with proper authority. The vantage point of the Puritans who had watched closely the discourse led by Sir Edmund Coke that shaped English common law had led them to be careful to ensure that the state be kept from intrusion upon the church, as that was the difficulty with which they had most to be concerned in England. The problem in Massachusetts Bay was to find a way to safeguard the church so that it would be allowed enough freedom from the authority of the state to determine its role and direction for itself, rather than giving in to state domination. "In old England [the clergy] had feared the state. In New England, with pursuivants and evil kings safely left behind, they could trust the magistrate. Once they had prophesied against the standing order. Now they were spokes men for the reigning values..."15 Thus, while all agreed that secular and ecclesiastical governments had to be in harmony and work together in many arenas to accomplish many of the same goals, they were careful to reflect that both were entirely separate entities, separately endowed and commissioned, and that therefore the church would have the ability to regulate itself, and the proper separation of the two was investigated and restated frequently during the early years of the colony.

In order to decide where the line of demarcation lay between the commonwealth and the ecclesiastical realms, it was necessary to feel assured as to the foundation of the authority for the state and the church. The state was believed to be derived from the will of God that good governors be set over the people; in this way the state obtained its power from God. However in the new land the much of the authority that underlay the development of the state was derived from the people who had compacted together to form the new commonwealth. In this way, the situation of the relationship of the people to the state differed dramatically from the case in England, where those born into the country were believed to be endowed with certain rights and privileges but the people's agreement with the laws was understood rather than openly pledged. All the colonists therefore had a stake in the administration of the state. Winthrop makes mention of the strong feelings evidenced by the voters on such occasions as in 1635, when they elected John Haynes to be governor, "partly, because the people would exercise their absolute power, etc."16 The people—at least the males who were church members—believed themselves to hold the power in the colony.

Given the beginnings of the political and constitutional crisis under way in England, it is perhaps not as remarkable as it would have been just a few years before, that the locus of practical authority rested in the people of the colony rather than in its leaders. Of course some of the reason for their democratic institutions stemmed not from a philosophical persuasion, but rather from the fact that the state was begun as a corporation, with its egalitarian organization. However, the idea that all freemen should share in the governance of the colony was accepted by both leaders and those who were led, as the proper foundation for their state. Even Winthrop's attempt to usurp authority had not eliminated the ordinary freeman from the process, merely removed him one degree from it. Freemen had all along been those who elected the Assistants, if not the Governor and Deputy Governor. And the fact that Winthrop did acquiesce in restoring their rights seems to have stemmed not only from a desire to curb unrest and lessen the risk of having the charter annulled, but also from a belief that he and the other offices had to obey the law. Just as Puritans had argued in Parliament that even the King was subject to the laws, no one could claim to have the final human authority in Boston, which was not in the end subject to the people.

The church was of course one of the primary reasons for the exodus to the new land, and was brought into being at the same time as the state. Its relationship to the state was of paramount significance to the Puritans, as they had intended from the first to establish a church in a different manner from that of England. Thus, while much of their understanding of the proper basis for and organization of a church had come with them from England, this was the first opportunity for them to examine the foundations for and operation of either institution, and to see in what ways cooperation between them would be effective. They fully expected the church to be established to function in concurrence with the state, but they also recognized all too well the differences between the two institutions and the ways in which the two had to be kept separate.

Just as the state derived its ultimate mandate from God, the church naturally derived its authority and power from God, and was intended to address the spiritual well-being of its members. Yet, in the new land it too derived much of its functional authority in a fairly democratic way from its membership. For in the new land it was confirmed that the model for churches would be one in which members of the community would form their democratically representative organization. Not merely the clergy, but the whole group evaluated new members and voted upon excommunications. Such decisions were decided by a majority vote which was then proclaimed by the minister.[17] Thus, the church in Massachusetts Bay was felt to conform far more closely to the ideal in which the church was an instrument of God operating through His people than was the Church of England, which had such close affinity to, even at times domination by, the state. In these ways in the new land the foundations and assumptions of power and authority of both the state and the church were made explicit in ways not necessary or possible in England with the result that both institu-

tions were organized in more democratic ways than in England, not because the beliefs of the derivation of ultimate authority differed so greatly
from those in England, but rather because conditions allowed it. The un-
written assumptions of freedoms and the vesting of authority in the people
held by Englishmen were allowed to guide the designing of the new organizational systems much more explicitly in the new land.

As the purpose of the state was to serve and govern the people in
order to keep the peace and promote the public welfare, and the purpose of
the church was to foster a proper understanding of the conditions for salvation and also to establish the earthly welfare of the people, the laws, rules,
regulations, and customs which guided both institutions were the means
used to secure these ends. The laws of the state carried out the desire of
the people for a well-regulated, peaceful state, and those of the church
nurtured the peace and well-being of the flock of the faithful. The laws
themselves then were integral to the purpose and the process of guarding
and securing the right and the righteous behavior of those under the care of
the church and the state.

The purpose of law as understood by the leaders of the Bay Colony
was similar in both civil and ecclesiastical institutions. In the church the
law (those rules and guidelines were found in the Bible) was intended to
demonstrate to the sinner first the errors of his ways and secondly to bring
him to a knowledge of and desire for Jesus Christ. The secular law was
intended by the state to ensure the public peace. Therefore, it also had a
double intent: to show the way to proper behavior, and to offer a yardstick
by which to measure behavior, as well. As both the civil law and the law
in the church served two purposes, they both acted as a guidepost as well as
a rule. The civil law was of course entirely separate from church rules, and
was to be used to protect the public peace; however because the person
lived in this world the civil peace was to be governed and aided by both
secular and ecclesiastic authorities. Indeed, most of the rules found in the
Bible were aimed at the regulation of society, and were not directed at the
spiritual world, which is why John Cotton was able to take the judicial
system he authored almost entirely from the Bible, allowing him to claim
the "complete sufficiency of the word of God alone to direct his people in
judgment of all causes, both civil and criminal."[18] Yet the colony had not
felt the same affection for reliance upon the Bible alone as a basis for its
laws as had John Cotton, and so had not expected to create a system of laws
based solely upon the Bible, and Cotton's laws were never to be implement-
ed.

Another difference between the colony and the mother country was
that the old ecclesiastical courts were not duplicated in Massachusetts Bay;

in England those courts had been responsible for church doctrine, and also marriages and punishment for sexual transgressions. In the new land however no such courts were created, and those matters were handled by the civil courts.[19] The church was still to look to the morals of its members however and a church member might find her or himself in the position of being tried by both courts, as was Anne Hutchinson. "Double jeopardy was not uncommon in Massachusetts, since the disciplinary verdicts of a congregation had no civil consequences, and most colonial Puritans thought the deterrents of secular law could be helpful in persuading men and women to turn from sin toward righteousness."[20]

It is perhaps not surprising that while much of the purpose of both civil and biblical law was to keep the civil peace, the church was to aid the secular courts in doing so. In England the church had been a tool of the Crown in keeping the public peace, and it continued to expect to perform that function in the new setting. Homilies were used to remind the faithful of their need for subjection, and the dire consequences of rebellion, and it was understood that citizens should be admonished from the pulpit toward behavior that would lead to a peaceful commonwealth.[21] After the threats to the social order deriving from Roger Williams' questioning of it the ministers of the Bay drew up "A Model of Church and Civil Power." Darret Rutman describes it as, "an ecclesiastical constitution based upon theories of church government discussed publicly and privately in England since the late 1590s."[22] In this document, of which we have fragments, quoted in the writings of Roger Williams in his long–running argument by letter with John Cotton, the statement is made that "God hath given a distinct power to Church and Common–weal, the one spiritual (called the Power of the Keys) the other Civil (called the Power of the Sword)...The leaders of the commonwealth must be the 'nursing fathers' of the church, defending 'the pure worship of God' with 'the power of the sword against all those who shall attempt to corrupt it.' "[23] It is clear from this excerpt that the leaders of the colony fully intended that the civil authorities must count as one of the responsibilities as "nursing fathers" to the infant colony that they defend both the state and the church from corruption. Hutchinson was seen as threatening both.

This is not to make the case, however, that the colony was run or intended to be a theocracy. It was not. The two spheres were to be separate. The English milieu out of which the "nursing fathers" of the colony had come, "considered the church and the state to be independent institutions, each with its own personnel and responsibilities. The church and the leaders of the colony were close cooperators, for each was charged with maintaining God's glory and truth in unadulterated form. What church and state had in common, though, did not obliterate the lines that separated them."24 Winthrop and Cotton as well as the other leaders of the colony dealt with the questions about the proper distance of the two institutions on a number of occasions, such as the trial of John Wheelwright, when a petition had been presented to the court making a request for closer cooperation. "The ministers, being called to give advice about the authority of the court in things concerning the churches..." were careful to insist that the proper distance be kept between the two, even when such distance diminished the role of the church in the running of the state.25 Even earlier John Cotton had preached a sermon in 1634 during a day of humiliation, fasting and prayer held for the purpose of seeking God's guidance with respect to the proper roles of the Magistrates and the rest of the people. In the sermon he outlined the roles of the magistracy, the ministry, and the people. He told the faithful that the strength of the magistracy was their authority, that of the people their liberty, and of the ministry their purity.26 Cotton was no doubt aware that Calvin too had decreed that as church and state had different functions, they also had different spheres of influence and legal parameters.27

Just as the church was not to be under the control of the state, the state was not to be considered to be less important, or under the control of, the church. The two were to work together in harmony, each recognizing the necessity and the role of the other; neither was to dominate. Winthrop wrote an "Essay Against the Power of the Church to Sit in Judgement on the Civil Magistracy" in November of 1637, during the time Hutchinson was given her trial by the state. In it he argues that the church does not have such power over the civil government.28 He wrote in his journal that after the trial of Anne Hutchinson, a number of the members of the Boston church "being highly offended with the governor for this proceeding, [they] were earnest with the elders to have him called to account for it."29 At this time he told the congregation that it simply was not lawful for the church to "call in question the proceedings of the civil court."30 The church, he went on to explain, had no authority to intervene in a civil case. Had he or any magistrate taken away a person's goods in a personal capacity, the church could raise the issue with him, but having done so as an officer of the court, the church had no jurisdiction to speak to the matter.31 The great theologian, William Ames, friend to most of the leaders of the Bay Colony, had felt the issue to be of enough importance to address it in his writing, *The Marrow of Theology*, first published in 1623. He emphasized that church and state were separate entities, although both were instituted by God for the ultimate good of the people. He pointed out that there were several differences between the church and the magistracy, but that while the ministry could only secure the good of the people by "ecclesiastical means," the magistracy "have the duty of securing the common good, both spiritual and corporal, of all those in their jurisdiction by political means and coercive power..."[32] John Cotton had made clear to Lord Saye and Sele in 1631 that "magistrates are neither chosen to office in the church, nor do govern by directions from the church, but by civil laws, and those enacted in general courts, and executed in courts of justice, by the governors and assistants. In all which, the church (as the church) hath nothing to do: only it prepareth fit instruments both to rule, and to choose rulers, which is no ambition in the church, nor dishonor to the commonwealth."[33]

The church was felt, however, by the zealous Puritans to be in a special sense the undergirding of the state. Winthrop and the other leaders of the colony would have agreed with John Preston's sermon of 1629, in which he called religion and zeal for religion, "the pillars that bear up the Church and Commonwealth..."[34] Thus, without the church to provide the foundation for the state, the state could not stand. The authority of the church provided that both institutions would look out for the peace and order of the society. Both institutions were given to the people by God for their well-being, and both, although with differing areas of responsibilities, could and would use their power to do so. It seems to have been understood by the magistrates and Governor, if not always by the people, where it would be proper to have overlap. For this reason, it seemed natural and right to the leaders of the Bay Colony that calumny of the ministers would be seen as a threat to the commonwealth. This of course was the tie to sedition in Hutchinson's trial. She was accused of "crying down the ministers," who could hardly perform their function as encouragers toward the peace without the respect and admiration of their congregants. If the average person on the street no longer trusted in the leadership of the ministry and its ability to lead in the paths of righteousness, how could the public good be exhorted? And who indeed could do it?

Questions of undergirding authority for the governance of the colony and for their legal system thus were resolved in the minds of those who were to sit in judgment upon Anne Hutchinson. The laws under which she would be judged and the procedure by which she would be tried however raise concerns of their own.

Notes

1. Hall, *Antinomian*, pp. 213–14.

2. Rugg, pp. 91–2.

3. "The Charter of the Colony of the Massachusetts Bay in New England: 1628–29" in *The Founding of Massachusetts: Historians and the Sources*, ed. Edmund S. Morgan, (New York: The Bobbs-Merrill Company, Inc., 1964), pp. 318, 319. For more discussion regarding the limits of the laws promulgated in Massachusetts Bay, see: Charles J. Hilkey, *Legal Development in Colonial Massachusetts, 1630–1686*, (New York: Columbia University Press, 1910), p.11.

4. John Winthrop, "A Model of Christian Charity," p. 202, in Morgan, *The Founding of Massachusetts,* pp.191–205

5. Winthrop, *Journal*, vol. 1. p. 135.

6. Haskins, *Law and Authority*, p. 121.

7. Winthrop, *Journal*, vol.1, p. 324.

8. Ibid.

9. Joseph H. Smith and Thomas G. Barnes, *The English Legal System: Carryover to the Colonies*, (Los Angeles: University of California, 1975), pp. 4, 5.

10. Robert B. Morris, *Studies in the History of American Law: With Special Reference to the Seventeenth and Eighteenth Centuries*, 2nd. ed. (Philadelphia: Joseph M. Mitchell Co., 1959), p. 19.

11. Quoted in Ibid.

12. Ibid. p. 15.

13. Smith and Barnes, p. 70.

14. Winthrop, *Journal*, vol. 1, pp. 211, 212.

15. David. D. Hall, *The Faithful Shepherd: A History of the New England Ministry in the Seventeenth Century* (Chapel Hill, NC: University of North Carolina Press, 1972), p. 121.

16. Winthrop, *Journal*, vol. 1, p. 149.

17. Stephen Botstein, *Early American Law and Society* (New York: Alfred A. Knopf, 1983), p. 24.

18. Morris, p. 29.

19. Botstein, p. 20.

20. Ibid., p. 25.

21. Christopher Hill, *Change and Continuity in Seventeenth-Century England* (Cambridge, MA: Harvard University Press, 1975), pp. 189–192.

22. Darret B. Rutman, *American Puritanism: Faith and Practice* (Philadelphia: J. B. Lippincott, 1970), p. 95.

23. Ibid.

24. John Dykstra Eusden, *Puritans, Lawyers, and Politics in Early Seventeenth-Century England* (n.p.: Archon Books, 1968), p. 33.

25. Winthrop, *Journal*, vol. 1, p. 210.

26. Hilkey, p. 24.

27. Hall, *Shepherd*, p. 123.

28. Lee Schweniger, *John Winthrop* (Boston: Twayne Publishers, 1990), p. 66.

29. Winthrop, *Journal*, vol. 1, p. 256.

30. Ibid.

31. Ibid., p. 57.

32. William Ames, *The Marrow of Theology*, ed. and trans. John Dykstra Eusden (Durham, NC: Labyrinth Press, 1983), pp. 311, 312.

33. Edmund S. Morgan, *Roger Williams: The Church and the State* (New York: Harcourt, Brace & World, Inc.), p. 76.

34. Eusden, p. 62.

Chapter Seven

"Prudential Rules":

Laws and Procedures

The leaders of the colony may have been comfortable with their understanding of the means, purposes, and basis of authority for the laws of the Massachusetts Bay Colony; however, although the power and spheres of influence of the leadership of the colony had been established, the actual structure of law under which Hutchinson was brought to trial was still uncodified and unsystematic.

Although it is obvious that Anne Hutchinson was brought to trial by the General Court for the purpose of ridding the colony of a disruptive influence, it was not the case that the outcome was all that mattered to the leaders of Massachusetts Bay. For albeit the system of laws for the colony had not yet been written, it is quite clear that the Magistrates who heard cases during the sessions of the General Court expected to decide their cases based upon reasonable and regular theories of jurisprudence. Much as they might have wished to rid themselves of a canker on the social body, they would have been horrified at the suggestion that this could happen without a fair trial. Winthrop himself wrote in his journal that Mrs. Hutchinson had almost secured a vote of not guilty, as they could not really prove anything against her, until they were aided by a providence of God, in allowing her to speak of her "revelations." In other words, he recognized that they could not have found her guilty without compelling proof. In her case, as in any other case, he would have argued that it would be unlawful to convict without proper procedure and indubitable proof of guilt.

Law was too integral to the lives and thinking of the Puritans in Massachusetts Bay to be trifled with by those invested with the power to use it. Winthrop wrote in "A Model of Christian Charity" of the importance of laws. He spoke of the "law of nature and the law of grace," by which he meant that God had from the beginning written into the hearts of all persons a knowledge of right behavior, and then had given further special directions to his saints.[1] Law was a gift from God for the regulation of all human endeavors, and not to be taken lightly. Laws indeed were the way in which God manifested His interest in, and regulation of, human affairs. He ruled through his church, but also through the laws of the land, which were based upon what Englishmen had called, "fundamental law," or those laws out of which the English common law was culled, and which were ascertained through the use of reason.[2]

Winthrop held the belief that the Magistrates were God's representatives upon earth, which was the basis upon which he argued that they needed their flexibility in rendering decisions and devising laws for the colony.[3] God had given two kinds of laws to humankind for the direction of human affairs, and the Christian must be careful to recognize and give obedience to both. Winthrop stated that both mercy and justice were the two rules "whereby we are to walk towards one another."[4] All laws were to incorporate both of these crucial elements, which would thereby ensure a godly commonwealth. Justice was central to the notion that the law in the new colony should reflect their new circumstances, and also God's plan for the "City on a Hill" to which the world would look for guidance. The law was the vehicle for securing justice for the individual and for the community. Winthrop himself had of course acted as a lawyer and a jurist for some years in England, and had been closely involved with the legislative process in London, "drafting legislation for a parliamentary committee" and sharing housing at the Inner Temple with other lawyers.[5] Because he had been a part of drafting at least one document to which we have access today which discussed alleged abuses by the king, he was well aware that such abuses must not be tolerated in Massachusetts, and justice must be the watchword.[6]

Furthermore justice, held Hugh Peter, was most crucial of all the attributes needed by a commonwealth. He stated unequivocally that justice was so vital to a commonwealth that even religion and mercy had to take a second place. Indeed he held that it is possible to have a commonwealth without the bulwark of the true religion, and that some states are even able to exist without a great deal of mercy, but a commonwealth will not exist for long without justice.[7] Winthrop described justice in "A Model of Christian Charity" as one of the requisites, along with mercy, which will hold together the commonwealth, as those who comprise the community seek to be "knit together."[8] He cited its importance as primary in that it would allow them to avoid the "shipwreck" of their whole venture.[9] Winthrop lays out in detail the reasons why love is the foundation for mercy, but he ends his dissertation upon the ideal commonwealth by reminding the reader that while justice indeed could and should be tempered with mercy, neither could be abandoned without jeopardizing the whole commonwealth. Clearly then one must be careful not to assume that in any particular case tried by the General Court Winthrop would be willing to jettison justice no matter how much he felt the commonwealth was threatened. Such action would be counterproductive. An individual action of his during the course of a trial such as that of Mrs. Hutchinson might not reflect careful weighing of justice versus expediency, but the intention of the trial had to be a search for justice, and not merely a hollow exercise.

Pragmatically, Winthrop had found that he was unable to control many of the colony's freemen and men of standing in the community when votes were taken having to do with Mrs. Hutchinson. He had opined that her party included, "some of all sorts, and quality, in all places to defend and Patronise them; Some of the Magistrates some Gentlemen, some Scholars, and men of learning, some Burgesses of our General Court, some of our Captains, and Soldiers, some chief men in Towns and some men eminent for Religion, parts and wit."10 For this reason as well, Winthrop was aware that all eyes would be upon them as they tried her, so he would have had to be scrupulous in attempting to assure that justice was served, or appeared to be served.

Justice was quite naturally tied to truth, which meant that the search for truth was paramount in a trial. That is why, although the colony's leaders wanted to use the Hutchinson trial to rid themselves of her threat, they recognized that the trial had to be a search for truth. Had it not been, Winthrop would hardly have been truthful enough to state in his record of the trial that Hutchinson had almost defeated their best efforts, until God stepped in with a providential sense of urgency on Hutchinson's part to state that she had had revelations. By stating that she had almost overwhelmed them, until God effectively took pity on the poor group of educated males and stepped in on their behalf, he gave credence to any who would claim that she was more intellectually agile than all of them put together, and only with a fortuitous intervention from God were they saved. This would not have been an easy statement to make, and had the importance of the trial been merely the verdict of guilt, he could have downplayed her role in defending herself, and the nearness of defeat.

Another consideration important to the colony's leaders was the limits of the law: Winthrop and the other legal minds were closely in tune with the latest English legal thinking concerning the limits of citizens' obligation to obey the law. While they were strongly determined that the law was a moral good and given by God to the people, their Puritan hearts also resonated to the arguments that the Christian must have a higher allegiance

than to the law. Those arguments made in England, although dealing with
the problems of the King's meddling in the church's affairs, also molded
their understanding of how far a citizen is compelled to go in obedience to
the law.[11] Roger Williams, having worked for Sir Edward Coke, who was
heavily involved in precisely those discussions in Parliament, stands out as
the one who was most aware of the considerations that had driven Puritans
within Parliament to state that the citizen must be allowed to obey a higher
law when necessary. However, other leaders of the Bay Colony, such as
John Winthrop, who had training and experience in the law also followed
those discussions closely. They recognized that they were obligated to,
"obey God even at the expense of disobeying men of high authority," and
that they should pray with the divine who prayed in Norwich in 1620,
"Bless the people and teach them to obey for conscience sake; and withall
wisely to know where, and how it is better to obey thee, then [sic] man."[12]
For Hutchinson, the issue was paramount. Like Williams, she would not
give an inch even when faced with banishment: she believed she had to
follow her conscience. Others in the colony were more willing to be
persuaded to see reason, especially when presented with the unpleasant
alternative. Hutchinson, Williams, Wheelwright, and a few others, however, would not compromise. This stance should have been recognized by the
leaders of the colony for what it was: the same stance that Puritans had
taken in England, when they refused to change their thinking because their
consciences would not allow them. Yet for all this, they did not hold with
the idea of freedom of conscience for others, much as they wanted it for
themselves. Several of the ministers, including Thomas Shepard, preached
sermons in which they vilified the idea of unlimited liberty of conscience.
John Norton, later the biographer of John Cotton, equated it with, "liberty
to blaspheme, a liberty to seduce others from the true God," and Nathaniel
Ward stated that those who preached "other Enthusiasms" could have "free
liberty to keep away from us."[13] For those like Hutchinson, freedom of
conscience was not offered nor did the leaders of the colony see a parallel
with the liberty they demanded for themselves. They were only able to see
the threat of disintegration of the colony.

It is commonly assumed that the laws of the colony, whether written
or understood, were based upon the Bible, and indeed when John Cotton
was asked to draw up a codification of laws, he did base it primarily, but
not entirely, upon the law of Moses. Many of the leaders of the colony,
including Cotton, had a good comprehension of theories of law, and its
relationship to politics and society. They intertwined their Puritan theological doctrines with this knowledge to give them a philosophy of how society
should be organized. For that reason none of them expected the magis-

trates of Massachusetts Bay Colony to depend only upon biblical teachings for derivation of decisions they handed down, nor were biblical teachings intended to provide the basis for the laws of the state. The legal opinions and practices that were developed in the colony, whether based upon judicial decisions or later, upon written laws, drew their authority from English common law, with biblical authority given as a "warrant," or further foundation, in many cases.[14] Thus their legal system as it developed was based primarily upon the English common law, and secondarily upon the Bible. One study describes an understanding of the system in this way:

> Early Massachusetts law was an amalgam of specific English rules and experience of English practice in the court of justices of the peace, of English boroughs, and of English manors, tested against and reconciled with the precepts of Hebraic law as understood from the Old Testament, and conditioned by the environment of the Bay Colony—both the natural ambience and the nature of the founders' community—a Godly commonwealth, to be structured *de novo* from top to bottom.[15]

The theories of law that they followed derived more from English common law than the Bible, undoubtedly because the founders were trained in the law and therefore were used to the arguments grounded in common law, and found them reasonable.[16]

Puritans felt much the same about the discussion of the law as with the discourse concerning theology. That is to say that they took both subjects quite seriously, and accepted that a correct interpretation of either was essential. Just as they needed to be in possession of the correct doctrinal interpretation, their belief that God's intentions for humanity were shown through laws, caused them to become "legalists par excellence."[17] Puritans in England and in New England as well formed their political thinking from reading biblical and civil laws. Both models formed critical parts of the political system: after all, while the laws written into the Bible had been given to "heathen," English laws had been fashioned by God for good Christians, as an anonymous writer pointed out in the early seventeenth century.[18] These laws were so perfect that while God had not personally dictated each of the laws of England, the writer "did imply that the Almighty could not have done better if He had tried."[19] Lawyers studied the law continuously like theologians studied Holy Writ, and indeed, in seeking a warrant for individual laws, were apt to quote scripture. And they looked, not to a wholistic system of laws, but to individual laws to guide them in their search for God's plan for humankind on earth. They were not seeking to discover overarching theories, but for God's intentions for humanity, revealed in particular laws.[20] This enabled them to derive "pithy axioms of the laws," which could guide them much as Justices of the Supreme Court today will be guided by the Constitution.[21] Such axioms as: "no man judge in his own case, no self-incrimination...no imprisonment without showing cause..." were extracted from individual laws and the Bible, and were, "distillations which made sense out of the scattered, sometimes contradictory laws."[22] These were the axioms that the lawyers of England had drawn out of the laws, and which men like Winthrop, Dudley, and the rest of the legally trained men in Massachusetts Bay Colony had learned as the maxims of English common law. Perhaps not surprisingly, a similar stance was taken by ministers in interpreting scripture. It was not to the separate strictures that one should point, but rather to the precept that could be drawn from the whole of scripture, and which are therefore eternal in their applicability.[23]

Like the system in Massachusetts Bay, English common law too was not based upon a written constitution or a precise and methodical code of laws, but was founded upon custom, judicial records, and written statutes; thus, it was in some ways inchoate, but also "adaptable and eclectic."[24] A background in the study and use of unsystematic legislation proved useful to Winthrop and the others as they devised a legal system for the colony; it meant that they could easily continue as they had started, with laws growing out of circumstances as they found them, rather than according to any system. Legal historian George Haskins makes the statement that the law of the colony was striking in the "autonomous course that it followed during the first decades of the colony's history."[25] In following this course the magistrates whose adjudications became the substance of the law were not directed wholly by precedent, biblical strictures, or theories of legal thought in England. This did, however, run counter to definitions of proper legal procedure as discussed by Coke, who had maintained that, "*melius est recurrere, quam male currere*," or, "it is better to turn back, than run ahead badly."[26] This makes it clear that the intention of the leaders of the colony, especially John Winthrop, to go their own way was unusual, to say the least.

As was the case in England, though, the aforementioned concept of "fundamental law" or "natural law" was essential to their understanding of the essence of proper legal systems. The seminal legal discourse that took place in England during the century dealt with English constitutional notions of the underpinnings of the law. For those Englishmen who entered into this discussion the concept of "fundamental" or "natural" law provided the framework into which such discourse could be held. Although those who were a part of these discussions equated the ideas with God's law, they did not mean that "fundamental law" was drawn from the

Bible, rather that it was intrinsic to human understanding, and in essence was superior to or formed a basis for biblical laws: laws given in the Bible were based upon it.[27] They believed that Englishmen were protected by the law, and all "fundamental" law was protective. They were protected by laws that were, to use the words of Lilburne in, *London's Liberty in Chains*, "such only as are agreeable to the Law Eternal, and not contrary to the word of God..."[28] The founders of Massachusetts Bay also incorporated such thinking into their own understanding of what constitutes the essence around which laws can be structured.

The laws of the colony thus were drawn from English common law, with careful analysis to ensure that they were in accordance with biblical injunctions as well. These were the bases for their law, and the legal system grew within these parameters. Its growth might in practice be less than systematic, but there were some curbs and guidelines. One of the protections upon which the colonists relied was written into Cotton's system of laws of 1634. This was the stipulation that the testimony of two witnesses be given in order to convict in a criminal case.[29] Such a requirement is of course based upon that demanded in the Bible as necessary for conviction, and was an issue raised by Hutchinson during her church trial. It seems to have been generally agreed that two witnesses were necessary in most cases, and in her civil trial Hutchinson insisted that allegations against her be confirmed by the sworn testimony of two witnesses based upon the biblical injunction. During her trial it became a problem for the prosecution, as it proved to be impossible to find the requisite two witnesses who could state that she had said in their presence that the ministers were preaching a covenant of works. Cotton himself admitted later that he had attempted to trap Hutchinson after the synod of 1637 and was frustrated by the fact that he was unable to catch her making unorthodox statements in the presence of two or more witnesses. Winthrop also noted that she and the others were careful not to make any indictable statements in front of witnesses.[30] Both Cotton and Winthrop assume that the reason they were unable to catch her saying heretical things in the presence of two witnesses was that she was too wily to be trapped: the simpler explanation that perhaps she was not making such statements to her friends does not seem to have occurred to them.

One expectation of the law grew out of the early jury system, where the jury was expected to give information regarding a crime, which was that anyone with knowledge of criminal behavior was to inform the authorities. Yet there were conditions under which one person should not be obligated to inform on another. William Ames wrote that a person who hears of an offence was not obligated to reveal it, "for he, whose offence is hidden, has he as yet right to preserve his fame, that it should not rashly be laid open."[31] Nor were wives forced to testify against their husbands, or parents to bring evidence about children.[32] These were felt to be situations that were contrary to nature. This sensitivity to human affections makes all the more stark the censure that John Cotton was to deliver to Hutchinson's son and son-in-law after her church trial, where he berated them for having stood by her.

The procedures followed in Hutchinson's trial followed the usual course for the most part, but not in all particulars. It was usual to have a pre-trial examination of a defendant, intended to wring a confession from the accused. The person would be examined be a Magistrate, and then be sent on to the court. At the pretrial examination the accused would be urged to confess.[33] While there was a strongly held belief that no one should be made to incriminate himself, there was no bar to cajoling or even threatening the accused into "voluntarily" doing so.[34] The technique was to interrogate the accused, and attempt to trip him up; the hope was that the person would confess to the crime, thereby saving time at the trial. The method had been relied upon heavily in England, and in New England was very effective as well. This procedural method was quite important to their theories and operation of justice because of the belief that the accused should not only be allowed but be expected to show remorse for his crime, and when this happened the court should show clemency. The system of justice depended strongly upon the concept of repentance by the defendant: often times the accused could save the state the expense and the community the trauma of a trial by pleading guilty and showing remorse for the crime, in which case punishment would be stayed. This concentration upon the importance of repentance to the judicial process was not only the case in criminal trials but also in ecclesiastical trials. In these cases it was not uncommon for the person to be excommunicated and then upon a show of remorse for the misdeed be accepted into the fold again.[35] If the magistrate or the court was able to wring a confession from the offender the person would be expected to make a public confession "as a final step in his exoneration."[36] Punishments for infractions of the law were severe, and included whipping and sitting in the stocks for stealing, public acknowledgment of slander (a punishment that would seem to be both well suited to the crime and a good antidote for it), whipping and sitting before the congregation with a piece of paper describing the crime for housebreaking and stealing on the Lord's day, death for rape, and public repentance where possible.[37] No doubt such harsh punishments also encouraged those accused of crimes to think more seriously of the possibility of repentance, and one can assume that the penalty for the crime may well have been mentioned by the judge examining the accused.

Hutchinson was tried during a regular session of the General Court, by the whole court, with Winthrop presiding. This was the usual procedure at the time, although there were instances in which juries were called to hear a case. However, in cases where the punishment would be severe, such as in capital cases, a jury often was not called. The reason for this appears to lie in the history of the growth of the use of juries. From the twelfth century on, when justice was served in England by having a representative of the King travel around the country to hear cases, a jury would be called to give evidence to aid the king's representative in deciding the case.[38] Only in the hundred or so years before the founding of New England had the responsibility of the jury changed to that of hearing and deciding cases rather than giving evidence. Although the practice of having a jury hear and decide a case was not yet universal, it was used in some cases by 1637, but rarely used in serious cases. It was unusual in serious cases because "New England magistrates consciously imitated what they evidently regarded as the most progressive and efficient feature of the whole system, the trend toward summary justice."[39] So, although the General Court had stated in 1634 that trials for banishment or where a life was at stake a jury would be called, the other alternative it allowed was that the General Court could hear such cases.[40] Banishment was often used as an alternative to capital punishment, and was therefore considered to be the equivalent of it. In 1641, when the codification of laws was completed for the colony, banishment was one of the punishments that was not to be meted out unless the person had been convicted of having broken a specific, serious, and written law.[41]

The General Court, by whom Anne Hutchinson was tried, was the final authority in the colony and did not allow appeals to the king. This was the highest judicial body in the land, and it acted as a court of appeals for the lower courts, whether Courts of Assistants, or the local courts that were instituted a few years after the Hutchinson trial.[42] The whole court heard and decided the case, with everyone who was part of the elected government acting as prosecutor and then participating in the final vote of guilt or acquittal. This also meant that any one of the men hearing the case could and did question the defendant, and, when the court decided it had heard enough, summarily voted on the guilt of the defendant. John M. Murrin, writing on court procedure of the time, says, "Criminal procedure during the early modern era was groping toward a distinction between the prosecutorial and adjudicative functions of the court. This difference could utterly collapse in major political trials in which the bench might insult the defendant and browbeat witnesses and jurors..."[43] Or, as stated even more strongly by W.S. Holdsworth, a trial conducted in England at the time was "an altercation between the accused, and the prosecutor and his witnesses."[44] Transcripts of Hutchinson's trials demonstrate that during the trials pressure was put upon her to recognize and repent of her sinful ways. This explains why the courts, both secular and ecclesiastical, spent so much time arguing vociferously and at length with her. The process of her trials, like those of others, was intended not simply to present evidence for conviction or acquittal, but to bring the evildoer to a change of ways. To that end it was not enough to elicit information from the defendant and witnesses, but also to argue and spar with the accused.

However, lest it be thought that all was confusion in the courtroom, Haskins reminds the reader that the early courts in Massachusetts were attempting to render justice, even where they disregarded the usual procedure followed under English common law. Haskins is convinced that Winthrop attempted to allow as much flexibility as possible in the courtroom proceedings as well as in rendering decisions. Their situation was in transition the way it was while they groped toward a system of laws and procedures that would be as appropriate to their new circumstances.[45] Another reason for Winthrop's insistence upon flexibility for the Magistrates may be found in his experience as a justice of the peace. For Haskins also notes that justices of the peace at the time in England interpreted the King's law with a great deal of freedom.[46] In 1637 Winthrop and the others were still attempting to adapt a much more conplex system of English laws, which was itself not uniform from place to place, with manorial courts, justices of the peace, courts of the shire and hundreds, courts leet and courts baron, and other legally and procedurally distinct methods in use. Therefore, one difference between the Massachusetts courts and those of England was the simplification of many legal procedures for the sake of rendering justice more efficiently and effectively. Because there were fewer layers and kinds of courts there was not as great a need for complex legal maneuvers, and because the legal system was in development the procedures were much less formal and simpler in the New World than in England.[47] Haskins states that procedure usually reflected that of the courts baron, but technicalities were often disregarded where it was felt prudent to do so in order to tailor the process to the needs of the case.[48]

At Hutchinson's trial the General Court heard the case without a formal pretrial examination, although there had been a number of times when she and John Cotton had been questioned. At any trial, if no confession had taken place at a pretrial examination of the accused he or she was questioned smartly by the judge and the rest of the court. "The ability of colonial judges to obtain a confession from the suspect, despite his initial reluctance, has probably been underestimated. A judge held the upper hand in the process."[49] At Hutchinson's trial no counsel was present for either side, which was the usual practice, and which gave the prosecutorial side an enormous advantage, as the men who sat on the court were educated, and Winthrop and others had legal training. In her case, Winthrop, governor of the Colony at the time of the trial, and therefore the one who led the questioning and judicial aspects of the trial, had the huge advantage of having acted as a justice of the peace in Suffolk County, and a judge of the court at Norwich borough.[50] Thomas Dudley, one of those who was most hostile toward Hutchinson, and a number of others had had some training in the law as well.[51] Hutchinson, needless to say, had not. And although, it appears likely that she consulted someone with such knowledge after the first day of the trial, it was rather her clever mind that enabled her to parry questions, insist on proper procedure, and in general to do as well as she did at her trials. In both trials she displayed an astonishing familiarity with the legal principles that governed her situation. One has to assume that most defendants would have fared far worse against the court, and indeed, the ease with which others were quickly tried and found guilty, as well as Winthrop's bewildered—if grudging—praise of Hutchinson, indicates that she was most unusual. Her trial was also atypical in that although she posed the threat of disintegration of the church at Boston, she "was in fact allowed considerable freedom in making her defense," according to Haskins.[52] In contrast, it was usual in such cases that defendants would not be allowed to cross-examine the witnesses for the defense; and that hearsay evidence would be admitted.[53]

Oath-taking, which became a serious issue at Hutchinson's trial—at her insistence—is another facet of the case that demonstrates both their attempts to follow proper procedure and their uncertainty as to how best to proceed. At the courts baron, which were held in England to enable those who were accused of offenses against the manor, twelve men of the manor heard cases, and decided them on the basis of sworn testimony from neighbors.[54] In such cases, any testimony that was false would easily be discovered by close neighbors. Justices of the peace had been given specific powers in 1590 to enforce their rulings, including the authority to doubly enforce oath-taking by requiring a surety bond.[55] The Puritans, however, were very careful about oath-taking, although they did require it at some points. Non-freemen who moved into towns were required to take oaths that they would abide by the laws of the area, for instance, and oaths were taken by those who were to give testimony as witnesses. Further, the

General Court itself "would not proceed to judgment in any course, civil or criminal, before the deputies had taken a solemn oath.[56]

However, there was a great deal of concern that one not take an oath in some instances. Self-incrimination was one area of legal thought that had been under discussion during the last century or so in England, with the result that there was general agreement in Massachusetts that torture should not be used to extract confessions, and the accused should not be forced to give testimony that would be self-incriminating. It was usual for an accused person to be examined without being expected to take an oath. This was in recognition of the fact that a person who was sworn could then be forced to incriminate himself.[57] Indeed, during the trial of John Wheelwright this issue came to the forefront. The Court informed Wheelwright that it possessed a written copy of his allegedly seditious sermon, and as he had declared that the copy was of his sermon, it would proceed, "*ex officio,*" and examine him. There was quite an outcry, however. Winthrop records that the members of the Court reacted angrily, as if Wheelwright were to be forced to incriminate himself. Winthrop says that he explained to those present that no overbearing control was intended, nor would the Court examine him, "by any compulsory means, as by oath, imprisonment, or the like, but only desired him for better satisfaction to answer some questions..."[58] Wheelwright's friends were furious, however, and claimed that the court was proceeding unlawfully,and intended to, "ensnare him, and make him accuse himself..."[59]

William Ames had found the topic of oaths to be of enough importance to demand a chapter in *The Marrow of Theology.* An oath was a serious matter, he explained, because, "in every oath there is contained implicitly or explicitly the utterance or calling down of a curse."[60] It was therefore a profound affair indeed to take an oath, and such action could not be undertaken lightly. For this reason any Puritan would be extremely fearful of taking an oath and then perjuring himself. For, the oath having been taken before God, this would be a deliberate sin against God, and would damn the person's soul to hell. For this reason, had Wheelwright been forced to take an oath, he would have had to tell the truth, and thereby possibly incriminate himself. During Hutchinson's trial she demanded that the ministers who accused her of libeling them take an oath, and they were extremely squeamish about doing so, because they feared that if their memories were inaccurate, they would be damning themselves. Ames' chapter in the *Marrow* that deals with oath-taking speaks to this very happpenstance. He states, "a man does not perjure himself, properly speaking, unless he swears against his conscience or knowingly and willingly departs from what he has lawfully sworn."[61] Given that Ames had spoken to the subject in his well-known work, one can assume that the ministers in fact doubted that their testimony was completely correct, which was why they demurred when asked to take the oath, rather than because they believed that God would damn them for an honest mistake.

Even if all procedures were carefully followed and all safeguards taken on behalf of the accused, to see that justice was rendered, ultimately the case against Hutchinson had to be based upon adequately proving that she was guilty of sedition, as charged. The charges against her were based upon maligning the ministers. There are two conditions that would have to have been met in order for her to have been proven guilty of sedition. First, the link between the church and the state would have to have been explicitly or implicitly made, in order for the relationship between sedition and maligning the ministers to stand. Secondly, it would then have to have been shown that she incited others to hostility toward the ministers, in their capacity as unofficial representatives of the government.

The connection between the ministers and the state was implicit in its undergirding of authority and in the organization of government as well. As the ministers were not allowed to hold state office, the colony had made it clear that it did not suppose itself to be a theocracy. The separation between the rulers and the clergy was distinct and intentional, and continued the thinking of the Puritan leaders who had considered the question in England. The intent was to have a separation between church and state, but the founding of the colony afforded them the opportunity to carefully delineate the size of the separation and its parameters: the separation was not complete, and the connections between the two were essential to the operation of the state.

One connection between the state and the church was the requirement that a man be admitted to a congregation before he could "be sworn to freemanship at its General Court."[62] While this guaranteed that the voters in the colony were all certified church members, it was not evidence of the kind of close intermingling of church and state that would have been the case had the clergy been in charge of state government. In fact, not only were the clergy not in control of state government, they were not in complete control of the churches, either, as church members were able to exercise some control over the ministers and the churches, in some cases. A case in point was when Winthrop, anxious not to have John Wheelwright as a third pastor in the Boston church found it necessary to appeal to the members of the church not to vote to have Wheelwright as another minister for the church. Had Winthrop not been able to convince the rank and file church members, Wheelwright might well have soon thereafter been exercising his oratorical gifts from the pulpit in Boston.

However, it is equally true that the clergy were allowed to have an unusually strong voice in determining policy. The code of laws drawn up by the group John Cotton chaired was not accepted by the colony; however that was not on grounds of its religious basis, but because Winthrop felt its penalties were too harsh. Yet Cotton was asked individually to perform this office because of his penetrating mental capacities, not because of his function as teacher of the church at Boston. The clergy had a function that in some ways parallels that of our Supreme Court: they were able to review laws and rules with a kind of veto power. The reason for their review was not whether ordinances were constitutional, since there was no constitution, nor was the consideration whether the laws might violate the charter of the colony, since the main consideration was whether ordinances and rulings were fair and just and the regard for the charter only came into play when some felt their rights had been abridged, but rather the question was whether the laws were in agreement with biblical strictures. Therefore in yet another twist in the vine of entanglement between church and state, the clergy, while part of the institution that could not challenge the proceedings of the civil court, could and did have a say in the suitability of the laws.

Therefore given the system of cooperation, if not entanglement, of church and state, it was not without the realm of reason for the General Court to base its charge of sedition on allegations that the ministers, leaders of one of the bastions of the society, had been maligned. It was reasonable for them to seek to prove that Hutchinson had endangered the state by maligning the minsters, because their reputations as godly men were indispensible to their review of laws for the state. The next requirement would be that they would have to prove that she had in fact done so, and this they attempted to do. The charge was that she had maligned the ministers by the claim that they were not orthodox in their preaching. Their doctrine being the original reason for the formation of the colony, her characterization of them as not completely orthodox was held to be sedition.

In the trial the case against Hutchinson was first made with the charge that she had been guilty of sedition by virtue of having agreed with and kept company with those who had signed the petition in favor of Wheelwright. She was able to make short work of that charge, on the basis that she had not signed the petition, and the fact of having kept company with someone who had signed it, in the absence of other proof, did not constitute seditious behavior. Once it became apparent to Winthrop that he could not hope to convict her on the ever so much more desirable charge of having committed sedition, "by proxy" so to speak, by linking her with Wheelwright, who had already been found guilty of the crime, he attempted to make his case based upon her maligning of the ministry. That charge was the one with more teeth in it. This was that she had violated the fifth commandment, against honoring one's parents, by maligning the ministers. The Puritans of the Bay Colony held that the commandment extended beyond one's biological parents to include anyone whom God had placed in authority, so that dishonoring those in charge of the community would equal dishonoring parents. Such a charge would be the same as sedition, as it would have undermined the leadership of the colony.

Her method of dealing with this charge was to argue that the passage in the writings of St. Paul that directs the believer to obey parents states, "obey them in the Lord," which is sometimes understood to mean that other authorities are to be considered "parents in the Lord." She stated however that the meaning of the passage was that obedience to authorities is to be given only in things that are religious, or, "in the Lord." Here she was able to carry the day, although she did not attempt to attack the charge at its weakest point, the equation of the breaking of the fifth commandment, understood in its broadest sense, with sedition. Sedition was the charge upon which the bulk of the trial turned. Winthrop had ministers who were ready to testify that she had told them, in confidence and at their urging it is true, that they were not as clear in their presentation of the covenant of grace as John Cotton. In this too, after much ado and many attempts, Winthrop was unable to find her guilty. At this point he allowed her to speak her piece, at which time she spoke of her "revelations." Although unable to persuade John Cotton to agree that her claims were heretical, the court moved to find her guilty on the basis of those claims.

Yet even had her claims to revelations from God been heretical, the trial should have stopped at that point—the state being unable to try a person for a doctrinal breach—and she should have been remanded for an ecclesiastical trial. Instead, the General Court took a vote, called her guilty, and banished her. And when she asked on what grounds she was guilty, Winthrop told her that the court knew, and was satisfied. He refused to answer this all-important question, the most crucial question of the trial: on what grounds did they, or could they, find her guilty? For in fact her claims to "immediate revelations" were not seditious. As will be seen, she stated that God brought Bible passages to her attention, and she acted upon her understanding of the passages. She did state that God would deal harshly with her accusers and judges for their treatment of her, and it could be claimed that this was seditious in that it dishonored the Magistrates. But that was not the claim upon which the court convicted her. It was her claim of revelations from God upon which they triumphantly seized, and used to her disadvantage. It was only after she had been sentenced to banishment that she was held over for a church trial, and that on different grounds.

Notes

1.Winthrop, "Charity," pp. 191, 192.

2. For further study on seventeenth century English understanding of the underpinnings of the relationship between the church and state, and the role of the law in the state, the reader is directed to Eusden.

3. Quoted in Haskins, *Law and Authority*, p. 44.

4. Ibid., p. 191.

5. James G. Moseley, *John Winthrop's World: History as a Story, The Story as History* (Madison WI: University of Wisconsin Press, 1992), pp. 29, 30.

6. Ibid. p. 31.

7. David Thomas Konig, *Law and Society in Puritan Massachusetts: Essex County, 1629–1692*, (Chapel Hill: The University of North Carolina Press, 1979), p. 18.

8. Winthrop, "A Model of Christian Charity," quoted in Morgan, *The Founding of Massachusetts*, p. 203.

9. Ibid.

10. Ibid. p. 208.

11. See especially Eusden's discussions of the relationship between the law courts and the Puritans.

12. Eusden, p. 116.

13. Both quotations are taken from Thomas Jefferson Wertenbaker, "The Fall of the Wilderness Zion," pp. 22–35, in *Puritanism in Early America*, ed. George M Waller (Boston: D.C. Heath and Company, 1950), p. 24.

14. Eusden, p. 5, Haskins, Law and Authority, pp. 4–7.

15. Smith and Barnes, p. 65.

16. Haskins, *Law and Authority*, p. 162, and chapter X, "After English Ways;" See also Eusden.

17. Eusden, p. 119.

18. Eusden, p. 122.

19. Eusden, p. 122.

20. See especially Eusden, pp. 121–135.

21. Eusden, p. 137.

22. Eusden, p. 137.

23. Eusden, p. 138.

24. Eusden, p. 46, see also pp. 94, 95, Haskins, Ibid., Christopher D. Felker, "Roger Williams's Uses of Legal Discourse: Testing Authority in Early New England," *New England Quarterly*, vol. 63, no. 4, (Dec. 1990), p. 627.

25. Haskins, *Law and Authority*, p. 114.

26. Quoted in Eusden, p. 95.

27. Richard B. Morris, *Studies in the History of American Law: With Special Reference to the Seventeenth and Eighteenth Centuries* (New York: Columbia University Press, 1930), p. 24.

28. Ibid.

29. Ibid. p. 125.

30. Hall, *Antinomian*, p. 210.

31. Quoted in David H. Flaherty, *Privacy in Colonial New England* (Charlottesville, VA: University Press of Virginia, 1972), p. 208.

32. Flaherty, p. 209.

33. Ibid., p. 227.

34. For a fuller discussion of self-incrimination, see Ibid., pp. 227-241.

35. Ibid., p. 159.

36. Ibid., p. 158.

37. Haskins, *Law and Authority*, p. 151, 175.

38. John M. Murrin, "Trial by Jury in Seventeenth-Century New England," in *Saints and Revolutionaries: Essays on Early American History*, ed. David D. Hall, John M. Murrin, Thad W. Tate (New York : W.W. Norton, 1986), pp. 152–197.

39. Murrin, p. 157.

40. Murrin, p. 161.

41. Haskins, *Law and Authority*, p. 128.

42. Hilkey, p. 31.

43. Murrin, p. 156.

44. W.S. Holdsworth, quoted in George Lee Haskins, *Law and Authority in Early Century Massachusetts: A Study in Tradition and Design* (Lanham, MD:University Press of America, 1960), p. 50.

45. I draw heavily upon Haskins' *Law and Authority,* chapter X, "After English Ways" in for clarification of Massachusetts legal systems at the time.

46. Haskins, *Law and Authority*, p. 174.

47. Peter Charles Hoffer, *Law and People in Colonial America* (Baltimore: The Johns Hopkins University Press, 1992), pp, 32, 33.

48. Haskins, *Law and Authority*, pp. 168, 9.

49. Flaherty, *Privacy*, p. 230.

50. Konig, *Law and Society*, p. 18.

51. Ibid.

52. Haskins, *Law and Authority*, p. 50.

53. Ibid.

54. Konig, *Law and Society*, p. 7.

55. Ibid. p. 14.

56. Hilkey, p. 32.

57. Flaherty, *Privacy*, p. 225.

58. Quoted in Haskins, *Law and Authority*, p. 201.

59. Ibid.

60. Ames, *Marrow*, p. 268.

61. Ibid., p. 269.

62. Konig, p. 23.

Chapter Eight

"Trouble Us No Further":
The Civil Trial

There are two extant versions of Anne Hutchinson's trial by the General Court. One, from the writings of John Winthrop, is shorter and sketchier, and comprises seventeen pages. The other, printed in a history of Massachusetts by Thomas Hutchinson, a great great grandson of Anne Hutchinson, is twenty five pages of much smaller type. It was copied from an earlier version by Timothy Weld, who took part in the trial. Both versions were evidently taken during the trial, and they agree substantially with one another. In some places the person who took the notes for John Winthrop left out some parts altogether, indicating in one place: "Divers other speeches passed to & fro about this matter..." while the longer version goes on for several pages about the issue.[1] As it is believed that the longer version was taken by Mr. Weld, both versions were written by those in opposition to Anne Hutchinson. Places that exhibit differences of note between the two versions will be addressed during the discussion of the trial. For the greatest percentage of the materials, the two versions agree well on what was said, with the Thomas Hutchinson version (hereinafter TH) almost invariably giving a longer variation of the questions and answers. One example will perhaps give the flavor of the differences. The Winthrop version (JW) reads in this way:

> *Court :* These seditious practices of theirs [those of her followers who signed a petition stating that they believed Wheelwright had been unjustly found guilty of sedition] have cast reproach and dishonour upon the Fathers of the commonwealth.
>
> *Hutch.:* Do I entertain, or maintain them in their actions, wherein they stand against any thing that God hath appointed?
>
> *Court:* Yes, you have justified Mr. *Wheelwright* his Sermon, for which you know he was convict of sedition, and you have likewise countenanced and encouraged those that had their hands to the Petition.
>
> *Hutch.:* I deny it, I am to obey you only in the Lord.[2]

The TH version of that part of the questioning reads:

> Gov: If his conscience comes into act in giving countenance and entertainment to him that hath broken the law he is guilty too. So if you do countenance those that are transgressors of the law you are in the same fact.
> Mrs. H: What law do they transgress?
> Gov: The law of God and of the state.
> Mrs. H: In what particular?
> Gov: Why in this among the rest, whereas the Lord doth say honour thy father and thy mother.
> Mrs. H: Aye Sir in the Lord.
> Gov: This honour you have broken in giving countenance to them.
> Mrs. H: In entertaining those did entertain them against any act (for there is the thing) or what God hath appointed?
> Gov: You knew that Mr. Wheelwright did preach this sermon and those that countenance him in this do break a law.
> Mrs. H: What law have I broken?
> Gov: Why the fifth commandment.
> Mrs. H: I deny that for he saith in the Lord.[3]

These excerpts will suffice to show the ways in which the two versions differ, but give essentially the same material. A careful comparison of the two versions demonstrates that they are comparable in substance.

The probable veracity of the transcripts can be addressed in another way. Puritans were quite adept at taking shorthand notes, as note-taking was encouraged during sermons, and was very common among the membership of the churches. A large percentage of the written sermons that were published during this time were taken, not from writings of the ministers themselves, but from notes taken by a listener, and sometimes, by no means always, edited by the minister who had given the sermon.[4] Most often sermons were written out by the minister as he prepared to preach them, although some of the colony's clergy such as Cotton and Wilson were able to preach extemporaneously. The laity were encouraged to take notes during the preaching of the sermons and to rehearse them on Sunday afternoon or during the week. Larzer Ziff's biography of John Cotton explains: "note-taking during sermons was regarded as a commendable practice which sharpened the note-taker's concentration and provided profit and enjoyment for groups within the congregation, who thereby filled the intervals between sermons with discussion of the doctrines recently opened by their preachers and with debates on obscure or ambiguous points."[5] The faithful would gather in homes to discuss the points raised in the sermons and receive further theological nourishment from them; this was the ostensible reason for the meetings of those who came to hear Anne Hutchinson explicate and comment upon sermons of the colony's ministers.

The ministers would arrange their sermons with careful Ramist logic, which enabled the hearer to follow and remember them easily.[6] This carefully organized structure enabled easier note-taking as well. As will be remembered, facility in taking shorthand had served Roger Williams well, and it was a skill that had no doubt proved useful in similar ways to many others in their daily professions as well as on Sunday mornings. For this reason the shorthand methods developed to enable sermon note-taking would have enabled those who transcribed the trials to take careful and fairly accurate notes.

Existent sermon notes indicate that shorthand methods of the time were predicated not upon learning a special easily employed system of notation as much as upon taking down key words, and reconstituting the whole sermons from those words. A comparison of several colonial sermons still in existence demonstrates that some note-takers took down more of the key words in sentences, thus giving a fuller version.[7] This would seem to have been the case at the trial as well. It is not entirely clear who took the notes: John Cotton maintains that one version of the transcripts was from Thomas Weld, and one from John Winthrop.[8] Discussion of the attribution of the "Short Story," now assumed to be the one from John Winthrop, can be found in John Stetson Barry's *History of Massachusetts: The Colonial Period.*[9] Thomas Hutchinson notes in his history of Massachusetts, written in the eighteenth century, that the "Short Story" of Anne Hutchinson is "commonly attributed" to Thomas Weld.[10] There is also discussion about the question of authorship and provenance of both the longer version of the trials, and of the "Short Story" in David Hall's documentary history of the Antinomian controversy.[11] Hall states confidently that his investigation has shown that Winthrop was the author of the "Short Story."[12]

There are some places in the transcripts in which the questions and answers are not in order, in some cases they are separated by several other lines of text, which requires a very close reading in order to determine the logic of the questioning.[13] However after the confusing transpositions in the transcripts have been rearranged, a sequence is found: one finds that the topics covered during the civil trial can be divided roughly into five parts. The first day three of the parts were covered:

1. Anne Hutchinson was brought before the court, and after the reading of the reasons for her being brought to trial, she asked for the charges against her to be named. By that she meant that she wished to know exactly what they claimed she had done that had occasioned her trial. At this point she made clear to Governor Winthrop that she believed that

she was being persecuted for "conscience" sake, or for her beliefs, rather than for any action of hers.

2. The next section of the trial dealt with Winthrop's claim that she had violated the fifth commandment, and was not honoring the ministers, as her parents "in the Lord" that God had placed over her. She argued that the commandment only expected her to obey those authorities in religious matters, not in civil ones. This led into a discussion about teaching in public, and the proper role of women.

3. The third part of the trial dealt with the most serious charge that Winthrop and the other authorities had, that she had breached the peace and slandered the ministers by claiming that the ministers were not preaching the true Gospel, but were preaching a covenant of works. This charge, of course, was very serious, for, while language such as "breaching the peace" was used, she was being tried for fomenting sedition. This section of the trial took the greatest part of the day, and several ministers testified against her, saying that she had indeed said that they preached a covenant of works. So, if she were to be allowed to convince large numbers of town's folk that their church leaders were unorthodox, or not true Christians, the stability of the state would be threatened. Such behavior could not be tolerated for long.

The second day of the trial covered two more areas:

4. The first part of the second day of the trial was concerned with Hutchinson's insistence that the ministers take an oath that their previous testimony had been truthful, and their various arguments that they should not have to take such an oath. The reason for their reluctance was that they believed that she had some sort of trick up her sleeve, as does indeed seem to have been the case. They were afraid that they would inadvertently tell an untruth because of inaccurate memories, and so damn themselves. It appears that she believed that they were not telling the story accurately, and so she too thought they would damn themselves if they gave the same testimony under oath. Their reluctance to do so indicates that they were not entirely comfortable with the testimony they had given.

5.   The final section of the trial came when Hutchinson felt confidant that she had won her case, as indeed it appears she had, and therefore she decided to tell them why she had been so sure of herself: God had showed her by several Bible verses that she had nothing to fear. The authorities, especially Deputy Governor Dudley, who was very clearly anxious to find her guilty, happily interpreted her answer as meaning that she was telling them that God spoke to her, and that God would provide a miracle to save her. This being interpreted as heresy, she was found guilty of sedition, and banished. She was remanded to Timothy Weld's

house, so that he could attempt to remonstrate with her during the time period of six months or so until she would have to undergo a church trial.

The civil trial took place during the regular session of the General Court, in November, 1637, with John Winthrop presiding over the General Court session, and leading the questioning of the defendant, as well. (The trial was of course not a civil action but a criminal trial: the term civil trial is generally used to differentiate it from her ecclesiastical trial.) In Winthrop's story of the trial he stated that while a number of men had been found guilty of sedition before her trial, she was the real problem for the community. He vehemently declared that while the men were "but young branches" it was necessary to deal with her last, because she was (as he quotes from the Aeneid) the "*Dux foemina facti.*"14   He noted that while her husband was "a peaceable man of good estate," she was a "woman of haughty and fierce carriage of a nimble wit and active spirit, and a very voluble tongue, more bold than a man, though in understanding and judgment, inferior to many women."15

Winthrop opened by announcing to Hutchinson:

> Mrs. Hutchinson, you are called here as one of those that have troubled the peace of the commonwealth and the churches here; you are known to be a woman that hath had a great share in the promoting and divulging of those opinions that are causes of this trouble... you have spoken divers things as we have been informed very prejudicial to the honour of the churches and ministers thereof, and you have maintained a meeting and an assembly in your house that hath been condemned by the general assembly as a thing not tolerable nor comely in the sight of God nor fitting for your sex, and notwithstanding that was cried down you have continued therefore we have thought good to send for you to understand how things are, that if you be in an erroneous way we may reduce you that you may become a profitable member here among us, otherwise if you be obstinate in your course that then the court may take such course that you may trouble us no further...16

Hutchinson replied to that, "I am called here to answer before you but I hear no things laid to my charge." This aggressive posture on her part was to last throughout the civil trial, and there are a number of places that indicate that the men were out of patience with her most of the time. Winthrop tells that she was asked next whether she would countenance "those seditious practices which have been censured here in this Court?" Hutchinson quickly replied to Winthrop that the court had no jurisdiction over her conscience. "That's a matter of conscience, Sir." Winthrop replied to this statement either, "No, your conscience you may keep to yourself"17 or, in the more acid version, "Your conscience you must keep or it must be kept for you.18 This set the tone for the proceedings. All during the trial the officers of the General Court were frustrated by her assurance, and by her skill in representing herself, especially as none of the men who had been tried before her showed as ready a wit as Hutchinson. Edmund Morgan states that the trial was "the least attractive episode in Winthrop's career. Anne Hutchinson was his intellectual superior in everything except political judgment, in everything except the sense of what was possible in this world." He goes on to discuss her ability at the trial, declaring that, "in nearly every exchange of words she defeated him, and the other members of the General Court with him."[19]

Hutchinson began by raising the point of conscience because she knew that it was not lawful for the court to try her for her thoughts and for following her conscience, and naturally Winthrop knew it, too. He wrote in his journal that the trial had not been about her beliefs, but her actions: "[they] began now to raise sedition amongst us, to the endangering [of] the common-wealth; Hereupon for these grounds named, [were they brought to trial] (and not for their opinions, as themselves falsely reported...)."[20] Besides Roger Williams's later accusation of John Cotton several of the leaders in England accused both Cotton and Winthrop of persecution of conscience. This made them both eager to deny in their writings about the case that they had done so. It was a troublesome concern, for it must be remembered that not only was such a charge odious to them personally, but it was the basis for the suggestion that the colony's charter should be revoked. Winthrop was therefore anxious to move from it to a charge with which he was more comfortable: the fifth commandment. Winthrop told Hutchinson that she had broken the commandment against obedience to parents by giving encouragement to those who had signed the petition declaring that Wheelwright had falsely been found guilty of sedition. She asked why she could not entertain those who had signed the petition without acquiring their guilt, and Winthrop accused her of having become guilty because she had not disagreed with them: "So if you do countenance those that are transgressors of the law you are in the same fact."[21]

She then asked what law they had broken, and was told that they—and she—had not given honor to their substitute parents, the authorities. She answered Winthrop, "I deny that for he saith in the Lord." Here she refers to Ephesians 6:1 where the apostle Paul says, "Children, obey your parents in the Lord, for this is right." Winthrop's inclusion of those authorities God has set over a person under the category of "parents" is not unusual for the time, which explains why she did not take issue with this interpreta-tion. However, her supposition as to the meaning of the verse that she cited in Ephesians as directing that one need only obey parents in things religious is not borne out by the context of the text, which gives instruction for proper Christian behavior in all circumstances, not only those circumstances where one is dealing with religious questions. It is surprising that Winthrop allowed her to make her argument based upon that reading of the verse.

Winthrop argued with her for a while about whether she was dishonoring the authorities by not keeping herself aloof from those whom he believed had been disobedient to the Magistrates. She was able to deflect every suggestion that she had disobeyed the law in any regard, so he changed the subject to that of the meetings she had held to discuss the Sunday sermon, and noted that she held them at a specific time each week. By this he was underscoring the implication that the meetings had not been casual ones, from time to time, but rather that they were planned meetings that took place on a regular schedule. This was intended to imply that the meetings had a subversive intent, and to disallow her claim, should she make it—and she did—that the meetings were merely unofficial, informal, friendly gatherings. For had they been merely congenial receptions, anything she happened to say there should not be taken to have been intended as formal teaching, only conversation. If her claim that her meetings were conversational rather than formal were accepted, any statements made during discussions at the meetings would of course be much less threatening to the commonwealth than would be what Winthrop characterized at the trial as "public assemblies": and of course less indictable.[22]

Hutchinson answered that it was completely lawful for her to hold such meetings, and that many others held them as well, asking, "and can you find a warrant for yourself and condemn me for the same thing?"[23] Winthrop was forced to agree that it was acceptable to hold meetings, but changed tack by bringing up the concern that she should not have been teaching men. This was intended to address the teachings of St. Paul regarding women's proper place in the worship service, which forbade them to teach men. Everyone knew that some of her meetings had been gatherings of men. He asked her by what authority she could teach, and she cited "a clear rule in Titus, that the elder women should instruct the younger and then I must have a time wherein I must do it."[24] "All this I grant, I grant you a time for it..." replied the irritated Winthrop. He then went on to press home his contention that she should not have been teaching men, as St. Paul did not allow it. Hutchinson rather cleverly replied that he must give her a rule that said she must send away men who came to her for instruction, and of course he could not do so. She added, "Do you think it not lawful for me to teach women and why do you call me to teach the court?" which garnered an irritated reply from Winthrop that she was not there to teach them, but to "lay open" her thinking.[25] In other words, he wished only to search for the truth. By this time he was impatiently sparring with her, and told her she needed to show a rule that said her teaching was acceptable. She replied, "I have done it." He petulantly returned, with almost childish reasoning, "I deny it because I have brought more arguments than you have." She stubbornly refused to acknowledge the unassailable logic of this, and gave him some of her own: "I say, to me it is a rule." And they went on for a while in this vein.

Winthrop told her that the verse she cited referred only to teaching about loving their husbands, but she maintained it meant "some public times." She refused to be daunted by his questions, and so he lectured her, telling her that families had been neglected because of her bad influence upon the women of Boston, and that she had been seducing "simple souls."26 She replied, "Sir, I do not believe that to be so." Finally, unable to curb himself, Winthrop threatened her with, "Well we see how it is we must therefore put it away from you or restrain you from maintaining this course." Undaunted, she replied, "If you have a rule for it from God's word you may." He shot back, "We are your judges, and not you ours, and we must compel you to it." She demurely returned, "If it please you by authority to put it down I will freely let you for I am subject to your authority."27 At this point Simon Bradstreet, one of the Assistants, intervened.

Bradstreet tried a new tack by appealing to her duty as a Christian not to give offense to others. This was based upon St. Paul's declaration in his first letter to the Corinthians, chapter eight, that while it was lawful for him to eat anything, even meat that had been offered to idols, he would not do so, as it gave offense to others. Bradstreet seems to have wished to find a way to secure an agreement from her that she would no longer hold such meetings; perhaps he hoped that if she would agree the court could finish with the case and not have to deal with her any longer. He asked her if she would be willing to give up her meetings on the grounds that they gave offense. She said, "Sir, in regard of myself I could, but for others I do not yet see light but shall further consider of it."28 She would have been willing to give up the meetings if they gave offense if she had only herself to consider, she felt, but it seemed to her that others needed the meetings. Bradstreet agreed that, "I am not against all women's meetings but do think them to be lawful."29 Deputy governor Dudley, worried that things were going her way, brought them back on track by asking whether men had come to the meetings. Upon questioning whether any women taught at the meetings for men, he was told that was never the case. That did not suit him, so he asserted that before she came "we were all in peace." She, however, had "vented divers of her strange opinions and had made parties in the country... and now she hath a potent party in the country. Now if all these things have endangered us as from that foundation and if she in particular hath disparaged all our ministers in the land that they have preached a covenant of works, and only Mr. Cotton a covenant of grace, why this is not to be suffered..."30 Indeed.

At this juncture things took an interesting turn: Hutchinson was not prepared to allow him to accuse her of misbehavior without a rebuttle. Hutchinson turned to Dudley and declared, "I pray Sir prove it that I said they preached nothing but a covenant of works." He disgustedly replied, "Nothing but a covenant of works, why a Jesuit may preach truth sometimes." Not at all daunted, she asked, "Did I ever say they preached a covenant of works then?"

"If they do not preach a covenant of grace clearly, then they preach a covenant of works."

"No sir, one may preach a covenant of grace more clearly than another, so I said." This was not going the way it should go. Dudley had a number of ministers standing by ready to give testimony of her effrontery to them and to their proper status in the community. She, however, continued to be uncooperative: "I did not come hither to answer to questions of that sort," she answered to one question from Dudley. She also insisted that he prove his allegations against her: "Aye, but that is to be proved first."

"I will prove this that you said the gospel in the letter and words holds forth nothing but a covenant of works and that all that do not hold as you do are in a covenant of works," he replied.31 Dudley was feeling smug; he believed he had her, now, and all of them were growing more than a little annoyed with her, as she insisted over and over that they must prove their claim that she had said the things they claimed. Dudley told her, "I will make it plain that you did say that the minister did preach a covenant of works...and that you said they were not able ministers of the new testament, but Mr. Cotton only."32 At her reply, "If I ever spake that I proved it by God's word," he was much improved in his temper. "Very well, very well..." he murmured.

Hutchinson however took the questions onto another track. She reminded the court that it was not enough to prove that she had told some people in private that some of the ministers were not as doctrinally pure as Cotton, they would have to prove that she did so publicly. There were two reasons for this. For one thing, in order to prove sedition, they needed to demonstrate that she had encouraged people to behave in ways that were dangerous to the public peace, or had undermined the ministers as part of the government of the colony, to the detriment of the colony. This could hardly be the case if she only mentioned in private to a friend that one

minister was doing a better job than another. In addition, if she had only
spoken in private to one person at a time, the requisite two witnesses that
Cotton had not been able to find could never be found. She noted, "It is
one thing for me to come before a public magistracy and there to speak
what they would have me to speak and another when a man comes to me in
a way of friendship privately..." Winthrop completely lost patience with
her at this juncture and interjected, "Only I would add this. It is well
discerned to the court that Mrs. Hutchinson can tell when to speak and
when to hold her tongue."[33]

The ministers who had been standing by ready to bring testimony
against her were now brought in, but they were extremely reluctant to do
so—"our brethren are very unwilling to answer, " Mr. Peter sadly told the
court. They were not looking forward to testifying now, as they could see
that Hutchinson was doing so well in her own behalf, and "that she was a
woman not only difficult in her opinions, but also of an intemperate spirit."[34] Peter gave a long history of the problems he and others had had
with her, how they had called upon Cotton to deal with her, and then the
ministers had spoken with her. She had made it very plain during that
meeting that she did not want to make comparisons between Cotton and the
other ministers, and felt that they were trying to entrap her. Peter put it,

> At the very first we gave her notice that such reports there were that she did
> conceive our ministry to be different from the ministry of the gospel and that
> we taught a covenant or works &c. and this was her table talk and therefore
> we desired her to clear herself and deal plainly. She was very tender
> [apprehensive] at first. Some of our brethren did desire to put this upon
> proof and then her words upon that were ["]The fear of man is a snare why
> should I be afraid.["] These were her words.[35]

He had persisted, though, and finally, "she answered that he preaches the
covenant of grace and you the covenant of works and that you are not able
ministers of the new testament..."[36] They had come to her in tears since
that time as well, he asserted.

To all of this she calmly replied, "if our pastor would shew his writings you should see what I said, and that many things are not so as is
reported." She told the court, according to Winthrop's version, that she
had a copy of Wilson's notes and she had studied them carefully, but did
not have them with her.[37] Unfortunately, Mr. Wilson, the pastor of her
church was also not able to produce his notes, saying that they were at
home, and that furthermore, "I must say that I did not write down all that
was said and did pass betwixt one and another..." It is noteworthy that the
court did not ask one or the other of them to produce the notes from at
home, which might have saved some time and difficulties in the long run.

The other ministers were called upon to give their testimony at this time, to corroborate what Hugh Peter had said, and Weld, minister of Roxbury, who was the one who took the notes from which Thomas Hutchinson's account is taken, George Phillips, minister of Watertown, Zechariah Simmes, minister of Charlestown, and Wilson, of Boston, all testified that she had cast aspersions on their ability to preach the clear gospel, telling them that Cotton preached the gospel more clearly than they and that they had not been sealed with the spirit. "And this I remember" said Weld, "she said we could not preach a covenant of grace because we were not sealed..."[38]

Simmes also told the court the story of how he had been concerned about her doctrinal purity when she had first come to New England, but that he had been reassured after she had been questioned. He gave a history of his dealings with her even as far back as when both were in England, and on the ship coming over to new England. He had been worried about some of her claims while on shipboard, and had raised those concerns when she had applied for admittance to the church. He said that he thought that the evidence of the other ministers was true, as far as he could remember, but added, "yet I do not think myself disparaged by her testimony and I would not trouble the court, only this one thing I shall put in, that Mr. Dudley and Mr. Haines were not wanting in the cause after I had given notice of her." Although Simmes was giving testimony that he knew would be prejudicial to her case he wanted it known that he had taken notice of the unusual prosecutorial zeal of Dudley and Haines. To this even Wilson, the minister whom she had wounded most, must have begun to sense the pricks of conscience at the proceedings, as he felt obliged to add that, "I desire you would give me leave to speak this word because of what has been said concerning her entrance into the church. There was some difficulty made, but in her answers she gave full satisfaction to our teacher [Cotton] and myself..."[39]

Mr. Shepard, minister at Cambridge, then spoke, although he said he was reluctant to do so, attesting that he agreed that what was said in private ought to remain private and said he felt that she had been in error in her speaking or "it may be but a slip of her tongue..." that she had said the ministers were not sealed of the Spirit.[40]   After him John Eliot, another minister at Roxbury, stated that he had taken a few notes about the conversations the ministers had had with her, and that "the substance" of it was correct. Thereupon Dudley, convinced that he had proved his case, stated, "You see they have proved this and you deny this, but it is clear. You said they preached a covenant of works and that they were not able ministers of the new testament..."[41]

Unrepentant, Hutchinson coolly gave back to these efforts to make her see reason, and to agree that the state had proved its case, "Prove that I said so." Winthrop asked, "Did you say so?" and she replied, "No sir it is your conclusion."[42] Exasperated, Dudley exploded, "What do I do charging of you if you deny what is so fully proved." Winthrop was as bewildered as Dudley at her answer to them. He said, "Here are six undeniable ministers who say it is true and yet you deny that you did say that they did preach a covenant of works and that they have spoken it..." Here she demonstrated that she could split hairs with the best of the theologians or lawyers. She "absolutely den[ied]" their testimony, going into some detail about the sequence of events. She reminded the court that she had been assured by the ministers that they came for "plain dealing and telling you our hearts."[43] She went on, "Then I said I would deal as plainly as I could, and whereas they say I said they were under a covenant of works and in the state of the apostles why these two speeches cross one another, I might say they might preach a covenant of works as did the apostles, but to preach a covenant of works and to be under a covenant of works is another business." And when Winthrop reminded her that six witnesses had given testimony that she had made statements of this kind about them, she left him non-plussed by saying, "I deny that these were the first words spoken." Peter soothingly said, "We do not desire to be so narrow to the court and the gentlewoman about times and seasons, whether first or after, but said it was."[44]

After a bit more discussion of the case with Dudley threatening to bring in written notes taken by one of the ministers, she acknowledged that she had made a distinction between the letter of the law and the letter of the gospel to one of the ministers, telling him that he was under the letter, and not the spirit, of the gospel. This, she maintained, was putting him under a covenant of works. She told the court that the minister in question had discussed this distinction with her at some length, where they had discussed the letter of the law and of the gospel. She maintained that he had finally come to agree with her reading of the scriptures in that regard, although he denied he was under a covenant of works.

It should be noted here that Hutchinson's differentiation between the "letter of the law" and the "letter of the gospel" which she states as different from the letter of the law, yet equally as damning, may have come from the marginal notes of her Geneva translation of the Bible. Winthrop mentions the "letter of the gospel," which he calls the "moral law," in his political treatise, "A Model of Christian Charity," and this letter of the gospel requires that the Christian person and Christian commonwealth practice mercy. However, the phrase was not one normally used, and certainly not to differentiate between the "spirit of the gospel" and the "letter of the gospel."[45] As the ministers were unable to understand her reference, yet she stuck to her interpretation, it may be that she had read of this idea in the notes in her Bible. As postulated earlier, Hutchinson may have imbibed the glosses along with the scripture verses in her reading, and formulated her understanding of the doctrines by use of the marginal notes as well as the verses themselves. Notes are found in the 1562 edition of the Geneva translation on the third chapter of Romans which discusses the law, and they may be what she used to aid her understanding of the text, and of the law. St. Paul discusses the law, which does not save, and the "law of faith" which saves. The gloss on verse 27 reads, "The Law of faith is the Gospel which offereth salvation with condition (if thou believest) which condition also Christ freely giveth to us. So the condition of the Law is (if thou doest all these things) the which only Christ hath fulfilled for us."[46] Another possible area of confusion relates to the "law of Christ" mentioned in Galations, chapter six. The gloss on verse two claims brotherly love is that which is meant by the law of Christ. Yet another possibility is found in the 1560 edition of the Geneva Bible at II Corinthians 3:6, which reads, "Who also hath made us able ministers of the New testament, not of the letter but of the Spirit; for the letter killeth, but the Spirit giveth life." If this is where she found the idea of distinguishing between the letter of the gospel and the spirit of the gospel the note that might have encouraged her in this thinking explains what the word, "Spirit" means as it is used in the verse. It reads, "Meaning, the spiritual doctrine, which is in our hearts." As her distinction is otherwise difficult to understand, and the ministers did not understand it, a plausible explanation is that perhaps one of these glosses is where she read something that seemed to make the differentiation.

After more discussion of the point, where the ministers were unable to find arguments against her claims, she had finally exhausted both the day and the patience of the court, so court was dismissed to allow Hutchinson an opportunity to see the error of her ways, and "a little more time to consider of it..." until the next morning.[47]

Notes

1. Hall, *Antinomian*, p. 264.

2. Winthrop, "A Short Story," in Hall, *Antinomian*, p. 267.

3. Thomas Hutchinson, *History of Massachusetts*, p. 367.

4. A discussion of the accuracy of published sermons can be found in Babette Levy's book on early new England sermons: *Preaching in the First Half-Century of New England's History* (Hartford: The American Society of Church History, 1945).

5. Ziff, *Career*, p. 106.

6. Levy, p. 81.

7. Winfried Herget, "Writing After the Ministers: The Significance of Sermon Notes," in *Studies in New England Puritanism* (Frankfurt am Main: Verlag Peter Lang, 1983), pp. 113–138.

8. Hall, *Antinomian*, p. 417.

9. John Stetson Barry, *The History of Massachusetts: The Colonial Period,* (Boston: Phillips, Sampson, and Company, 1857), p. 258, n. 2.

10. Hutchinson, *Papers*, p. 71.

11. Hall, *Antinomian*, pp. 199–200, 311, 439.

12. Ibid., p. 200.

13. David Hall has edited the trials and his notes and discussion aid the reader greatly in following the material. However, problems inherent in the material make it difficult work to sort through them.

14. *Aeneid*, Bk. 1, line 364, "the woman the leader in the act," quoted in Hall, *Antinomian*, p. 262.

15. Hall, *Antinomian*, p. 263. All citations from the transcripts will be taken from Hall, unless otherwise noted.

16. Ibid.,p. 312.

17. Ibid., p. 266.

18. Ibid., p. 312.

19. Morgan, *Dilemma,* p. 147.

20. Hall, *Antinomian*, p. 313.

21. Ibid., p. 313.

22. Ibid., p. 319.

23. Ibid., p. 314.

24. Ibid. p. 315.

25. Ibid.

26. Ibid., p. 316.

27. Ibid.

28. Ibid. p. 317.

29. Ibid.

30. Ibid. p. 318.

31. Ibid.

32. Ibid. pp. 318, 319.

33. Ibid. p. 319.

34. Ibid., p. 320.

35. Ibid., p. 321.

36. Ibid.

37. Ibid., p. 271.

38. Ibid., p. 321.

39. Ibid., p. 323.

40. Ibid. p. 324.

41. Ibid.

42. Ibid.

43. Ibid., pp. 324, 325.

44. Ibid. p. 325.

45. Morgan, *Founding*, p. 191.

46. *The Newe Testament of Ovr Lord Iesus Christ: Conferred diligently with the Greke, and Best Approued Translations* (Geneva: Conrad Badius, Printer, 1557), a facsimile reprint (London: Samuel Bagster and Sons, nd), Romans 3:27.

47. Hall, *Antinomian,* p. 326.

Chapter Nine

The Civil Trial: Day Two

The next day Winthrop gave a little precis of the previous day's questioning. He pointed out that "there were divers things laid to her charge, her ordinary meetings about religious exercises, her speeches in derogation of the ministers among us, and the weakening of the hands and hearts of the people towards them. "Here was sufficient proof made of that which she was accused..." and so on. [1] He then began the day's proceedings by asking if anyone wished to speak, and Hutchinson went on the offensive, claiming that the ministers had come "in their own cause," rather than hers, and should be made to take an oath that they were speaking the truth. Winthrop states that she said, "they ought not to be informers and witnesses both." [2] She may have been coached by someone who had some legal knowledge, given that she led off with this demand, and the requirement became a real sticking point with them. She said, "Now the Lord hath said that an oath is the end of all controversy; though there be a sufficient number of witnesses yet they are not according to the word, therefore I desire they may speak upon oath." Here she was quoting Hebrews, chapter six, verse sixteen, which states that an oath "is the end of all strife." Winthrop went back and forth with her, declaring that the court could decide whether an oath was needed. She told him she had again reread some of Mr. Wilson's notes, and had found that the testimony given by the ministers had been inaccurate. She had not brought the notes with her, and Wilson could not supply them either. Once again it is hard to understand why no one seems to have felt the notes were vital to the case, for the notes were never produced; or perhaps they did not wish to have them in the courtroom at all.

Hutchinson continued to press for an oath, but several members of the court worried that if the ministers swore to tell the truth and then remembered imperfectly, giving inaccurate testimony, they would be in a state of sin. To that Hutchinson gave short shrift: "That is not the thing. If they accuse me I desire it may be upon oath."[3] Court members continued to aver that they were perfectly satisfied with testimony that was not sworn, but Hutchinson stood firm. Winthrop asked the court to tell him if they were satisfied, but several spoke up at his question to say they were not, one also quoting Hebrews 6:16, so he asked Hutchinson, "If the ministers shall take an oath will you sit down satisfied?" She obstinately replied that oaths or not, she would not be satisfied unless they told the story correctly as she saw it.[4] There was "a parley between the deputy governor and Mr. Stoughton about the oath," and more hopeful suggestions to Hutchinson about how oaths were not really needed. Discussion continued about the need for oaths, and Mrs. Hutchinson said she could prove what she had said by Wilson's notes, whereupon Mr. Simmes asked to have them produced. But Mr. Endicot claimed this lack of trust was prejudicial toward the ministers. At this a reassuring statement was given by Roger Harlakenden that, "I would have the spectators take notice that the court doth not suspect the evidence that is given in."[5]

It had by now become clear to all the ministers that Hutchinson had some reason to be quite confident that should they swear to their previous testimony, they would find themselves in an uncomfortable situation.

"After that they have taken an oath, I will make good what I say," Hutchinson confidently informed them.[6] This did not sound promising. They argued with her some more, and could not agree among the members of the court just exactly what had been said by the ministers. They badgered her:

"You lifted up your eyes as if you took God to witness that you came to entrap none and yet you will have them swear." She reminded them of what the ministers had testified that she had said, and stated that she had not been accurately quoted.

"Aye, that was the thing that I do deny they were my words and they were not spoken at the first as they do allege." Her point seems to be that the time and place when she made certain statements was important to the case the state was bringing against her, and her defense. If she had made statements when she believed that she was speaking to a friend, and casually, she should have been able to make claims about other people that she could not expect to claim in public. The men either did not understand what she was getting at, or felt that this kind of scruple was no defense. Mr. Peter, again impatient with this kind of thing, and eager to get back to what he felt was the heart of the matter, exclaimed, "We cannot tell what was first or last, we suppose that an oath is an end of all strife and we are tender of it, yet this is the main thing against her that she charged us to be unable ministers of the gospel and to preach a covenant of works."7

They debated more among themselves, when Mr. Coggeshall, a follower of Hutchinson, interjected that Cotton should be called before the ministers were sworn. This seems to have been an attempt to relieve the ministers of the necessity of being sworn in, as Coggeshall probably felt that Cotton's testimony would be powerful enough that the others would no longer be needed. However, this suggestion was not received well, as it seemed to them to imply that Cotton's testimony would be more believable than that of the other ministers. In fact, when finally they had heard Cotton, his testimony gave the other ministers a chance to modify their previous testimony, so that this tactic worked for the ministers rather than against them. Coggeshall was asked whether he agreed with the testimony that had been given, and he announced that Hutchinson had not been accurately quoted: "I dare say that she did not say all that which they lay against her."8 Mr. Peter was furious: "How dare you look into the court to say such a word?" Coggeshall used Hutchinson's tactics: "Mr. Peters [sic] takes upon him to forbid me. I shall be silent."9 Others were asked what they could remember, as the anxiety level of the court rose. Hutchinson questioned some of the ministers about how the discussion had gone when they spoke with her. They could not remember some things about which she reminded them. At last Cotton was called.

Cotton began with the unpromising note that he had not expected to be called, and so "did not labour to call to remembrance what was done."10 However, he did remember that while Hutchinson had said that their ministry differed from his, it was only that she had told one or another of the ministers that, "You preach of the seal of the spirit upon a work and he upon free grace without a work or without respect to a work, he preaches the seal of the spirit upon free grace and you upon a work." He repeated several times that he had told her he was unhappy about her having drawn comparisons between him and the other ministers, but in the end, "this was the sum of the difference...And I must say that I did not find her saying they were under a covenant of works, nor that she said they did preach a covenant of works."11 Peter, with patience greatly in evidence, reminded "Our reverend teacher..." that, "she spake plump that we were not sealed." To his disgust, Cotton, the debater, allowed as how she had said, "you were not sealed with the seal of the spirit." Peter was not ready to let this go by, and sneered, "There was a double seal found out that day which never was." Cotton's reply to this also not gratifying Peter, he snapped, "So that was the ground of our discourse concerning the great seal and the little seal."12 More confusion about who said exactly what ensued, but if anything was unmistakable by this time it was that no one could be exactly sure that Hutchinson had actually said other than that there were some rather fuzzy differences between the ministers. Winthrop could not believe that this could be true. After all, why would the elders have questioned her in the first place, "if they saw not some cause [?]"13

Winthrop knew that he had lost. There had to be some reason they were here, he felt, but they had gotten nowhere with her. She had parried his questions, demonstrated that his legal grounds were shaky, and now showed that his witnesses had exaggerated her statements. Hutchinson too recognized that she had confirmed that they had brought her up on charges they were unable to establish. They could prove nothing against her because anything she had said about the ministers had been negligible. She had known it would turn out thus; her Bible reading had led her to conclude that they would not be able to prove wrongdoing against her. So, confident that she had proved her case, she decided to tell them why she had been so confident. Winthrop says he tried to quiet her; the longer version of the trial record does not so indicate. Hutchinson finally spoke out, and confidently made the statement that gave them their chance.

She began by telling them of her history; she had been so troubled by what she saw in the church in England that she had "like to have turned separatist." Praying and fasting to find God's will, *this scripture was brought unto me..."* that those who deny Christ were of the antichrist. And who did she think was the antichrist?

> *The Lord knows that I could not open scripture*: he must by his prophetical office open it unto me. So after that being unsatisfied in the thing, the Lord was pleased to *bring this scripture out of the Hebrews*. He that denies the testament denies the testator, and *in this did open unto me* and give me to see that those which did not teach the new covenant had the spirit of antichrist, and upon this *he did discover the ministry unto me* and ever since, I bless the Lord, he hath let me see which was the clear ministry and which the wrong. Since that time I confess I have been more choice and he hath left me to distinguish between the voice of my beloved and the voice of Moses, the voice of John Baptist and the voice of antichrist, for all those voices are spoken of in scripture... [italics added]14

God brought scriptures to her mind, enabling her to distinguish among ministries. By God's opening of biblical passages, she felt, she was able to tell which ministers were preaching the teachings of Moses, or John the Baptist, those who were chronologically before Christ, and therefore under the covenant of works, and which preached Christ's gospel. She spoke of verses: John 4:3, Hebrews 9:16, I John 2:18, quoted above, as well as Isaiah 46:12, 13; and Isaiah 30:20. And how, she was asked, could she be sure that it was God who had told her these things? In the same way that Abraham knew that it was God who spoke to him, "so to me by an immediate revelation."[15]   Winthrop's version is the more detailed here, and he has her replying, "I will give you one place more which the Lord brought to me by immediate revelations, and that doth concern you all, it is in Dan[iel] 6."[16]

Here at last was the opportunity they needed. They leapt upon this. Dudley exulted: "How! an immediate revelation." They had her now: the claim to immediate, or unmediated, revelations would brand her a blasphemer. But, when asked what she meant she went on to explain that this was done, "By the voice of his own spirit to my soul. I will give you another scripture, Jer. 46. 27, 28—*out of which the Lord shewed me* what he would do for me and the rest of his servants..." [italics added] As Edmund Morgan notes, her claim that God gave her guidance through the scriptures was no more than any Puritan would claim.[17]   Yet her hearers turned it against her.

This was the turning point in the trial. The claim of immediate revelations on her part at last gave the members of the court the ammunition for which they were looking. Winthrop claimed that it was God's providential hand that caused her to blaspheme, and say that He was speaking to her directly.[18] However, such a claim of divine guidance was neither heresy nor blasphemy: what was the crucial matter was how one came to such assurance. If a Christian heard voices telling of God's intentions, that was not allowable; any assurances of a specific nature must come out of scripture, just as any assurances whether of general or specific nature were to come. For this reason, when Hutchinson stated that she had had an immediate revelation, that is, a revelation given directly by God, and unmediated by other means, it was taken—quite happily—by those concerned to mean that she was hearing voices rather than reading scripture. Indeed, she herself referred to the voice of God that spoke to Abraham when he was about to sacrifice Isaac. However, a look at her example reminds one that the voice Abraham heard was mediated: an angel spoke to Abraham, as recorded in Genesis 22:10, and Abraham was not at all sure of the truth of what he heard until he saw the ram that had been provided as the substitutionary sacrifice. While this difference might seem to be hair-splitting to the modern reader, it was germane to the case at hand, because it was absolutely necessary to understand what she meant by an immediate revelation, if she was to be held accountable for having made a heretical claim.

The court was anxious to find her guilty, and Winthrop waxed ecstatic later when he wrote of the opportunity this admission of hers had given them. He sarcastically wrote of how, "she can fetch a revelation that shall reach the Magistrates and the whole Court, and the succeeding generations, and she hath Scripture for it also, Daniel must be a type of Mistress Hutchinson...and all must sort to this conclusion, she must be delivered by a miracle...See the impudent boldness of a proud dame..."[19]   The most charitable interpretation one can make of the behavior of the members of the court is that in their eagerness they neglected to think through her claim, and interpreted it not as their recordings of the trial indicate she made it, but in the most prejudicial way possible.   Nowhere did she state that her revelation was unmediated, rather the reverse, she always made it plain that she was speaking of God's "opening" of the scriptures, or His word, to her, and was careful to indicate to them that she could not open scripture on her own, but only with God's help.   However, they chose not to understand her, and decided to believe that she meant that God spoke to her with no scripture or other medium involved.

What she had said when asked what she meant by an immediate revelation was that the Lord showed her His meaning just as He showed other Christians: by speaking through the scriptures: "By the voice of his own spirit to my soul. I will give you another scripture, Jer. 46. 27, 28—*out of which the Lord showed me* what he would do for me and the rest of his servants..." [italics added].   The Lord spoke to her soul by the scriptures, and showed her what was in store for her and the others.   She did not contend that God had spoken to her aloud, but rather that He spoke to her soul through the scriptures.

It might be well to reiterate here that Puritans used highly personal and intimate language when speaking of their relationship with God, and with Christ. It is often a bit jarring to read some of the figurative language used to describe their intense feelings and their sense of closeness to Christ. It was not unusual for a person to claim that, "I saw the Lord gave me a heart to receive Christ with a naked hand, even naked Christ..." as Thomas Shepard wrote in his autobiography.[20] Their imagery was sometimes marital in nature, such as the following: "and hence I saw with sadness my widow-like separation and disunion from my Husband and my God, and that we two were now parted that had been nearer together once."[21]   Such imagery was based on the feeling of a passionate personal relationship to their Savior, and so did not seem strange to Puritan writers. It was metaphorical, and was understood to be so. Anne Hutchinson's statement of God speaking to her through the scripture must be read in this light, and should as a matter of course have been taken in this way by the court, just as such exclamations in sermons by Shepard, Cotton, and others would be taken.

Hutchinson spoke to the court of her early years, when she wrestled (as Shepard had) with her personal "atheism" or unbelief. God had showed her passages of scripture that led her to believe she was in His care and he would continue to care for her. God had also led her to the realization that she must follow Cotton to New England, she said. She spoke aggressively, and reminded the court that whatever they chose to do with her, Christ had the ultimate power over her body and soul. Going on, she said, "if you go on in this course you begin you will bring a curse upon you and your posterity, and the mouth of the Lord hath spoken it." This was strong stuff, and they resented it. She claimed that God had protected her thus far, and would continue to do so, and so they should stop persecuting her. She then went on to say, "I was then much troubled...This place in Daniel was brought to me," that, as in the case of Daniel, God would deliver her.[22] Daniel had been delivered by a miracle, she was reminded. Is that what she expected, too? "I look that the Lord should deliver me by his providence."[23]

This caused William Bartholomew, a deputy to the court from Ipswich, to stand up and regale the court with his fears concerning her orthodoxy. He had spoken with her while she was still in London, when she told him that she knew for a fact that England would be destroyed, which was why she was planning to travel to Massachusetts Bay. He was worried: "I speak as a member of the court. I fear that her revelations will deceive."[24] She had told him that nothing of importance had ever happened to her without it having been revealed to her beforehand. She was told that England would be destroyed, which caused her to feel she must leave the country. He had also, he noted, heard her claim that Thomas Hooker had asserted in a sermon that God had told him He was about to destroy England for the sins of the English people. Mr. Eliot, a friend of Thomas Hooker, was quick to state however that Hooker would not have said such a thing.[25]

Interestingly, Hooker does appear to have made exactly this claim in his sermon preached shortly before he left for New England. Hooker said:

> What if I should tell you what God told me yesternight that he would destroy England and lay it waste? What say you to this, my beloved? It is my message, by meditation in God's word, that he bid me do to you and he expects an answer from you. I do my message as God commanded me. What sayest thou unto it, England? I must return an answer to my master that sent me, yea, this present night I must return an answer; for the Lord hath appointed a set time, saying, Exodus 9:5, *Tomorrow the Lord will do this thing in the land.*[26]

Yet, those present in the court were so eager to find her guilty that they accepted Bartholomew's claim that she excused herself by making wild claims about others. Apparently none of those present except Hutchinson admitted to remembering the sermon by Hooker, nor did they check on it by asking Hooker, and so Eliot was believed.

Now the dialogue turned to the meaning of the word providence. Mr. Endicott pointed out to the court that these allegations against her were just that, but he believed that "I think it is a special providence of God to hear what she hath said."[27]   He went on about the brazenness of her assertion that God would perform a miracle on her behalf: "I hope the court takes notice of the vanity of it and heat of her spirit." Then he turned to Cotton to ask if she got her ideas from him, and whether he could assure them about the meaning of such a statement. Cotton pointed out to them that Hutchinson had every right according to Puritan doctrinal theory, to pray for and even expect, God's providence. While there could be room for disagreement about whether one should feel overconfident of such aid in any particular undertaking, as this would be presuming a knowledge of God's will, such dependence upon God, and assurance of His aid was not outside the mainstream of Puritan Christian thought. The question was whether she was looking to be saved from whatever the court could do to her by some sort of miracle that God would perform for her.

Mr. Endicott gloated, "She saith she now suffers and let us do what we will she shall be delivered by a miracle."[28]   Cotton was moved to point out to the court in his pedantic and long-winded way that she had not claimed that God would work a miracle in her behalf. He also spoke to them about revelations, saying: "there are two sorts of revelations," one of which is simply God speaking to the believer "in the ministry of his word...in some chapter or verse and whenever it comes it comes flying upon the wings of the spirit." All right, then, what about that "providence," he was asked. He explained to them that he felt if she had used the word, "miracle" he would have been concerned, but the providence of God would be acceptable. He went on: "Though the word revelation be rare in common speech and we make it uncouth in our ordinary expressions, yet notwithstanding, being understood in the scripture sense I think they are not only lawful but such as Christians may receive and God bear witness to it in his word, and usually he doth express it in the ministry of the word, and doth accompany it by his spirit, or else it is in the reading of the word..."[29]

"I should desire to know whether the sentence of the court will bring her to any calamity, and then I would know of her whether she expects to be delivered from that calamity by a miracle or a providence of God."[30] His reticence to make a plain statement about her declaration of hope in a providence of God is the more surprising when one realizes that he had made God's special—not general—providence in leading his children one of the points of the sermon he delivered to Winthrop's company as they were leaving England. He had said at that time, "Secondly, when some special providence of God leads a man unto such a course [of leaving his homeland for a new country] *I will instruct, and guide thee with mine eye*....First, if God give a man an inclination to this or that course, for that is the spirit of man; and *God is the father of spirits*..."[31] He himself had counseled Winthrop and the rest that they could feel comfortable leaving England and knowing they were doing God's bidding, because God had demonstrated to them that he was leading them. That demonstration was a "special providence of God," in that they felt in their hearts that they should go. And did Cotton believe in her revelations? "That she may have some special providence of God to help her is a thing that I cannot bear witness against."[32]   Cotton, though repeatedly pressed to come out strongly against her, could not bring himself to do that; he could not tell them for certain that God would not deliver her—anymore, presumably, than they could.

Asked once again about how God would help her, Hutchinson stated that it was God's providence she expected; and when asked to choose between the words "miracle" and "providence" she did not use the word miracle. But, Winthrop had heard enough to realize that once again she seemed to be about to escape the wrath of the court. He wrote in his journal that while of course she was guilty, they "were not furnished with proof sufficient to proceed against her..."[33] And, like Endicot earlier, the record shows that he had no compunction against stating, "Now the mercy of God *by a providence* hath answered our desires and made her to lay open her self..." [italics added]. Winthrop could claim that God had answered their desires by a providence, but for Hutchinson to claim that he would deliver her by His providence was heresy. He went over the evidence that the court had against her.

> The groundwork of her revelations is the immediate revelation of the spirit and not by the ministry of the word, and that is the means by which she hath very much abused the country that they shall look for revelations and are not bound to the ministry of the word, but God will teach them by immediate revelations and this hath been the ground of all these tumults and troubles, and I would that those were all cut off from us that trouble us, for this is the thing that hath been the root of all the mischief.[34]

(Here Winthrop quotes the Apostle Paul, who being so angry at those who insisted on circumcision as a requirement for membership in the church that he makes a kind of pun, saying that those who insist on circumcision should—in language more polite than the more pungent language used by St. Paul—emasculate themselves, and thereby cut themselves off from the church.)[35] The members of the court were quick to agree that they all consented with Winthrop in her guilt. Indeed, "it is the most desperate enthusiasm in the world..." added Winthrop.[36] And, should Cotton have ideas of speaking in her behalf, Endicott let him know that he was not certain but that Cotton too was a heretic. Was he for her or against her, he was asked. "This is what I said Sir, and my answer is plain that if she doth look for deliverance from the hand of God by his providence, and the revelation be in a word or according to a word, that I cannot deny." If she was guided by the words of scripture he did not see that as heretical. Endicott then announced that he was "comfortable" with Cotton.[37]

Dudley, though, was not, and shifted his attack to Cotton. Cotton explained his position to him: that if she had not been quoting the Bible she would have been depending on herself alone, and that would be wrong, but as "the revelation be in a word or according to a word," he had no problem with her statements. Dudley would have none of that. "Sir, you weary me and do not satisfy me."[38] Cotton was worried now. "I pray Sir give me leave to express my self. In that sense that she speaks I dare not bear witness against it."[39] Mr. Nowell felt that Cotton was being deluded by the devil. Winthrop felt that, "the enthusiasts and Anabaptists had never the like."[40] Dudley was sorry that, "Mr. Cotton should stand to justify her." And several of the men present began to argue with Cotton, making it plain that they were most unhappy that he did not wholeheartedly agree that Hutchinson was in the wrong. Mr. Collicut, one of the deputies, asked for Cotton to explain himself further: "It is a great burden to us that we differ from Mr. Cotton and that he should justify these revelations. I would entreat him to answer concerning that about the destruction of England."[41] Here, however, Winthrop intervened. He realized that it would not be expedient to go after Cotton, and he had no intention of doing so. He reminded the court, therefore, that "Mr. Cotton is not called to answer to any thing but we are to deal with the party here standing before us." Instead, he and others raised the question of how she should be dealt with, now that they had decided her guilt.

Coddington, one of her followers, had a question for them. Before they proceeded to censuring her, he wanted to know: what if she had only been speaking to her family, and someone else had happened to be present. Would that have been seditious? Winthrop, who could see where that was leading, and who had no intention that anyone should remind them of the original charges against Hutchinson—which had not been proved—scolded Coddington for interrupting them. Coddington continued: he had not seen "any clear witness against her," and he reminded them that this would make their finding of guilt unlawful.

> You know it is a rule of the court that no man may be a judge and an accuser too. I do not speak to disparage our elders and their callings, but I do not see any thing that they accuse her of witnessed against her, and therefore I do not see how she should be censured for that. And for the other thing which hath fallen from her occasionally by the spirit of god, you know the spirit of God witnesses with our spirits, and there is no truth in scripture but God bears witnesses with our spirit... therefore I would entreat you to consider whether those things you have alleged against her deserve such censure as you are about to pass...42

To Winthrop's exasperated reply that the things she had just said were reason enough, Coddington spoke out: "I beseech you do not speak so to force things along...I pray consider what you do, for here is no law of God or man broken."

Deputy Governor Dudley, apparently tired of the whole discussion, declared that he wanted things hurried up, or: "we shall all be sick with fasting."43 But several of the men present had problems with proceeding further, so two of the ministers announced that they were now willing to swear to their testimony in order to prove that she had been stirring up the populace by maligning them. They were asked to swear "to the truth and nothing but the truth as far as you know. So help you God."44 One wonders why the oath could not have been administered in this way, with "as far as you know" in the first place, but perhaps no one thought of it until then. Eliot and Weld then testified that she had said they were not able ministers, and that there was a "broad difference" between them and Cotton.

After a few more attempts by Coddington to point out that nothing had been proved against her, the rest said they were now satisfied, and ready to censure her. "Therefore if it be the mind of the court that Mrs. Hutchinson for these things that appear before us is unfit for our society, and if it be the mind of the court that she shall be banished out of our liberties and imprisoned till she be sent away, let them hold up their hands," said Winthrop.45 Three men did not hold up their hands: Coddington, Colburn, and Jennison.

Winthrop pronounced the sentence: "Mrs. Hutchinson, the sentence of the court you hear is that you are banished from out of our jurisdiction as being a woman not fit for our society, and are to be imprisoned till the court shall send you away." When she asked on what grounds she had been found guilty: "I desire to know wherefore I am banished?" Winthrop ended the day with the reply, "Say no more, the court knows wherefore

and is satisfied."[46] She must have been weary indeed, not to have fought
that answer, as she had answered every point raised against her so well up
to that moment. After finding her guilty the Court stated:

> Whereas the opinions and revelations of Mr. Wheelwright and Mrs.
> Hutchinson have seduced and led into dangerous errors many of the people
> here in New England, insomuch as there is just cause of suspicion that they,
> as others in Germany, in former times, may upon some revelation, make
> some sudden eruption upon those that differ from them in judgment, for
> prevention whereof it is ordered, that all those whose names are underwrit-
> ten shall (upon warning given or left at their dwelling houses) before the
> 30th of this month of November, deliver at Mr. Cane's house at Boston, all
> such guns, pistols, swords, powder, shot, and match as they shall be
> owners of, or have in their custody.[47]

The Pequot massacre had occurred so recently and even the impounding of
ammunition was a terribly serious punishment: men depended upon their
weapons to hunt for food, and for protection for their families. It must
have seemed seriously likely to the Court that an insurrection was imma-
nent.

Hutchinson was sent to live at Mr. Weld's house until the next March,
when she would undergo examination by the church. This was apparently
intended to give Cotton a chance to remonstrate with her, which is surprising, given that members of the court were so unsatisfied at his rather
pedantic and lukewarm defense of her. Her church trial was to go in much
the same way as had the trial by the General Court.

Notes

1. Hall, *Antinomian*, p. 326.

2. Ibid., p. 271.

3. Ibid., p. 327.

4. Ibid., p. 328.

5. Ibid., p. 329.

6. Ibid., p. 330.

7. Ibid., p. 331.

8. Ibid., p. 332.

9. Ibid., p. 333.

10. Ibid.

11. Ibid. p. 334.

12. Ibid. p. 335.

13. Ibid., p. 336.

14. Ibid.

15. Ibid. p. 337.

16. Ibid. p. 273.

17. Morgan, *Dilemma*, p. 151.

18. Hall, *Antinomian*, p. 274.

19. Ibid., p. 375.

20. Shepard, *Plot,* p. 47.

21. Shepard, *Plot*, p. 98.

22. Hall, *Antinomian,* p. 337.

23. Ibid., p. 338.

24. Ibid., p. 338.

25. Ibid., p. 339.

26. Hooker, "Danger of Desertion," quoted in *Puritans in America: A Narrative Anthology,* ed. Alan Heimert and Andrew Delbanco (Cambridge, MA: Harvard University Press, 1985), p. 68.

27. Hall, Antinomian, p. 340.

28. Ibid.

29. Ibid.

30. Ibid.

31. Cotton, "God's Promise to His Plantation," in *Old South Leaflets*, vol. 53 (Boston: Division of the Old South Work, 1896), p. 10.

32. Ibid., p. 341.

33. Ibid.

34. Ibid., 341, 342.

35. I would they were even cut off which trouble you. Gal. 5:12.   (Winthrop was quoting from the King James version.)

36. Hall, *Antinomian*, p. 342.

37. Ibid.

38. Ibid.

39. Ibid.

40. Ibid.

41. Ibid., p. 343.

42. Ibid., p. 344, 345.

43. Ibid., p. 345.

44. Ibid., p. 346.

45. Ibid., p. 347.

46. Ibid., p. 348.

47. *Records of the State of Massachusetts*, vol. I, quoted in Erickson, p. 92.

Chapter Ten

"I Cast You Out":

The Ecclesiastical Trial

The ecclesiastical trial was an examination of Anne Hutchinson by the church at Boston, with its function to question her as to the orthodoxy of her beliefs and to persuade her to change them, if necessary. The hope was that she would repent of any errors she held, at which point she could be happily embraced as a member in good standing once again. "Puritans were primarily concerned with the need for repentance; the penitent offender was welcomed back into the fold."[1] Even in civil matters the defendant who confessed was treated as a reformed sinner, and given a lighter sentence, or no sentence; in a church trial such repentance was paramount.

It was important to follow proper procedure in the church trial as well as in the civil one, and Cotton and others spent no small amount of time debating how—and sometimes whether—to proceed. John Cotton, as her minister, was expected to lead the questioning, and if possible bring her to see her errors. However, Cotton's behavior at this trial was strikingly different from his behavior at the civil trial six months before. By this time he had changed from rather passive observer and reluctant witness for Anne Hutchinson during her civil trial to an eager prosecutor, and conducted the trial very zealously. Charges against her were contained on two lists which had been drawn up containing questions about Hutchinson's doctrinal views for her to answer. Because not all of the questions were asked of her at her trial, the actual substance of the trial revolved around only three of the first questions from the two sets of questions put to her.

The first list of nine questions was drawn up by Thomas Shepard, minister of the church at Cambridge, who had already become so involved in her situation, and Edmund Frost, an elder in that church.[2] The Second list of seven questions was drawn up by Mr. Weld and Mr. Eliot, the ministers from Roxbury. The direction of the questions raised at the trial revolved around the difference between the words, "soul" and "spirit" and the resurrection of the body, and were based on statements the ministers believed she had made earlier about her beliefs. After much discussion of the first two of these questions, and some little explanation of the passages of the Bible in question, she agreed with her accusers that she had been mistaken about her understanding of several passages of the Bible. The third passage, however, was never clarified to her in a way that was convincing to her, and the men questioning her had by that time lost patience with her, so she was admonished at the end of the first day.

The second day of the trial, held one week after the first, her son-in-law and son, as members of the church, argued that they were not convinced that she should be admonished, as she had admitted that she had seen her errors. There was a great deal of discussion as to whether the vote of the church against her was required to be unanimous, as her son-in-law, Thomas Savage, contended. Cotton made an argument that the vote should be unanimous if possible, but if certain persons who were close to the accused refused to be persuaded of her guilt just because of their filial affection, when all other members had been persuaded, that much unanimity was enough. She was then to be excommunicated.

The trial began on March 15, 1638, when Hutchinson was examined in Boston about her "divers Errors and unsound Opinions which she held."[3] The first order of business was for the ruling elders of the Boston church to explain the proceedings to the congregation and observers. The observers and church members were admonished to remember to "deny all Relations of Father, Mother, Sister, Brother, Friend, Enemy...and let all be carried by the Rules of Gods Word..."[4] Next the lists of Hutchinson's errors were read to her. Hutchinson was suffering from some kind of physical disability at the time; possibly she was pregnant, although she had been kept at Mr. Weld's house for six months. She had what has been described as a miscarriage three months later, expelling what was believed at the time to be a "monster," and what Emery Battis has described as a hydatidiform mole. Whatever Hutchinson's problem was, she was too weak to stand during the trial, as a person under examination was expected to do, and was not even present until after the beginning of the trial. Elder Thomas Oliver told the congregation that, "I am to acquaint all this Congregation, that whereas our Sister Hutchinson was not here at the Beginning of the Exercise, it was not out of any Contempt or Neglect to the Ordinance, but because she hath been long under Durance. She is so weak that she conceives herself not fit nor able to have been here so long together. This she sent to our Elders."[5] Her statement as rendered by Elder Oliver suggests that she felt weak from lack of exercise; whatever the cause it is probable that her physical weakness led her to her abject "repentance" of her errors later in the trial, for during the first day she showed as much fire in her argumentations as she had during her civil trial.

Elder Thomas Leveritt followed Oliver's explanation to the assembly of Hutchinson's illness with a request of the members of the congregation to sit in an easily identifiable group so that when they would be called upon to vote upon a question their votes could easily be counted. Then he read the questions to Hutchinson, telling her, "I must request you in the name of the Church to declare whether you hold them or renounce them as they be read to you."6   This reading of each question was required to give her the opportunity to answer each one, and to renounce them and repent of her errors. It was apparently not the first time she had been made aware of the questions, for Winthrop says in his short version of the trial that she had also received the lists in writing before the trial.7   The lists read as follows. The first list, from Shepard and Frost:8

> 1. That the Souls...of all men by Nature are mortal. Ecclesiastes 3.18-21
> 2. That those that ... are united to Christ have 2 Bodies, Christ's and a new Body and you knew not how Christ should be united to our fleshly Bodies. 1 Corinthians 6.19
> 3. That our Bodies shall not rise...with Christ Jesus, not the same Bodies at the last day. 1 Corinthians 15.4.
> 4. That the Resurrection mentioned...is not of our Resurrection at the last day but of our Union to Christ Jesus. 1 Corinthians 15
> 5. That there be no created graces in the human Nature of Christ nor in Believers after Union.
> 6. That you had no scripture to Warrant Christ being now in Heaven in his human Nature.
> 7. That the Disciples were not converted at Christ's Death.
> 8. That there is no Kingdom of Heaven but Christ Jesus.
> 9. That the first Thing we receive for our Assurance is our Election.

Eliot and Weld's list was quite different in its line of inquiry, and reflects questions given earlier to John Cotton:

> 1. That Sanctification can be no Evidence of a good Estate in no wise.
> 2. That her Revelations about future Events are to be believed as well as Scripture because the same holy Ghost did indict both.
> 3. That Abraham was not in saving Estate till he offered Isaac and so saving the firmness of God's Election he might have perished eternally for any Work of Grace that was in him.
> 4. That an Hypocrite may have the Righteousness of Adam and perish.
> 5. That we are not bound to the Law, not as a Rule of Life.
> 6. That not being bound to the Law, no Transgression of the Law is

7. That you see no Warrant in Scripture to prove that the Image of God in
Adam was Righteousness and true Holiness.[9]

It is rather startling that the two lists differ so, as each was intended to
represent her main doctrinal errors. It is difficult to understand why the
ministers did not recognize the problems presented by having two lists that
deal with entirely different concerns, yet are supposed to have been drawn
up by ministers who had spoken with her at some length about her beliefs;
this issue does not seem to have bothered anyone present at the trial.

After the lists had been read aloud, Hutchinson was asked if she held
these opinions or not and replied in the same feisty manner as she had
during the earlier trial, "If this be Error then it is mine and I ought to lay
it down. If it be truth it is not mine but Christ Jesus and then I am not to
lay it down."[10]   She then went on to ask by "what Rule of the Word"
accusations could be brought against her as she had discussed things privately with some of the Elders, who had assured her they were not trying to
trap her. She stated that she should have had a chance to defend herself
privately before being brought before the church. "I think it is a Breach of
Church Rule, to bring a Thing in Public before they have dealt with me in
private."[11] When asked by Shepard if she was accusing any specific person
of having treated her in this way, she reminded him that she could not
accuse an elder unless she had two or three witnesses to the matter of which
she spoke, which she did not.

Cotton turned to Shepard, asking if he could speak to the issue, and
Shepard stated that he had been the one to tell her he was not trying to trap
her. He had been asked to talk to her, and had spoken with her privately,
he said. Sent to speak to her a second time "by special providences of
God..." he had then stated that he did not intend to trap her. To that end
he had told no one of what she had told him; but upon thinking the matter
over he changed his mind based upon what he conceived to be the seriousness of her charges, deciding that the most loving thing he could do was to
bring her before the church to answer for her statements. Shepard admitted that while he had indeed told her that she had no need to fear he would
make public what she said to him, he subsequently decided that she was so
dangerous he could not keep his word. Then he added that she should not
accuse him of failing to deal with her privately, as he had done so:

> But seeing the Fluentness of her Tongue and her Willingness to open herself
> and to divulge her Opinions and to sow her seed in us that are but highway
> side and Strangers to her and therefore would do much more to her own
> Jealousy and to them that are more nearly like to her, for I account her a very
> dangerous Woman to sow her corrupt opinions to the infection of many and
> therefore the more need you have to look to her. And therefore at my third

Coming to her I told her that I came to deal with her and labour to reduce her from her Errors and to bear witness against them therefore I do marvel that she will say that we bring it into public before I dealt with her in private. Hebrews 4.12.12

She, of course, had pointed out that if his private conversation with her had led him to believe that she was in such serious error, according to biblical teachings, two elders should have dealt with her on those specific issues about which Shepard was concerned.

With this interchange the trial began in earnest. Hutchinson stated, as she continued to state throughout the trial, that she did not actually believe many of the things of which she had been accused, but had only asked Shepard to explain some vexing questions found in Ecclesiastes 3:18-21, and that she was merely questioning the meaning of the passage in Ecclesiastes.13 Shepard responded to this with, "I would have this Congregation know that the vilest Errors that ever was brought into the Church was brought by way of Questions 42.7" It is not known to what reference Shepard was pointing as proof of the dangers of raising questions. However, his outburst helped to set the tone for the trial. Cotton replied to Shepard, "Brother we consent with you. Therefore Sister Hutchinson it will be most satisfactory to the Congregation for you to answer to the Things as they are objected against you in order." She asked that they be read again, and Cotton replied, "Your first opinion laid to your Charge is That the souls of all men by nature are mortal and die like Beasts, and for that you allege Ecclesiastes 3.18-21." The discussion of this passage and several similar ones that raised related concerns in her mind formed the large part of the trial; for this reason, it would be well to look at the passage in question, and its background.

The text in question is poetry from the "Wisdom" literature of the Bible, and raises questions about the meaning of humankind's life on earth; it is from the part of Ecclesiastes that speaks of the "appointed time." The tradition from which this literature comes is derived heavily from Greek philosophy of the third or second century B.C., when the book is believed to have been written.14 The Wisdom literature is heavily reflective of the philosophy of the Greeks, although it is now believed that the books were written in Aramaic and incorporate Hebrew thinking as well. Ecclesiastes 3:18-21 reads as follows, with the text taken from the Geneva translation of the Bible:

18.   I considered in mine heart, the state of the children of men that God had purged them: yet to see to, they are in themselves as beasts.

19.   For the conditions of the children of men, and the conditions of beasts are even as one condition unto them. As the one dieth, so dieth the other: for they have all one breath, and there is no excellency of man above

the beast; for all is vanity.

    20. All go to one place, and all was of the dust, and all shall return to the dust.

    21. Who knoweth whether the spirit of man ascend upward, and the spirit of the beast descend downward to the earth?[15]

This passage follows the well-known text dealing with a "time to be born and a time to die; a time to plant, and a time to pluck up that which is planted..." Qohelet, or the Teacher, as the writer of Ecclesiastes was known, was discussing the ways in which the times of all people have been decided ahead of their existence by God, who ordains all things. The passage continues to take up the theme of God's judgment of the wicked, and this is where the verses quoted come in. Hutchinson was correct in reading these verses as stating that humans are no different from animals, and that the wicked, at least, will die, and return to dust in the ground. Verse twenty-two continues the theme to close out the chapter with: "Therefore I see that there is nothing better, than that a man should rejoice in his affairs, because that is his portion. For who shall bring him to see what shall be after him?" All is vanity, so humankind should "do good in his life," as verse twelve states, and then "eat and drink," as verse thirteen suggests.[16]

The literature that reflects the Greek philosophy of that period has caused no end of difficulties for those who have sought to read the Bible literally, because of the pessimism and uncheerful resignation found in many of the passages. Hutchinson had come upon passages that are difficult for those who expect discussions of immortality, such as found in the New Testament, to grasp. She was able to recognize those differences, however. She had steeped herself in the Bible, and was led by her studies to question the ministers about the resurrection and the immortality of the soul, based on her careful examination of a number of Bible verses that can be confusing when read in English. One of the areas that caused her to question the meaning of the verses had to do with the fact that two words, "soul" and "spirit" are used, and that the two have different meanings. She asked for an explication of the differences between the words "soul" and "spirit," noting that while verse twenty-one indicates that the spirit will not live on after death, in other places the word soul is used when that soul would appear to be immortal. She had discovered that the two words are used to mean different things judging by their uses, and that their meanings contradict and conflict with one another. Sometimes, she noted, "soul" is used in places—such as in Matthew 10:28—when contextually "spirit" is meant. Therefore, she asked the assembled ministers, most especially Cotton, to explain the verses and what they meant.

When she first raised the uncertainty she had about the two words Cotton, as her pastor, should have tried to explain to her that the biblical languages, the Greek of the New Testament and the Old Testament Septuagint, and the Hebrew of the Old Testament, have more than one word to express the ideas of "life," "immortality," and "breath," or "aliveness." The words have caused translators and exegetes no little difficulty. Cotton should have told her that the Greeks did indeed differentiate between "soul" and "spirit," and he could even have mentioned that Christians have difficulty in translation and exegesis of the words. One of them, *pneuma*, means "wind, air in motion," "breath," "the substance, spirit," or "a spirit or spiritual being," and it is translated spirit.[17]   The second, *psyche*, means "breath; the principle of animal life; the life," and is translated soul.[18] The Hebrew also uses more than one word to express the meanings of "soul" or "immortal soul," and "breath," "life," or "life force." Two corresponding words, which are *ruach*, and *nephesh*, which are translated as spirit and soul respectively, are often used.   Different translations of verse nineteen use the term, "breath of life," "spirit," and, "soul."[19] The term, *hebel*, or breath is also used, and it is sometimes translated as such, making the last line of verse nineteen, "all is but a breath." It also connotes "futile," "vain," "fleeting," and is usually translated, "vanity."[20]

As will be recalled, Cotton and the rest of the men educated at Oxford or Cambridge had studied Greek and Hebrew for several years. In reference to Ecclesiastes 3:21 Cotton was to note in sermons published in 1640 that the difference between what happens to a man or an animal after death "is not known or acknowledged, discerned, or considered by men generally, to wit, not by natural man at all."[21] In this he demonstrates that he was aware of the exegetical problems of the passage.

On the other hand, though Hutchinson did not understand why the two words were used she was able to read the Bible passages and interpret correctly the meanings of the two words, soul and spirit. She had been able to ferret out the meaning of the passages; having done so, was perplexed by that meaning. It was this questioning that had caused the ministers to fear her influence, and led her to her predicament. She was not willing to allow the ministers or any one else to be the arbiters of the meaning of the scriptures for her. Rather than remaining passively complacent that the ministers had interpreted scripture, making it unnecessary for her to understand it, she questioned any passage she did not understand. Here, interestingly, she reflects the claims of her father who during questioning by the Bishop of London in 1578 refused to accept that the clergy (of whom he was one) were the only ones capable of interpreting scripture. He replied to one question from the bishop, "What, can an ignorant Minister see more in those things than a book-learned parishioner?"22 It is not hard to imagine that her father had taught her well that she should search the scriptures, and she had tried to do so.

She therefore led off the examination by referring to part of the passage of Ecclesiastes in question. She asked, "I desire that place might be answered: the spirit that God gives returns." [to the earth, and does not rise upward to heaven.] Cotton quoted Ecclesiastes 12:7 in rebuttal, that "Man's spirit doth not return to Dust as man's body doth but to God." Then he added, "The soul of man is immortal."23 Here was the crux of the matter, for Cotton had used both the terms "soul" and "spirit" as if the two were interchangeable. Yet she had read verses that stated differently.

"Every Man consists of Soul and Body," she probed. "Now Adam dies not except his soul and Body die. And in Hebrews 4 the word [of God] is lively in operation, and divides between soul and spirit: So that the Spirit that God gives man, returns to God indeed, but the Soul dies and That is the spirit Ecclesiastes speaks of, and not of the Soul. Luke 19.10."24 In this explanation Hutchinson pointed out to Cotton that in Hebrews there is a clear differentiation between the two terms. She had read carefully a number of verses that refer to both soul and spirit, or to one or the other, giving each word a separate meaning, including Hebrews 4:12, which reads: "For the word of God is lively and mighty in operation, and sharper than any two-edged sword: & entereth through, even unto the dividing asunder of the soul and the spirit..." (Geneva, 1560).

It simply is not credible that Cotton would not have known the difference between the two words, and to have understood why she was having difficulty. As all of the ministers present, and John Winthrop as well, had been trained in biblical languages any of them should have been able to see immediately what the problem was with Hutchinson's understanding of the passages. Later in the trial, John Davenport, who had been visiting John Cotton, did try to give her an explanation. While his explanation was obscure, and did not address the fact that there are different words in Greek and in Hebrew which are used to mean quite different things, she accepted it, and declared herself satisfied with his explanation of the words. Cotton, however, argued with her that she was wrong, and made no effort to clarify passages that are difficult for any Christian who seeks to read the Bible literally, as of course the Puritans did. As her pastor, Cotton was leading the questioning with the assumption that he was trying to educate her, and if possible bring her back into the fold. Yet it would seem that from the beginning of the questioning, he was on the attack, and attempting to distance himself from her rather than to bring her to an understanding of her errors.

Rather, after some discussion with her of the question of usages of soul and spirit, he again confused the issue by saying to her, "That in Ecclesiastes proveth that the soul is the Gift of God and that it hath no relation so such fading and destroying matter as his Body was made of. Matthew 10. 28, 1 Thessalonians 5: 23."[25] However, the citations do not demonstrate what Cotton claimed. For, while Ecclesiastes 12:7 speaks of the "spirit" returning to God, the meaning of the Hebrew is "breath," and the passage has the literal meaning of God sucking out the breath He had originally given. The citation of Matthew 10:28 is especially interesting, as it states that believers should, "fear ye not them which kill the body, but are not able to kill the soul; but rather fear him, which is able to destroy both soul and body in hell" (Geneva translation, 1557). Far from demonstrating that the body and soul are quite different and distinct, the verse says the opposite, that both can be destroyed in hell. I Thessalonians 5:23 is also a poor choice for Cotton, as it uses both *pneuma* and *psyche*: "May now the very God of peace sanctify you throughout: I pray God that your whole spirit and soul and body, may be kept blameless unto the coming of our Lord Jesus Christ" (Geneva translation, 1589). One can assume that Cotton would think it good form to use scripture to explain scripture, but he was trained in disputation at Emmanual College, as well as being a scholar of Greek and Hebrew, and should have been able to deal with the questions more ably than that.

Hutchinson and Cotton continued to argue back and forth on this a bit, and then she asked for clarification of the passage from Thessalonians that he had cited: "Then you have both a Soul and Spirit that shall be saved. I desire you to answer that in 1 Thessalonians 5.23. Your whole spirit Soul and Body, and that in Psalms he hath redeemed his soul from hell"[26] Again, Cotton gave her no answer to that question; he did not explain to her the meaning of either of the verses. Rather, at this interchange Cotton tired of the discussion of the terms, and lost all patience with her refusal to see things the way he stated they were rather than what she could see for herself. He accused her of shutting her eyes to the truth, and stated that all of the passages he had cited prove the immortality of the soul. "Sister, do not shut your Eyes against the Truth. All these places prove that the soul is Immortal."[27] The statement from Cotton comes across as if he were desperately fighting to make her see reason, and has been misinterpreted in this way by many scholars.[28] However, that is not what the allegation of Cotton demonstrates, but that he was angry at her for continuing to insist on an explanation. He wanted her to accept his word that soul and spirit mean the same thing in these passages—which they do not. To Cotton's frustration, Hutchinson replied to his outburst, "The Spirit is immortal indeed but prove that the Soul is." Then she added, "For that place in Matthew which you bring of Casting the soul into hell is meant of the Spirit." Here she is incorrect: the word used is, "*psyche*." She seems to have been arguing that in other places the Bible states that the spirit is immortal; it must be assumed that "spirit" was intended by the author of the gospel of Matthew. She would take his word for nothing, nor would she be cowed by his assertions, only persuaded by reason. Cotton angrily told her, "These are principles of our Christian Faith, and not denied."

Cotton then did make some effort to explain the differences, but did not give enough information to satisfy her. He said, "The Spirit is sometimes put for the Conscience and for the Gifts of the Spirit that fits the soul for God's Service." This was the extent of explanation of the soul/spirit problem he was to give her. In response she reminded him that, "The holy Ghost makes this Distinction between the soul and Body and not I."29

At this juncture Winthrop saw that she had reason to be unclear about these distinctions, and tried to mediate. The Governor had begun to see that her difficulties were real ones and explained her difficulties to the assembly by telling them that she misunderstood the results of Adam's sin, and stating that Adam's sin caused a separation of soul and body and not a total annihilation of the soul. "She thinks that the Soul is annihilated by the Judgment that was sentenced upon Adam. Her Error springs from her Mistaking of the Curse of God upon Adam, for that Curse doth not imply Annihilation of the soul and body, but only a dissolution of the Soul and Body."30 She seems to have found something to her liking in Winthrop's next statement that, "As the Body remains an Earthly substance after Dissolution, so the Soul remains a spiritual Substance after the Curse, though we see not what substance it is turned into after Dissolution."31 Her answer to this is most revealing. She replied, "I will take that into Consideration for it is of more weight to me than any thing which yet hath been spoken." She was not simply being stubborn, but was struggling to understand. She was ready to consider an explanation that was given to her if it dealt with the questions she raised. Upon receiving an explanation that made sense to her, she replied that such an elucidation was what she had been seeking, and that finally one of the vexing questions in her mind had been cleared up to some degree.

And so they proceeded. But Mr. Elliot broke in to accuse her of believing that the soul is "Nothing but a Breath & so vanisheth..." This statement is of interest; the last few words of Ecclesiastes 3:19 can be translated in this way, in which case it would not have been strange for her to believe it.32 Cotton then explained her concerns as he understood them to the assembly. He described her thinking in as negative terms as possible:

The Sum of her Opinion is that the souls of men by Creation is no other or better than the souls of beasts which die and are mortal, but are made immortal by the Redemption of Christ Jesus, to which hath been answered that soul is Immortal by Creation and some places brought to prove that they are, namely, the souls of the wicked [are] cast into Hell forever, and the souls of the godly are kept in a blameless frame unto Immortal Glory.[33]

Mr. Wilson then took up the cudgel, but in doing so he made an interesting observation. "It was usual in the former Times when any Blasphemy or Idolatry was held forth they did use to rent their Garments and tear their hair of their heads in sign of Loathing. And if we deny the Resurrection of the Body then let us turn Epicures. Let us eat and drink and do any Thing, tomorrow we shall die:..." Here Wilson is quoting I Corinthians 15:22, "If I have fought with beasts at Ephesus after the manner of men, what advantageth it me, if the dead be not raised up? Let us eat & drink: for tomorrow we shall die." This passage echoes Isaiah 22:13, "And, Joy and gladness, slaying oxen and killing sheep, eating flesh, and drinking wine, eating and drinking: for tomorrow we shall die" (both from Geneva, 1560). These passages and other similar ones found in Ecclesiastes chapter three and Ecclesiastes chapter eight, direct that people should endeavor to enjoy life, and are a reflection of the Greek philosophy of the Epicureans. They are paraphrased and presented in the New Testament as philosophy that followers of Christ would not wish to emulate. Wilson therefore knew the whole passage about which she had been inquiring, and knew the historical background of the philosophy reflected in the Biblical text. Yet, he was calling her a heretic for having brought up a passage of scripture that did indeed have overtones of Epicurean philosophy in it. Just how much of this would she have understood? None at all. Her questions indicate that she did not know the language out of which the Bible had been translated, or the original meanings of the words she was questioning, and she certainly did not realize that Wilson was accusing her of a position her church considered heretical but which is none the less reflected in certain writings of the Bible. Cotton, however, and the rest of the ministers would have to have been aware of all that was being said in the statement of Wilson. He was the preacher noted for his classical quotes and his great learning. Neither he nor any one other of the ministers spoke up for her.

Hutchinson's son-in-law, Thomas Savage, tried to defend her at this juncture by arguing with several of those in charge who felt that enough had been said on that question, and that things should move along. He argued that if she was not convinced of her error, more time should be spent on the point rather than moving on. Cotton and Wilson would have none of that. They accused him of not being Christian enough to "forsake Father and Mother, Wife and children for Christ Jesus 1 Corinthians 5:12," and Cotton concluded with a reference to her "damnable Errors."[34] They then took a vote that she had heard enough arguments to be expected to have been convinced on the first point, and went on. The next point dealt with her understanding of how the soul becomes immortal. She was accused of believing that the soul was not created an immortal soul, but becomes immortal when redeemed by Christ at the time of union with Christ. This apparently followed from her reading of the previous verses of scripture that the spirit is not immortal, although the soul is.

Cotton then said, "I would ask our sister this Question, whether the Soul, body and spirit be not Immortal 1 Peter 3.19."[35]   I Peter 3:19 is interpreted to refer the time after Jesus's death but before his resurrection, when he was believed to have preached to those in hell, and reads, "By the which he also went, & preached to the spirits that were in prison." (Geneva, 1562). She replied to that, "It is more than I know. How do we prove that both soul and body are saved?"[36] Wilson answered her, "*I pray God keep your whole body* soul and body may be kept blameless to Salvation." This quote is part of I Thessalonians 5:23. She pointed out that the verse in fact reads, "may be kept blameless to the coming of Jesus Christ, not to Salvation."[37] When asked what she believed was meant she said it referred to, "his coming to us in Union."

Hutchinson asserted that a verse, apparently Romans 6:4, 5, referred to Christ's coming to be in union with the believer, rather than the usual assumption that it refers to the second coming.[38] Romans 6:4, 5 speaks of being buried with Christ through baptism, and just as he was raised up, the Christian should then also "walk in newness of life." It may be well to return here to the marginal notes to these and many other verses in many of the editions of the Geneva translation. Just as suggested in the previous chapter, these notes may have influenced Hutchinson's thinking about the doctrines under question. She may have imbibed the glosses along with the scripture verses, and formulated her understanding of the doctrines by use of the marginal notes as well as the verses themselves. The particular verses she cited have a gloss, probably by Calvin, in the 1577 edition that discusses sanctification in terms that could lead to the assumption that the resurrection of Christ is the same as his coming into union with the believer. This possibility is of utmost importance for the trial, because it was one of the points that was argued the longest by Hutchinson and the ministers, and helps to explain where her confusion may have come from, and why she felt certain in her arguments. While she nowhere argued that the glosses should be used to explain scripture, and in fact stated at one point that she wanted to have God's word to prove a point, Cotton was attempting to make, and not man's word, it is still likely that she would have held such marginal explanations to be closer to sacred word than anything anyone else could tell her. They certainly would have reinforced ideas she had formed from her scripture reading. The notes to Romans 6:4,5 read:

> There are three parts of this Sanctification: to wit, the death of the old man of sin, his burial, and *the resurrection of the new man,* descending into us from the virtue of the death burial and resurrection of Christ, of which benefit our baptism is the sign and pledge. Gal. 3. 27. To the end that growing up in one with him we should receive his strength, to quench sin in us, and to make us new men...They are said of Paul to be dead to sin, which are in such sort made partakers of the virtue of Christ, that natural corruption is dead in them, that is, the force of it is put out, and it bringeth not forth his bitter fruits: And on the other side, they are said to live to sin, which are in the flesh, that is, whom the spirit of God hath not delivered from the slavery of the corruption of nature. (Geneva, 1560, italics added)

These notes reinforce the ideas that there are separate bodies, and also that the resurrection is accomplished when the person is united with Christ. Wilson, however, was horrified at this suggestion, calling it "no less than Sadducism and Atheism and therefore to be detested."[39]

Hutchinson returned that she had not spoken of this idea at her earlier trial, and asked on what basis she had been banished. She also raised a question as to how the voting should properly take place. No one answered her question about how she had been banished, but Davenport next refuted strongly the idea that the soul is not immortal, citing an unspecified Pope Adrian, who, he claimed, had stated that he did not believe that the soul is immortal, although he agreed that the scriptures claimed it to be so. He then went into a discussion about voting, upholding the practice of having all the church members vote on whether discussion should continue.

Cotton then moved to the second question for her, asking whether souls are immortal "by creation" or are made so by Christ's redemption. She chose the second, which brought down Cotton's wrath. So Davenport explained to her that, "the soul cannot have Immortality in itself but from God from whom it hath its being."[40] Having thought through the implications of this Hutchinson exclaimed, "I thank the Lord I have Light. And I see more Light a great deal by Mr. Davenport's opening of it." This exclamation certainly lends weight to her and her relatives' claims that she was merely raising questions for the purpose of understanding the scriptures, rather than perversely insisting on unorthodox interpretations of doctrine, let alone sectarianism.

When asked by Cotton if this meant she reversed her previous position she replied in cautious legal style, "So far as I understand Mr. Davenport. I Pray let some body open this. How the soul is Immortal by Creation." A great deal more discussion of the method by which souls are made immor-

tal ensued. Davenport explained to her that there were differences between the "Life of the Soul and the Life of the Body," and gave her the
particulars on the differences. He told her: "That Word Spirit in Ecclesiastes is meant the soul, and that Spirit in Thessalonians is not the substance of
the soul but a Quality of it. That soul which Christ speaks of in Matthew
He casts both soul and Body into Hell there soul is not meant spirit but
soul."[41] She declared she was now convinced on the issue as Davenport
had explained it: "I am clear on this now." Davenport: "Then you
renounce what you held in both those points." Hutchinson: "Yes, I do,
taking Soul as Mr. Davenport doth. So there was my Mistake. I took Soul
for Life."[42] Davenport explained more about the meanings of spirit and
soul: "The Spirit is not a Third Substance but the Bent and Inclination of
the soul and all the faculties thereof. Now this is not a substance differing
from the soul, and that Spirit in Ecclesiastes is meant of the Soul, the Spirit
returns to God that gave it, that is, the soul or substance thereof." Again,
her reply is significant: "I do not differ from Mr. Davenport, as he
expresseth himself." After more discussion and questions to her she exclaimed, "Now Mr. Davenport hath opened it, it is clear to me or God by
him hath given me Light."[43] It is hard to imagine her repeatedly making
such statements unless she was telling the truth: she did not hold differing
opinions from them; she had not been able to explain herself clearly.

Cotton, rather than rejoicing that his pupil had now come to see the
light, staggered her with this question: "Sister speak to this: Whether you
conceive that the divine and gracious Qualities of the souls of Believers be
Immortal or no and shall go with the soul into Heaven and whether you
think the Evil Qualities of the souls of wicked men and their Evil Disposi-
tions shall go with their Souls to Hell or no."[44] Her reply was an understandable, "I know not presently what to say to this." Davenport, who at
this point seemed to be the one most willing to attempt to explain the issues
to her, and eager to have her understand what was being said, questioned
her, "You do then consent to the two first Questions that the Coming of
Christ in Thessalonians to the soul is not meant of Christ's Coming in
Union but of his Coming at the day of Judgment." She replied, "I do not
acknowledge it to be an Error but a Mistake. I do acknowledge my Expression to be erroneous but my Judgment was not Erroneous, for I held
before as you did but could not express it so."[45] This statement was one
she tried to repeat later, and it was always ignored or deliberately misunderstood. She was struggling to express to them that in some points of doctrine she agreed with them where they alleged that she disagreed, but that
she could not always articulate her understanding in correct theological

terms. She was asking them to understand that she was not always able to verbalize her thinking in terms they would consider accurate.

She went on to raise more concern:, "John 12 (1) Corinthians 4.16. 3 Things. That men when they believe have a New Body and they have 2 bodies (1 Corinthians 15.44.37)." The twelfth chapter of John deals with the raising of Lazarus, and contains verse 24: "Verily verily I say unto you, except the wheat corn fall into the ground and die, it bideth alone: but if it die, it bringeth forth much fruit." This passage is taken to be a prophesy of Jesus, and of his death and resurrection. When Cotton asked her to agree to his explanations of the Bible passages she had cited, having to do with the differing bodies believers have before and after the resurrection, she carefully stated, "I mean as that Scripture means 1 Corinthians 4.16."[46] As I Corinthians 4:16 has very little to say, and nothing to this point, it is most likely that she was referring to II Corinthians 4:16, which reads, "Therefore, we faint not, but though our outward man perish, yet the inward man is renewed daily."[47] Cotton replied, "You say you do not know whether Jesus Christ be united to this body of ours or...our fleshly bodies. There lies the scruple and the absurdity of it." He continued, "Therefore, remember, both soul and body are united to Christ..."

Now she turned to Davenport for more explanation. She asked, "I desire you to speak to that place in 1 Corinthians 15.37.44 for I do question whether the same Bodies that dies, shall rise again."[48] The passage reads:

> 37. And that which thou sowest, thou sowest not that body that shall be, but bare corn, I mean either of wheat, or of some other.
>
> 38. But God giveth it a body at his pleasure, to every seed his own body.
>
> 39. All flesh is not one manner of flesh but there is one manner [of] flesh of men, another manner [of] flesh of beasts, another of fishes, and another of birds.
>
> 40. There are also celestial bodies, and there are bodies terrestrial; but the glory of the celestial is one and the glory of the terrestrial is another.
>
> 41. There is one manner [of] glory of the sun, and another glory of the moon, & another glory of the stars. For one star differeth from another in glory.
>
> 42. So is the resurrection of the dead. The body is sown in corruption, and riseth in incorruption.
>
> 43. It is sown in dishonour, and riseth in honour: it is sown in weakness, and riseth in power.
>
> 44. It is sown a natural body, and riseth a spiritual body. There is a natural body, & there is a spiritual body." (Geneva, 1557)

Once again it is useful to look at the marginal glosses to these verses. The first, interestingly enough says, "There is one substance as touching the flesh both of man and beast, but the difference is as touching the quality."

The second says, "Even as the sun and moon being of one substance differ in dignity: so in the resurrection our bodies shall have more excellent qualities than they have now." The last says of verse 44, "Not changing the substance, but made partaker of the divine nature" (Geneva, 1560). While any of these might be quite clear to someone like Cotton or Davenport, it is not at all difficult to see how a layperson like Hutchinson could read any of them as referring to differing bodies, even as they agree that humans and beasts are the same. It is entirely possible she did.

Davenport then discussed several passages that deal with natural bodies, spiritual bodies, and the resurrection, attempting to convince her that the fleshly body is raised, but Hutchinson argued that the passages state that the heavenly body is different. During this discussion Hutchinson averred, "I do not believe that Christ Jesus is united to our Bodies." Brother Wilson expostulated, "God forbid."[49] This after Cotton had admonished her to remember that Christ is united both to body and soul.

She was questioned about possible "familist" beliefs, having to do with licentious behavior, which would necessarily follow from the conclusion that the resurrection is past, according to Davenport. She denied any such, and stated that she did not wish to put any construction on any Bible verse that would lead to such thinking, "for I abhor that Practice."[50] Questioned about the resurrection she refused to declare that she held a position different from theirs. Mr. Leveritt interjected, "But our sister doth not deny the Resurrection of the Body."[51] "No," replied Hutchinson. Tempers again began to rise. Even Davenport was moved to declare, "You tell us of a new Body and of 2 bodies; that is three. Now which of these Bodies do you hold shall rise again." Eliot put in, "We are altogether unsatisfied with her answers and we think it is very dangerous to dispute the Question so long in this Congregation...we much fear her spirit."[52] She had them worried that the congregation would agree with her. Several of the men tried to convince her that her "scruples" made her a "dangerous Heretic," but she answered, "I confess if there be no Resurrection than all is in vain, both preaching and all. I scruple not the Resurrection but what Body shall rise, it shall rise, that is in Christ we shall rise." And to questioning by Winthrop about the body that rises at the resurrection she answered, "I know not but that they may be the same Bodies." Getting what he felt was reluctant agreement from her said that "the point is at an End."[53] Unfortunately, she was not willing to leave the point until sure she really did feel persuaded, so the questioning continued for a while on the question of what body rises at the resurrection.

The men had lost their patience with her by now, however. She had the temerity to tell them that she was not sure that the "very Bodies" of

Moses, Elijah and Enoch had been taken up into heaven. Davenport, evidently feeling that he had patiently explained things to her long enough, could take her scruples no longer. He said, "These are Opinions that cannot be borne. They shake the very foundation of our faith and tends to the Overthrow of all Religion. They are not slight matters [but] of great Weight and Consequence."[54] The ministers called for a vote signifying that the members of the congregation felt had enough arguments had been given her to have convinced her of her errors. Wilson described her opinions as "gross and damnable Heresies."

They called for a vote that the members of the church were convinced that she had been in error. Her son tried to argue that they could not vote, but was argued down. She attempted to interject that, "I consent to them [the arguments made to her] as far as I know that there is a Resurrection, etc.," but they were having none of that now. They wished to vote whether she agreed with them or not, and Shepard warned the congregation against holding such "dangerous and fearful Errors which she hath drunk in."[55] Her son-in-law, Sergeant Savage, also attempted to argue that she should be given more time and arguments, especially as she had been led to see the light on some matters, but Cotton stepped in to make it clear that "whereas you say she seeks Light and Information...you hear that there hath been much pains taken and many Arguments brought not only from ourselves but from diverse of the Elders of other Churches...and yet she persists in her Opinion..."[56] Cotton creatively allowed that "your Mother though she be not accused of any thing in point of fact or practice neither for my own part do I know there is any cause. Yet she may hold Errors as dangerous and of worse Consequence than matters of practice can be, and therefore I see not but the church may proceed to Admonition."[57] Here he admitted that nothing had been proven against her of fact or of her practice, but since "she may hold Errors" he was eager to proceed against her. Edward Gibbons reminded them that she had been willing to change her mind about some of her, "Error or Mistake as she calls it in some of the points..." so that they should not "wait a little longer to see if God will not help her to see the rest and to acknowledge them."[58] But Mr. Simmes, who had borne witness against her in the civil trial, allowed that "I am much grieved to hear so many in this Congregation should stand up and declare themselves unwilling that Mrs. Hutchinson should be proceeded against for such dangerous Errors."[59] Davenport admitted that any who had problems with the proceedings should be able to air them. Elder Oliver argued that the Bible required unanimity for a congregation to censure a member. Cotton, however, said there had been discussions enough. (It may be well to note here that when the Boston church had attempted to censure Mr.

Wilson, they were not allowed to do so because the vote was not unanimous.) "If yet some brethren persist in their Dissent upon no Ground but for by Respects of their own or out of natural affection then the Church is not to stay her proceeding for that."[60]   So much for unanimity.

Cotton proceeded to the very long admonition, beginning by admonishing her son and son-in-law because they had argued that the church should give her more time. He accused them of having, "cast down her Name and Credit" and of trampling on the crown of Jesus by defending her, and becoming "instruments of hardening her Heart and Nourishing her in her unsound Opinions by your pleading for her and hindering the proceedings of the Church..." He told them they had not been loving children, but "you have proved Vipers to Eat through the very Bowels of your Mother, to her Ruin..."[61] After more of that line, he proceeded to warn the other women of the church that no matter what good things Hutchinson had done for them, they should search their souls to see "if you have drunk in with this good any Evil or Poison," and if so, to "make speed to vomit it up again." After all, "you see she is but a Woman, and many unsound and dangerous principles are held by her..."[62]

Then he directed himself to Hutchinson. "It is true that when you came first over into this Country we heard some thing of some opinions that you held..."[63]   However, he had worked with her, noting the good she did with the women of the town, and seeing her "sharp apprehension" and her ability to articulate the word. But now, she had misled souls around her, and she could not avoid seeing that if she held to her unsound beliefs the result would be "that filthy Sin of the Community of Women and all promiscuous and filthy coming together of men and Women without Distinction or Relation of Marriage, will necessarily follow."[64]

When he had proceeded that far, Hutchinson interrupted him, stating that she had something she must say, and was afraid she would forget it if she waited for him to finish. She said, "All that I would say is this that I did not hold any of these Things before my Imprisonment."[65] Cotton agreed with her that he had not heard any of the things charged against her until recently, but went on at some length to tell her she had been acting out of pride and dishonoring the church. Shepard, however, was outraged by Cotton's seeming to agree that she had not held any questionable opinions until recently. Further he was not convinced that she had been admonished enough. He sarcastically began, "Lest the Crown should be set on her Head in the day of her Humiliation I desire Leave to speak one Word..."[66] Then he went on at some length about how she had "forwardly expressed herself to me" saying that he had told her he did not wish to trap her. He also was upset that she claimed not to have held any of the opinions ascribed to her before her incarceration. He was quite sure that if she had expressed herself fully to him she would have declared, "these very opinions." Eliot also felt that he had been troubled by such thoughts.[67] Hutchinson was told to come back a week later for more examination.

The next examination was held, "one Thursday Lecture day after Sermon: March: 22th. 1638, before all the Elders of other Churches, and the Face of the Country."[68] By then things had changed considerably. In contrast to her demeanor at her earlier appearances in civil and church courts, Hutchinson came to the second day of questioning completely cowed. She had stayed at John Cotton's house during that week, and he seems to have convinced her to admit all her "errors," and repent of them. She was ready to admit anything, and repent of everything. She did so, but to no avail. Another list of allegations was read, containing accusations that she believed that: "Those that have Union with Christ shall not rise in these Bodies," that the resurrection discussed in I Corinthians 15 refers to the "union with Christ Jesus," and that "there is no created Graces in Believers after Union.... and several similar questions."[69] She was told that she had been admonished because of the first three questions on the list, having to do with the resurrection of the body, and that she must now again address herself to them.

This time her answers were very different in tone. She had now been convinced that she had been wrong. She said she had been "deeply deceived" and that now she could "better see" the doctrines.[70] "Thus she answered to the first sixteen objections," going through them one by one and repudiating them all.[71] She declared, "Though I never doubted that the Soul was Immortal yet...Things I renounce, as that the Soul was purchased to eternal pain." She told them that, "I acknowledge my Mistake of Believers having two Bodies. So now I see that the Apostle in I Corinthians 6.14.15 speaks of persons in one place and of bodies in another." She noted specifically that, "I acknowledge and I do thank God that I better see that Christ is united to our Fleshly Bodies as I Corinthians 6.18.19. I do acknowledge that the same Body that lies in the Grave shall rise again and renounce the former as erroneous Isaiah 11.2."[72] She explained that, "For no Graces being in Believers I desire that to be understood that they are *not in us but as they flow from Christ...*" And she continued in this vein, specifying each "error," and repudiating it. Asked to address Mr. Weld's list, she went through it as well. She made a general repudiation: "For these Scriptures that I used at the Court in Censuring the Country I confess I did it rashly and out of heat of Spirit and unadvisedly, and have cause to be sorry for my unreverent Carriage to them and I am heartily sorry that any Thing I have said have drawn any from hearing any of the Elders of the Bay." She specifically repudiated antinomianism: "I deny it, that not being bound to the Law it is no Transgression to break it..."73

But it was not enough. Wilson had "one Thing that will be necessary for you Sister to answer..." Pointing out that she had claimed that she had only held the opinions after she had been kept at Cotton's house, he questioned her about when she began to hold the unsound opinions. She apologized humbly to them, taking responsibility upon herself for the "errors" and for speaking "rashly and unadvisedly." "I do not allow the slighting of Ministers nor of the Scriptures...If Mr. Shepard doth conceive that I have any of these things in my mind then he is deceived."74 Cotton was asked to repeat her speech, as not everyone had heard. He said that she maintained that she had not fallen into error until recently, that she "doth utterly disallow herself and condemn herself for that Carriage; and she confesseth the Root of all was the height and Pride of her Spirit," and that she was sorry for "her slighting the Ministers."

Shepard, though, was having none of that. "She shall cast Shame upon others and say they are mistaken, and to turn off many of those gross Errors with so slight an Answer as *your Mistake*...I confess I am wholly unsatisfied in her Expressions to some of the Errors. Any Heretic may bring a sly Interpretation...I am unsatisfied, I should be glad to see any Repentance in her: that might give me Satisfaction."75 Eliot agreed, so Cotton went after her again. Again Hutchinson said that she had been mistaken, and that she had not expressed herself clearly: "I confess my Expressions was that way but it was never my Judgment." But it was no longer enough for them. Cotton said, "there is 2 things to be cleared, 1. what you do now hold. 2ly what you did hold."76 She tried once again to explain to them that she had not been able to express herself clearly before, "My Judgment is not altered though my Expression alters." But this time they not only refused to understand her but they turned this against her, interpreting this to mean that she still held the erroneous beliefs, but was now expressing them in orthodox terms. Wilson: "This you say is most dangerous, for if your Judgment all this while be not altered but only your Expressions, when your Expressions are so contrary to the Truth."

A critical juncture was reached when Mr. Simmes said of her, "I should be glad to see any Humiliation in Mrs. Hutchinson...for I fear these are no new Things but she hath anciently held them and had need to be humbled for her former Doctrines and for her abuse of diverse Scriptures. And if she held no new Thing yet she ought to be humbled for what she hath held formerly..."77 Evidently, they had decided that nothing she could say would save her. Literally, they would have her be damned if she did or if she did not. They went on in this vein for some length of time, alleging that she had spoken admiringly of a female minister in Ely, and "that I believe that she thinks vile thoughts of us." Wilson was able to vent his anger at her for having slighted the ministers, even though she had already apologized for that sin. He was particularly upset that she had been "crying down them as Nobodies."[78]

Finally Shepard stated that there had been enough witnesses, but then Hutchinson interjected that Cotton had always known what she believed. Several of the others jumped upon that, and reminded the court that it was true that she had always said that Cotton and she agreed on everything.[79] She was questioned more about "created graces," without being given opportunity to answer the various questions put to her. Several others took the chance to get a word or two in, including Mr. Peter, who reprimanded Hutchinson that "You have rather been a Husband than a Wife and a preacher than a hearer; and a Magistrate than a Subject."[80] Shepard, again attempting to bring things to a close, announced that he felt that she had never been a Christian at all, that "she all this while hath not altered her Judgment, but only her Expressions," and so, he "would have the Congregation judge whether ever there was any Grace in her heart or no..."[81] The ministers all agreed that she was a liar, "a dangerous Instrument of the Devil raised up by Satan amongst us to raise up Divisions and Contentions..." and an "Evil Woman, guilty of such foul Evils."[82]

Only one seemed to question how things had come to this pass. Elder Oliver noted that "I did not think the Church would have come thus far so soon, especially seeing when I talked with her in the morning I saw her to come off so freely in her Confession of her sin in Condemning Magistrates and Ministers."[83] Indeed. As Eliot replied to that, it was "a wonderful Wisdom of God" that had brought them to that point. Cotton summed up this effusion of condemnation against the woman who had repented of all the opinions they had accused her of holding, and apologized for all actions that had seemed to bring calumny on the ministers. He now said, "The matter is now translated, [changed] the last day she was dealt with in point of Doctrine, now she is dealt with in point of practice."[84] He went on to state that witnesses had proved she was not really repentant but lying. So much for the statements of the ministers that they only wanted to convince her of her errors.

Someone, horrified at this turn of affairs, asked, "I desire to be satisfied in this how the Church may proceed to Excommunication when the Scripture sayeth he that confesseth and forsakes sin shall have Mercy, and whether we should not bear with Patience the contrary minded."[85] But Cotton was quick with an answer that amazes: "Confession of Sin there is meant with all the Aggravations of it...which yet hath not appeared to us.

And by bearing with the contrary minded is meant of those that are without [the church]."[86] Others had reservations. Cotton answered all of them. Shepard answered "many of the Brethren" who wished to have only a second admonition rather than excommunication.[87] Several men gave reasons to wait. Cotton however insisted there should be no delay, arguing that, "as in Acts 5. as soon as ever Annanias had told a Lie the Church cast them out."[88] Cotton turned to Wilson, as pastor of the congregation, to pronounce the excommunication:

> Forasmuch as you, Mrs. Hutchinson, have highly transgressed and offended and forasmuch as you have so many ways troubled the Church with your Errors and have drawn away many a poor soul and have upheld your Revelation: and forasmuch as you have made a Lie, etc. Therefore in the name of our Lord Jesus Christ and in the name of the Church I do not only pronounce you worthy to be cast out, but I do cast you out and in the name of Christ I do deliver you up to Satan that you may learn no more to blaspheme to seduce and to lie. And I do account you from this time forth to be a Heathen and a Publican and so to be held of all the Brethren and Sisters of the Congregation, and of others. Therefore I command you in the name of Christ Jesus and of this Church as a Leper to withdraw your self out of the Congregation; that as formerly you have despised and condemned the Holy Ordinances of God and turned your Back on them, so you may now have no part in them nor benefit by them.[89]

Notes

1. Flaherty, *Privacy*, p. 159.

2. Hall, *Antinomian*, p. 351.

3. Ibid., p. 350.

4. Ibid., p. 351.

5. Ibid.

6. Ibid.

7. Ibid., p. 303.

8. The ellipses indicate citations of scripture, which have been moved to the end of the question, for the sake of clarity.

9. Hall, *Antinomian* , pp. 351, 352.

10. Ibid., p. 352.

11. Ibid., p. 353.

12. Ibid., pp. 353, 354. (The citation is out of place here. The verse is quoted— but not cited—by Hutchinson later.)

13. Ibid., p. 354.

14. The brief explanation given here is merely intended to underscore the problems faced by the untutored, such as Anne Hutchinson. For fuller discussions of the book of Ecclesiastes, its origins and its meaning the reader is directed to: Elias Bickerman, *Four Strange Books of the Bible* (New York: Schocken Books, 1967); Frank Zimmermann, *The Inner World of Qohelet* (New York: KTAV Publishing House, 1973); and James L. Crenshaw, *Ecclesiastes: A Commentary* (Philadelphia: The Westminster Press, 1987).

15. Geneva *Bible*, 1577 edition.

16. 12: I know that there is nothing good in them, but to rejoice and to do good in [t]his life. 13: And also that every man eateth and drinketh, and seeth the commodity of all his labor: this is the gift of God. Ecclesiastes 3: 12, 13, Geneva, 1577 ed.

17. Thomas Sheldon Green, *A Greek-English Lexicon to the New Testament* (Grand Rapids: Zondervan Publishing Co., 1970), p. 149.

18. Ibid., p. 207.

19. For the first two see: R.B.Y. Scott, trans., ed.,*The Anchor Bible: Proverbs, Ecclesiastes* (Garden City, NY: Doubleday & Company, 1965). For the third see: Zimmermann, p. 167.

20. Zimmermann., p. 144.

21. Quoted in Emerson, p. 95.

22. Marbury's transcript of his questioning by the Bishop is reprinted in the *Proceedings of the Massachusetts Historical Society*, vol. 48, 1914-1915, pp. 280-287. The quote is from p. 285.

23. Hall, *Antinomian*, p. 354.

24. Ibid.

25. Ibid., 355.

26. Ibid., p. 355.

27. Ibid.

28. Emery Battis cited it, in his well-researched biography of Hutchinson; Stephen Foster, and Larzer Ziff have cited it. All of them took the statement at face value as vindicating Cotton, and demonstrating his futile attempts to persuade her to see reason. Battis says that Cotton "implored" her; Ziff states that, "he showed her many places of scripture contrary to her opinion..." (Battis, p. 238; Larzer Ziff, *The Career of John Cotton: Puritanism and the American Experience* (Princeton: Princeton University Press, 1962), p. 143;) Foster states it strongly: "One can sense the grief and shock in his remonstrance: 'Sister, do not shut your eyes Against the Truth. All these places prove that the soul is Immortal.' " (Stephen Foster, "New England and the Challenge of Heresy, 1637-1660: The Puritan Crisis in a Transatlantic Perspective" *William and Mary Quarterly*, vol. 38, 1981, p. 625.)
   In his introduction to the church trial, David Hall says, "Those who prosecuted Mrs. Hutchinson hoped that she would confess her errors, as, for a moment, she did. But in the end she stood her ground and the church had no other choice than to cast her out." (Hall, *Antinomian*, p. 350) Emery Battis, in his biography of Hutchinson states, "In the last analysis she could not concede that she was really and wholly wrong and that the ministers were unimpeachably right. This inability to unlearn the questions she had asked was to prove her undoing." (Battis, p. 241) J. F. Maclear, in his article, "Anne Hutchinson and the Mortalist Heresy," makes the most damning claim of all: "Her defensive claim that her views were perplexities rather than convictions may have been genuine, and certainly her mortalist ideas appeared confused and still ill formed. But Anne was also stubborn, and in spite of her concessions the elders, at the end of the trial, were convinced that she taught only a spiritual resurrection in this life." (Maclear, p. 88) Maclear believes that she had somehow come into contact with preaching or teaching of the mortalist heresy, the belief that there is no resurrection, and the soul dies at the time of death of the body. He, then, accuses her of confusion and stubbornness, and possibly of lying about her motives. In his article on Hutchinson, Maclear does not take into account that there is a difference between the use of the words "soul" and "spirit" in the Bible, and thus his confusion about her answers. The interpretation that she was at best stubborn and at worst disingenuous is shared by all scholars. None has recognized that she was correct in her reading of the texts, and that there were perfectly rational and not terribly complex answers to her questions.

29. Hall, *Antinomian*, p. 355.

30. Ibid., p. 356.

31. Ibid.

32. Scott gives this translation of verse 19: "For the fate of men and the fate of animals is the same; as one dies, so dies the other, for all have the same breath of life. Man has no superiority over the beast, for all are a breath that vanishes." P. 222.

33. Hall, *Antinomian*, p. 356.

34. Ibid., p. 357.

35. Ibid.

36. Ibid.

37. Ibid., p. 358.

38. Hutchinson is quoted as citing "1 46 6," and this is believed to refer to Romans 6:4. Hall says Adams believes it to be such, and the context supports this understanding. Ibid., p. 358.

39. Ibid.

40. Ibid., p. 359.

41. Ibid., p. 360.

42. Ibid.

43. Ibid.

44. Ibid.

45. Ibid., p. 361.

46. Ibid.

47. Geneva translation, 1557 edition.

48. Hall, *Antinomian*, p. 361.

49. Ibid., pp. 361-2.

50. Ibid., p. 362.

51. Ibid., p. 363.

52. Ibid.

53. Ibid., p. 364.

54. Ibid.

55. Ibid., p. 365.

56. Ibid., p. 366.

57. Ibid.

58. Ibid., pp. 366, 367.

59. Ibid., p. 367.

60. Ibid., p. 368.

61. Ibid., p. 369.

62. Ibid., p. 370.

63. Ibid.

64. Ibid., p. 372.

65. Ibid., p. 372.

66. Ibid., p. 373.

67. Ibid., p. 374.

68. Ibid.

69. Ibid.

70. Ibid., p. 375.

71. Ibid., p. 376.

72. Ibid., p. 375.

73. Ibid., p. 376.

74. Ibid., p. 377.

75. Ibid.

76. Ibid., p. 378.

77. Ibid., p. 379.

78. Ibid., p. 380.

79. Ibid., p. 381.

80. Ibid., p. 383.

81. Ibid.

82. Ibid., p. 384, 5.

83. Ibid., p. 385.

84. Ibid.

85. Ibid., p. 386.

86. Ibid.

87. Ibid.

88. Ibid., p. 387.

89. Ibid., p. 388.

Chapter Eleven

Reprise: Was She Guilty?

This study cannot be concluded without inquiring: was she guilty? The answer is: even employing the legal and ecclesiastical frameworks of their times, she was not. In the civil trial the court was unable to prove charges of sedition, even sedition quite broadly defined. The definition of the charges against her in the history of the time written by William Hubbard, one of the first Harvard graduates, states:

> it was laid to her charge, that she had a great hand in the public disturbance of the country, partly by erroneous opinions, which she broached and divulged, and partly by countenancing, and encouraging such as sowed sedition therein, and partly by casting reproach upon the faithful ministers of the country, and their ministry; thereby weakening their hands in the day of the Lord, and raising prejudice against them in the hearts of the people.[1]

The papers of Thomas Hutchinson, Governor of Massachusetts and great-great grandson of Anne and William Hutchinson, include the petition signed on behalf of John Wheelwright. Quotes from it indicate what the people of Boston felt was a proper definition of the burden of proof for sedition: "either the person condemned must be culpable of some sedition fact or his doctrines must be seditious or must breed sedition in the hearts of his hearers."[2] The first of these explanations would include the charges against Anne Hutchinson, and the second could be read to do so if one remembers that the relationship of the ministry to the governing powers was quite close. However, nothing in either of these definitions was proven against her.

Even John Winthrop admitted in his writings about the case that the General Court was never able to prove the civil case against her with respect to the ministers, or the other charge, that she incited to sedition when she had contact with those who had signed a petition claiming that

John Wheelwright was not guilty of sedition. That was why he was so grateful for the providential statements regarding "revelations." Having gotten to the point at which it was obvious to everyone that the trial was essentially over, her claim that she had felt so sure of herself because God had revealed to her that they could not hurt her gave Winthrop and the court a vision of a whole new possibility. In response to her—undoubtedly smug—claims to God's opening of scripture for her Winthrop and the others chose to believe that Hutchinson was asserting that God spoke to her directly, through a voice, or some other means, a heretical claim. However, her claims of "revelations" were not heretical, as John Cotton explained to them, because she quoted the Bible verses that God "opened" to her, a practice shared by all of them. Winthrop also claimed that she said that God would save her through a miracle, although further questioning by John Cotton made it plain that she had not said so. She was not proven guilty of heresy, even by their strict standards.

She was not guilty of claims of direct revelations and of expecting a miracle from God on her behalf. But what if she had been? Would she then have been guilty of sedition? No, she would not. That was why Winthrop did not respond to her question of what she had been found guilty, but merely said that the court knew and was satisfied; he knew very well that his court could not convict her *only* of a religious infraction. The General Court could only try her on a civil (secular) charge, which was why she was charged with sedition. Even if she had claimed that Michael and all his angels were waiting in the anteroom to come to her defense, she was not guilty of a civil crime. Thus, although they convicted her, they did not prove her guilty. She was not proven guilty of any of the charges.

The church trial is based upon doctrinal questions and church procedure, but the answer to her guilt on those charges is also negative. During the first day's proceedings she asked questions of the ministers, and the questions that she had were not mere quibbles; had they been answered fully and carefully she might have understood the explanations and accepted them. She was willing to accept the exegesis given her, so there is no reason to believe that she would not have done so with a better explanation.

At the second day of that trial—after having spent a week with John Cotton—she recanted, and was willing to forswear every question she had raised, giving as explanation that things had now been explained to her to her satisfaction, or that her position had been shown to her as being incorrect. She stated that she had not meant to malign the clergy, and did not believe that anyone should do so. She referred to most of her previous opinions as "mistakes" rather than "errors," which was significant, in that she did so consistently when she wanted to minimize her lapses. She also noted that if Mr. Shepard thought that she had held any of the opinions before her incarceration, he was incorrect; she had merely been asking questions. In this way, she explained away her statement that she had not held any of the offending opinions earlier, as Shepard and others had claimed. She acknowledged that she had been deceived and mistaken. Her claim that she had not held these opinions before the examination by the church is borne out by the fact that she was not accused of holding such opinions until the church trial. All earlier lists of questions for her or John Cotton dealt with preparationist themes. Further, she maintained that she was raising questions in regard to puzzling biblical passages, and her willingness to disavow those points confirms this.

As several of those present attempted to argue—to no avail—this should have ended the matter. It did not. Shepard, Dudley, Eliot, Peter, and others claimed that they did not see repentance in her face, and that therefore her recantation was not acceptable, and that she was a liar for having said that she did not hold any of the offending opinions before she had been confined. Obviously at that point it really did not matter to them what she said or did. They should not have excommunicated her after she had recanted; as her brother-in-law, Richard Scott, asked, "I desire to propound this one Scruple which keeps me that I cannot so freely in my spirit give way to Excommunication. Whether it were not better to give her a little time to consider of the Things that is...vised against her, because she is not yet convinced of her Lie and so things is with her in Distraction, and she cannot recollect her Thoughts."[3] Shepard and Cotton argued that she was obstinate in her lying, although they noted that "many of the brethren" wanted to wait for the excommunication. But Cotton insisted that she should be cast out immediately. At that point she was excommunicated. It was clear to "many of the brethren" it should not happen, and it is apparent today that she did not receive an honest trial.

She was undoubtedly an opinionated, perhaps even at times obnoxious, woman. That was not a matter for excommunication. If she did in fact harbor any heretical opinions, it was never proven. To the extent that she held opinions disagreeable to the church at Boston, she repented of them, even if some of the brethren did not like her facial expression. There was no proof that she had lied; Shepard seems to have gone out of his way to construe questions as tenets dearly held. It appeared all along that she was questioning the ministers in order to have the points explained to her; when the points were explained, she said she was clear on them and accepted their explanations. Further, she stated several times that she had been unable to explain her theological position properly, which is not an unreasonable claim for her to make. The points she questioned were difficult and abstruse. In addition, it is more than possible that she was confused by marginal notes in her Bible, which would also have required explanation from the ministers to clarify for her.   She should not have been excommunicated; they did not provide any proof that she should be cast out from among them.

The answer to the overarching question about Anne Hutchinson then is that there is no evidence that she was in fact guilty of the charges against her.   However, because the ministers of the colony, and Winthrop, Dudley, and the other representatives of the General Court recognized the need to intertwine covenant theology and covenanted civil order, they could not tolerate her threat.   She was waging a war against their understanding of the perfect civil order, but she was waging it with an older Calvinistic theology, one that she firmly believed should, and would, be protected by God.   She did not expect a miracle, but she had every confidence that he would provide for her protection in some providential way.   They had to rid themselves of her to protect their own interpretation of orthodoxy.

There remain questions that should be raised with respect to the trials:

a) Was she in fact an Antinomian?

b) Why did she make the statements that were used by her prosecutors just when she appeared to have won at the first trial, and could have gotten by with an admonition at the second?

c) Was Anne Hutchinson persecuted because she was a woman?

d) What would have happened in the colony if she had not been tried?

Was she in fact, whether proven or not, an Antinomian? Historians and scholars have maintained she was.[4] All however, have relied upon the verdicts of the trials, and upon the allegations against her, rather than her own words, to demonstrate that she was an Antinomian.[5] A closer look at her trials reveals however that it is most likely she was just what she pleaded at her church trial: a woman who had many questions about the meaning of the scriptures, and had been raising questions with Thomas Shepard on several places in scripture that were puzzling to her, who would not be put off with hesitant or inconclusive answers, and, most damning of all, who trumpeted her questions about theological inconsistencies to all and sundry.

If she did not hold unorthodox positions, why did she behave the way she did at the end of each of her trials? Why did she make statements that allowed them to rid themselves of her?[6] Her explanations after the civil trial seem to have welled up from a need to tell the men where she stood, possibly in hopes of convincing them: when they all knew it was over, she felt able to do what she had been eager to do all along, tell them of her special insights from God. Anne Hutchinson was not a woman to keep still; her discussions on board ship and at her weekly meetings make that plain. She was driven to tell the truth as she saw it. Her control of the civil trial came at the expense of her ability to hold forth, and once she felt confident that she would not be convicted, she had to relay to them the advantage of her superior insights into scripture. Perhaps she believed they would be persuaded. Her question as to on what grounds she was found guilty seems as if it came from someone who was truly bewildered by what happened: she had been confident she would go free.

At her second trial she also lost her chance to avoid excommunication. At the opening of the second day of questioning she apologized for all the unpleasantness she had caused, and repudiated all heterodoxy. But then she insisted she had not held those opinions earlier: why? One explanation of those claims presents an interesting answer to the question of her motivation for the statement. This interpretation comes from John Winthrop's "Short Story" of the events, recorded in his *Journal*. Winthrop felt that her claim indicated that she was accusing the leaders of the colony of having tortured her when she was under arrest. He declares that:

> She asked for what errors she had been banished, professing withall that she held none of these things she was now charged with, before her imprisonment; (supposing that whatsoever should be found amiss would be imputed to that, but it was answered as the truth was, that she was not put to durance, but only a favorable confinement, so as all of her Family and divers others, resorted to her at their pleasure).[7]

This is an interesting concern, especially as she was so physically frail at her church trial, and obviously acquiescent in her bearing at the second day of the trial. Whether others had expressed concern about possible mistreatment of her, just as some voiced apprehension about Wheelwright's treatment during his trial, Winthrop does not indicate. He does seem to be quite eager to impress the reader with the positive nature of her house arrest, "a favorable confinement," however.

It is more likely however, that once again, she could not resist explaining herself to them. Given that accusation of the mortality of the soul had not been made earlier, it is likely she really was exploring new questions that had recently occurred to her when she discoursed during the week with Thomas Shepard. But she was never given the opportunity to discuss her thinking on the matters that had been of such concern for the previous years: the church trial dealt only with the new questions listed by Shepard. She was not asked the questions from the other list that raised to issues dealing with predestination, justification/sanctification, and obedience to the law: the very areas of concern that had caused all the original commotion, and led to the rift between Cotton and the other ministers. Thus the most important questions of all were never asked of her. In reply to the theological points that were alleged against her, she saw herself as merely persistently asking questions. Shepard saw her suggesting heresy: it was Shepard, after all, who had lectured the congregation that horrible doctrinal falsities had been brought into the church by way of questions. Undoubtedly she had raised those concerns during her discussions with Shepard, by way of questions, which is why he was so angry with her for reminding the church that she had not held those tenets before. Thus, she could repudiate the beliefs, if indeed she had ever held them, because Davenport had explained them to her, but she could not resist pointing out that she had not held the beliefs before that time. She may have intended to explain that her questions were merely that: however, Shepard's credibility was at stake, and his fury rained down upon her. Again, her need to try to relate fully her thinking seems to have been her undoing. She was far more effective in defending herself when she spoke little.

Further, did she become an Antinomian later, after having been banished? It is impossible to tell. Winthrop and some others wrote of her in the most derogatory terms, interpreting anything she said as upholding their original impressions. Perhaps, by that time, she had gone over to "unorthodox" beliefs, once she no longer had John Cotton to keep her within the pale. There is precious little evidence to indicate she had become anything but a vocal thorn in the side of Massachusetts Bay.

The question whether she was treated more harshly by the powers of Massachusetts Bay because she was a woman is quite regularly asked by people who hear the story, and often the assumption is that Anne Hutchinson was treated more ruthlessly than a man would have been in the same circumstance. Upon careful review of the facts of the story the answer to the question seems to be, no, she was not treated differently at her trials from the way a man would have been. Roger Williams, tried two years before her, was like her a pesky gadfly banished by the Massachusetts Bay Colony for his refusal to repudiate his unorthodox beliefs. It is fair to assume that the experience the colony had had with him made the magistracy even more anxious than it would otherwise have been to rid the colony of troublemakers. Given his earlier test of their patience, there was actually a certain amount of restraint shown Hutchinson. Banishment was a substitute for the death penalty, and one result of Hutchinson's succeeding Williams chronologically could have been a decision on the part of the authorities to give her the harsher penalty: death. That was indeed the penalty some years later when Mary Dyer was hanged for obstinately insisting on being a Quaker. Obviously by that time the colony had lost whatever patience it still retained during Anne Hutchinson's time.

It is possible that she was treated differently from the way a man would have been before her trials. That is to say, a man might have been called to task sooner than she was if he had held meetings in his house in the manner she did. A man might have been taken more seriously as a threat to the colony sooner than she was. This is likely the case, as Roger Williams was disciplined sooner in the game: his threat was nipped in the bud much more quickly than hers. Probably the suggestion that a woman would be the cause of many folks going astray—even the governor, after all—was so foreign to the leadership of Massachusetts Bay that it was felt best to leave her alone so that the enthusiasm for her meetings would die out. But once her trials were underway, there would appear to be no difference in the way in which she was treated from the way in which one would expect a man to have been treated. Her arguments were taken seriously, and had she not felt triumphant enough at the end of her civil trial to declare that she had assurance from God that they could not hurt her, she would have frustrated their attempts to convict her. She was most certainly not treated any less seriously than a man would have been in like circumstances; her claims were given due weight, and she was finally able to force the court to have the ministers testify against her under oath, although neither the ministers themselves nor the rest of the leaders were eager for them to do so. At her church trial all her questions were answered by John Davenport with some thought, although not always completely, and though at times Cotton and others lost patience with her, there is no suggestion that the reason was merely because she was a woman.[8] It would appear that any uneducated person, man or woman, would have been treated similarly. A man who had been educated would not have raised some of the questions she did, because he would have studied Greek and possibly Hebrew, and would have known the answers to some of the questions; an uneducated man would not, and there is no reason to suppose the ministers and Winthrop would have answered a man's questions any more straightforwardly than they did hers. The outcome of the trial was a foregone conclusion, even to a greater extent than that of the civil trial; it was only necessary in both cases to find a reason to declare the court satisfied, and then to stop the proceedings. That is exactly what happened at both trials, although she came close to foiling them at the first one.

At times during both trials, and at the admonition at the end of the first day of the church trial, the fact that Anne Hutchinson was a woman was mentioned. She was told that she had not behaved in the way that a good woman should; she should have been under her husband's tutelage.

She was also told that she had not comported herself properly in holding her meetings, but she was able to convince the court that she had not violated any of St. Paul's commands in doing so, and the court grudgingly agreed. The women present were admonished not to act as she did, or to give weight to her teachings, and there were unpleasant references to their inability to judge her teachings for themselves. However, it is not unlikely that uneducated men would have been warned not to listen to other uneducated men who might be preaching to them. These reprimands do not contradict the judgment that she was not treated or judged more harshly during either of her trials because she was a woman. She was given a chance to defend herself—the same unfair chance that a man in similar circumstances would have been given. She was taken seriously: she was not ridiculed as being a woman and therefore unable to understand what was being said to her. She was able to force the court into having the ministers testify under oath. There would seem to be no basis for claiming that she was persecuted because she was a woman.

The last question to be dealt with is what would have happened in the colony had she been left alone. Needless to state, this is conjecture, but it is not uninteresting to speculate upon the question. Could the colony have withstood the civil unrest caused by her declaring that the ministers were not preaching the gospel clearly? Only if Winthrop, Cotton, and more particularly Shepard and Hooker and the others had been willing to allow freedom of conscience and more separation of church and state. Roger Williams was willing to allow those ideas because he felt that since only God could judge any person's heart it was impossible to have a pure church on earth: therefore, one could not set up the state in any way that assumed church membership. Rhode Island was able to weather similar problems to those facing Massachusetts Bay, so one can assume that the allowing of freedom of conscience itself would not necessarily have led to the disintegration of the Bay Colony. Eventually of course the leaders of the Bay colony were forced in that direction, but it would indeed have been painful to have had to move that way as soon as 1637.

Possibly if all the ministers had been willing to agree, at that first synod of theirs in summer, 1637, that they would allow for some differences in doctrine, she could have been allowed to be left unmolested. Had they agreed then to have a (formal or informal) platform of agreement, with some room for disagreement, perhaps it could have worked. Instead of insisting on perfect uniformity, they could have set forth a platform of agreement with basic tenets, and allowed for some differences in interpretation. Cotton would have liked to have had some flexibility; perhaps things might have been different if he had remained firm on that one idea, and insisted that flexibility was needed in interpreting doctrine. Or, if he had moved during that summer, and taken Hutchinson and her followers with him, he could have set up another town in the area, with more tolerance there. He did neither, and capitulated to the ministers' demands instead. The game was lost for Anne Hutchinson when he did so.

Notes

1. William Hubbard, *A General History of New England: From the Discovery to MDCLXXX*, (Cambridge, MA: Massachusetts Historical Society, 1815), p. 284.

2. Hutchinson, *Papers*, p. 72.

3. Hall, *Antinomian*, p. 386.

4. Edmund S. Morgan , in his oft-quoted look at the Hutchinson trials in the article in the *New England Quarterly* in 1937 cited earlier, maintained stoutly that while we may be appalled at the trials to which Hutchinson was subjected, there can be no disagreeing with their verdict. (That was the purpose of the article—to show that she had been guilty, by Puritan standards.) Samuel Eliot Morison's history of Harvard dismissed Hutchinson as a rather confused troublemaker whose unfortunate treatment was the necessary price to be paid for the founding of Harvard College.

5. K. B. Stoever's work, *A Faire and Easy Way to Heaven: Covenant Theology and Antinomianism in Early Massachusetts*, mentioned earlier, devotes a considerable number of pages to analyzing the theology of the time, and some of the allegations against Hutchinson. He relies heavily upon the lists of questions and accusations, and assumes her Antinomianism based upon them and the fact that there were sects in England that held to tenets it was alleged she held. He does not demonstrate any connection between her and the sects whose tenets he assumes she held. He does use one statement attributed to her from the trials, that there is a difference between the spirit and the letter of the Gospel, as evidence that she was Antinomian. Her statement is difficult to comprehend, but did not excite much interest at the trial, so apparently the ministers did not interpret it as evidence of sectarianism.

6. Scholars have interpreted her claims to God's guidance as meaning that she was using religious rather than legal language, that by pouring forth her beliefs she made the trial "a cleansing ritual," and that she "reject[ed] the legal process and decid[ed] to defy the state in her own religious terms."   Ann Fairfax Withington and Jack Schwartz, "The Political Trial of Anne Hutchinson" *New England Quarterly* 41 (1978): 226-240. Quotes from p. 238.

7. Winthrop, *Journal*, vol. 1, p. 247.

8. Hull, in her study of women and the legal system in colonial times, states that Hutchinson "suffered for [her] independence of mind," and believes that she was treated unfairly because of her sex, but her study finds that in general, "the criminal justice system treated women fairly: it did not impose special burdens upon them, nor did it prejudge their guilt," pp. 12, 140. Although Hutchinson's guilt was prejudged, it is difficult that a man would have been treated differently, had all other facts of the case been the same.

Chapter Twelve

Epilogue

Hutchinson's trials ended the period of raw beginning and innocence for the colony. Although they could not know it, by forcing the leaders to deliberate carefully on their positions on law and doctrine, on relationships with the mother country and with surrounding colonies, the trials brought to a close the initial struggle toward erecting their hoped-for utopia, their "city on a hill." The initial period of exploration of the potential of the new model of society, during which they assayed their "Model of Christian Charity," was at an end. They had completed their initial attempts to hold together a community with Christian charity and found that it was not possible to do so. The intertwining of ecclesiastical and secular authority they had envisioned as comprising a heavenly ideal for the last days of the earth had proved unworkable.

Events moved quickly after the trials as the colony attempted to deal with some of the matters that had come to the fore. Winthrop quickly wrote a pamphlet excoriating Hutchinson and exonerating the leadership of Boston, and the colony moved to purge itself of all those it felt were still contaminated with her ideas. One of those who was caught in the colony's efforts to purge itself of heretical leanings was her friend, Mary Dyer. Dyer was the wife of a milliner, and had been a loyal follower of Hutchinson. At the end of her ecclesiastical trial, after the pronouncement of excommunication, Hutchinson's good friend Mary Dyer had stood up and walked out of the church with her, knowing that she too would likely be forced to leave the colony, but also demonstrating that she was ready to stand with her friend and their beliefs. When a stranger to the vicinity asked who that woman was, he was told that she was the woman who had given birth to a "monster." The facts surrounding that birth made the good people of Boston all the more sure they had found evil in both Dyer and Hutchinson.

Hutchinson had been one of the two midwives present to deliver Dyer of the "monster." Although Dyer had had two children, her third labor was early, and difficult: she had finally given birth to an extremely malformed, and dead, child. Hutchinson feared accusations from the citizens of Boston that the deformed stillbirth portended evil, so she asked John Cotton for advice. Given the circumstances of the birth he told her to conceal the nature of the miscarriage. He reported later that he was acting on the desires he himself would have had in such a situation. He wrote that he himself would want the thing concealed if it were his problem, for exactly the same reasons Anne was concerned. On his advice, she buried the fetus and swore the other women present to secrecy. As one might expect, the whole town had been whispering ever since about the horrible news.[1] Now the question of what had happened at the delivery came out into the open after Hutchinson's trial, and one of the elders asked Hutchinson about the case. She told him what had happened. Winthrop was quite upset, and inquired of Cotton about the case, which forced Cotton to admit his part in it.[2] Winthrop became so disturbed about the matter that he consulted with the other magistrates and some elders, and finally they decided to have the fetus disinterred in order to see if it was indeed some sort of sign from God. Winthrop described the fetus in ghoulish detail: "The wife of one William Dyer...was delivered of a large woman child, it was stillborn, about two months before her time, the child having life a few hours before the delivery, but so monstrous and misshapen, as the like hath scarce been heard of: it had no head but a face which stood so low upon the breast, as the ears (which were like an Ape's) grew upon the shoulders." He went on to declare that the fetus had claws, holes like mouths, and spines upon its back, with other deformations. Most importantly of all, of course, he stated that this birth proved that the devil had some hand in the matter, and noted with satisfaction that the father of the fetus, having come back to town just after the birth, had been called before the church to explain some of his unorthodox religious opinions.[3]

Mary and William Dyer left Boston after the trials and went to Rhode Island where she later became a Quaker, and "one of the most ardent and fearless proselytizers of the 'inner light'."[4] The colony saw further proof in her case of the serious implications of the growth of heretical beliefs, and fearing those consequences, began to mete out death sentences to Quakers and Baptists in the years following. Mary was persecuted for her beliefs when she attempted to return to Boston and on one occasion imprisoned. Finally she returned to Boston in 1660 to be hanged for her beliefs rather than repudiate them or run from Boston any longer.

Meanwhile Anne Hutchinson and her husband, along with her younger children and two of her older sons, left the colony and went to Rhode Island. She went by boat to Mt. Wollaston, where she and William had a house, intending to go to live at Piscataqua, where her brother-in-law, John Wheelwright, had gone. Changing her mind as to her destination, she went on foot to Portsmouth, Rhode Island, to a place suggested by Roger Williams. She felt so beleaguered by her treatment from Governor Winthrop that she longed for the return of Harry Vane, even going so far as to tell Roger Williams that she almost felt she was ready to leave and return to England if Vane did not come back.[5]

Hutchinson herself suffered a miscarriage a few months after leaving Boston. She too was believed to have given birth to a "monster," to the great satisfaction of the magistracy in Boston. Cotton and Winthrop were so interested in the mass that was aborted that they asked the physician who had been called to help Hutchinson to recount for them in detail the composition of the substance of which she was delivered. He declared it to be made up of a large number of lumps of fetal material, which allowed them to claim that she had given birth to a mass of thirty-eight monsters, which Cotton and Winthrop then proclaimed to be a sign of God's anger at Hutchinson. They decided that she had promulgated exactly thirty-eight "errors," which God had expelled from her in the form of the mass. This circumstance enabled Cotton and Winthrop to hold her up as having incurred God's wrath, and themselves up as having tried valiantly to uphold His laws on earth. The actual likely composition of the mass of which she was delivered has been researched by Emery Battis, and his medical advisor felt that it fit the description of a hydatidiform mole, or a mass containing partially formed fetal material.[6]

The colony was able to purge itself of all vestiges of tainted thinking by banishing several of Hutchinson's friends shortly after her. In addition a number of others whose theology was suspect were sent away from Salem.[7] Anne was encouraged in her banishment when her sister Katherine Scott came to live in Providence, and others of the group that had been banished with her formed a small assembly there. During this time Anne continued her influence in the community, preaching and, according to John Winthrop, urging the families who lived near her to "have no magistracy," which enraged him when he heard of it. He was much gratified to discover that an earthquake was sent by God at one time when she and some of her followers were praying. Her leadership continued in Rhode Island, and her husband was selected to be the only magistrate of her town (apparently they needed at least one) in 1639.

Winthrop and the other Bostonians kept a close eye on all the goings-on of Hutchinson's group in Rhode Island, and were annoyed with the little church that she and the others near her had gathered together; he and the leaders of the Boston church felt that the Rhode Island church was not lawful. The reason for this was that, although some of the members of the new church had been excommunicated from the Boston church, others had merely left it without resigning their membership, and therefore were nominally still members in Boston. All of these events merely served to exacerbate the hard feelings that were already evident in the dealings of the Boston church with Hutchinson and her followers. Winthrop and the other magistrates did not feel they could simply leave the Hutchinsonian Rhode Islanders alone, which stemmed from their belief that they should continue to encourage those who had fallen away from the true church to repent of their errors, so as not to be destined for eternal perdition. So, they continued to contact them and rebuke them.

In 1640 the Boston church sent a group of emissaries to discuss orthodoxy with Mrs. Hutchinson, and see if they could persuade her to repent of her ways. "When they came first unto her, she asked from whom they came, and what was their business. They answered, 'We are come in the name of the Lord Jesus, from the Church of Christ at Boston, to labor to convince you of' etc. At that word she (being filled with as much disdain in her countenance, as bitterness in her spirit) replied, 'What, from the Church of Boston? I know no such Church, neither will I own it. Call it the Whore and Strumpet of Boston, no Church of Christ'."[8] Having heard her opinion of them and their church, the men tried to influence her husband, who told them that "he was more nearly tied to his wife than to the church; he thought her to be a dear saint and servant of God."[9] Bravely they attempted to hold a discussion with Anne, but she insisted that the dialogue could not be conducted unless notes were taken. This was undoubtedly due to her recognition that the notes of her discussions with the ministers had never been produced during her civil trial. She undoubtedly felt that had the court directed that the written record of her communications with the ministers be produced, perhaps her case might have been aided enormously. In any case, her call for a written record insulted the men, and they left Rhode Island. Returning to Boston, they reported on the unhappy meeting. John Cotton became quite distressed over the report, and announced to the congregation that, "They were in a Covenant with us as a wife to the Husband, but like a Harlot she will be gone for all her covenant."[10] This rather telling *cri de coeur* demonstrates not only the depth of his anguish over her unruly behavior but the simile also reveals rather forcefully his feelings of personal rejection.

One of the members of the Boston church was especially upset at her unwillingness to open a dialogue with her former church. This was Thomas Leverett, who was now the ruling elder of the Boston church, but who had once supported Hutchinson. He was so angry that he wrote to her and called her haughty, a Jezebel, and ridiculed her former reputation. She wrote back a letter that was full of the wit and cleverness she showed to such advantage at her civil trial, pointing out that he had misquoted the Bible, and that as he himself had once believed her interpretation of doctrine, he was displaying serious inconsistencies in his behavior. His response to her too would seem to indicate that he was angry and disappointed at Hutchinson herself, rather than merely cross at her unorthodox beliefs.[11] The Boston church at last became so outraged with her refusal to discuss issues with them and her condemnation of their congregation that they concluded the best course of action was to refuse to have anything to do with the little Rhode Island group, which would perhaps have been the better plan from the first.

In 1641 the magistracy in Boston tried to fine her son, Francis, and son-in-law, William Collins, ostensibly for holding to the same heretical opinions as Mrs. Hutchinson. Actually, however, this was an attempt to compensate the town for the cost of her trials, according to Winthrop's account of the matter.[12] The young men held out, however, even to the extent of going to jail rather than paying the hefty fines, and were released without paying their fines or recanting—the bond they had posted was confiscated for their fines. They were banished and told never to return.

During their years in Rhode Island, Hutchinson and the supporters from Boston who had migrated with her did not always continue to agree; often these staunch individualists became unwilling to be led by Hutchinson or anyone else, and like Mary Dyer went in new directions in their doctrinal thinking. Some of them even returned to England: one of her most vocal supporters, Coddington, became a fifth monarchist agitator there. Winthrop maintained that the group promulgated "new heresies" all the time. He lists such "heresies" as refusing to wear arms, becoming Anabaptist, and maintaining that no church since those founded by the apostles was a true church.[13]

By 1642 the political difficulties of the Rhode Islanders and their relationships to the colony of Massachusetts Bay were intensifying. Winthrop had an opportunity to try to extend Massachusetts Bay to include land around Providence, which would involve the possibility of including Aquidneck, where Hutchinson and her family and friends were living. The situation became very serious for the Hutchinsons and friends when Massachusetts Bay cut off trade with them, which forced them to trade only with the Dutch. At the same time rumors flew that Massachusetts Bay might be in league with the Narragansetts, Indians who were unfriendly to the Rhode Islanders. Life became very hard personally for Hutchinson during this period, because her devoted husband William died, and Anne felt she could not battle these events without his support, moral and practical. Feeling unable to handle these developments alone, she determined to leave Rhode Island to avert having to deal with Massachusetts Bay. At last she decided to take the children living with or near her and move to New York. She left Rhode Island in the summer of 1642 with fifteen other people, including her son-in-law and his wife, and the other five of her children still living with her. The area where they went in New York was Dutch territory, and an area near there was known as Anne's Hoeck, near Hutchinson's Creek, on Pelham Bay, which were named after her. Although legend has told of her having lived at Anne's Hoeck, (neck) the evidence suggests that she lived nearer the coast in Eastchester.14 She took a business partner, Captain James Sands, in order to have him build her a house, but the house-building was interrupted several times by Native Americans who attempted to stop the process and make the Europeans go away. About a year later a group of Narragansetts came to Hutchinson's home demanding to speak with her. This group was angry because the European settlers who had built homes there had thereby caused desecration of their burial grounds. Arriving at her home they asked that the dogs be tied up. Suspecting no trouble, this was done. But once her canine defenders were unable to help, Anne and her family had no protection. The Narragansetts were then able to kill Anne and all of her children but one daughter, whom they took captive. She remained their prisoner for four years.15

Upon hearing of the massacre, Winthrop noted sagely that the group of Indians who killed Hutchinson had not behaved so violently before that time. As with her miscarriage, he felt the slaughter of her family had been a sign of God's judgment.16 It is ironic to think that Winthrop would take this attitude regarding the aggressions of Native Americans. They had acted because their religious beliefs had been violated: they felt their consecrated ground had been defiled by the Europeans. Yet he took their actions as signs of the Europeans' God's displeasure over heterodoxy on Hutchinson's part.

During the years following Hutchinson's trials the Bay Colony was to feel the effects of the Antinomian controversy in many ways: politically, legally, socially, in their relations with England, and religiously. It should perhaps not be surprising that this is the case: the trials raised penetrating considerations of issues deeply embedded in the political and religious thinking of the group of emigrants who had begun the colony. Separation of church and state, freedom of speech, the right to a fair (civil) trial, the proper behavior of women, appropriate political representation, the position of the individual within the state, were all areas touched upon in one way or another in the challenge brought by Anne Hutchinson. The colony had to regroup itself after the trials: the threat of schism was also a peril to the fabric of the society, and as one might expect, the wounds were not easily healed. God showed his unhappiness with the state of things by sending a heavy snowstorm in the winter after Hutchinson was banished, and the people of the colony showed their disregard for the authorities and the proper order by donning expensive and fashionable clothing.[17] It was necessary to call a fast because of widespread cases of smallpox, as well as "decay in the power of religion."[18] The colony was in turbulence, and "the devil would never cease to disturb our peace, and to raise up instruments one after another," John Winthrop reported.[19]

Crime increased in the area, especially among women. Women were whipped or excommunicated for defiance of the authorities, and for publicly defending Anne Hutchinson; wives perceived to be improperly unsubmissive were excommunicated, for idleness, and for "prophesying" in mixed company.[20] Many of the crimes committed during the six years after the trials were very serious. Murders and attempted murders, even of husbands and children, were added to the more common swearing, promiscuity, and adultery charges.[21] One woman murdered her three-year-old child because she had received revelations from God that she should do so.[22] At least one study of the increase in crime attributes it directly to the women's response to Hutchinson's trials, and fear on the part of the men that women were no longer tractable.[23] The percentage of women who were charged in court with such crimes increased significantly after the trials, from less than 2% of such crimes in the period from 1630–1634 to 7.2% in 1635–39.[24]

An attempt to regularize the legal situation finally took shape in 1641, with the codification of laws for the colony, called the "Body of Liberties of the People of Massachusetts." The call for the codification of the laws had been issued in 1634, and the process had begun at that time, but the Antinomian controversy had raised more concerns on the part of the people. The attempt of Henry Vane to circumvent the election process in 1637 as he battled the older leaders of the colony had alerted the freemen to the possibility that a "majority living at the capital" could usurp their voting responsibilities and privileges if allowed to do so.[25] They had thus been made aware that they had to keep a jealous eye on all legal process. After Hutchinson's civil trial a large number of people had been forced to turn over their weapons and ammunition, which caused worries among the people that the authorities could disarm them and render them impotent against animal and human marauders. Indeed, the petition against the guilty finding against John Wheelwright underscores how worried the people became about the use of banishment or the death penalty. Its use against Hutchinson also emphasized the need of the protection of written laws.

As pressure grew for written laws, Winthrop was forced to agree to such protection for the people. However, the occasion that finally prompted the General Court to complete the revision of the laws was the obstinacy of Governor Bellingham's dealing with the rest of the General Court rather than more threats to the liberties of the people; clearly such codification was sorely needed by all sections of the community.[26] The set of laws that was ultimately accepted by the colony had been drafted by Nathaniel Ward, who had been minister at Ipswich, and who had had legal training in common law. Among other protections for the people, in the "Body of Liberties" it was declared that, "No man's life shall be taken away, no man's honour or good name shall be stained, no man's person shall be arrested, restrained, banished, dismembered, nor any ways punished...unless it be by virtue or equity of some express law of the Country warranting the same, established by a general Court and sufficiently published..."[27]

For a number of years after the trials religious persecution became much more common, even to the extent that the death penalty was meted out. Women who did not show proper submission were especially targeted for punishment by the colony's churches, and John Cotton wrote of the need for women to remember their station. He reminded them that they were especially liable to commit doctrinal lapses.[28] Such oppression of women continued for some time in spite of repeated notices from various men in England that such conduct was unpalatable. Anabaptists and Quakers were the usual recipients of this treatment, but several women and some men who had been followers of Hutchinson also found the colony to be harsh in its punishments for misbehavior. One such was Captain Underhill, who claimed that while smoking some tobacco he had been given assurance that he was of the elect, with the result that he would never have to worry about his spiritual condition again. He took this to mean that he had no need to concern himself about the law. In 1638 he was accused of having visited a beautiful, sociable married woman every day behind closed doors, and later he admitted that he had been committing adultery with her. His behavior has been held up as an example of the thinking and as a result of the preaching of Anne Hutchinson.[29]

During these years the colony continued to worry about the perception of it held by the powers in England, as there were rumblings of unhappiness there about the behavior of the leaders of the colony, and more threats to recall the colony's charter, based upon England's perception of the colony as a place that persecuted people for conscience. Cotton and Winthrop continued to spend time writing letters and even books defending the conduct of the colony on these matters, and Roger Williams and others fanned the flames of such concerns among the English leaders. As a matter of fact, Williams had his correspondence with Cotton published in England. Several men questioned the fairness of the laws of the colony and the punishments meted out to dissidents, which reinforced the notion that the colony's charter should be revoked.

More and more, however, the colony thought of itself as separate and distinct from England, able to govern itself as it pleased. The growing prosperity of the colony contributed to a feeling of independence on the part of the colonists, and over time they became more willing to make decisions based only on what they considered best for themselves. The self-image of the colony as a legal entity separate from England grew as the years passed, and the colonists' experiences in the new land made them feel more and more at home there. Thus, the colony also increasingly saw itself as having a right to the land in the new country. This attitude on their part then obviated the necessity of securing it in any way from the Native Americans, and they insisted upon more and more control over the tribes near them. One such practice was that of insisting upon trying Native Americans suspected of criminal activities, rather than asking that the Native Americans do so in tribal courts. Some, such as William Pynchon, decried the Europeans' right to do so, but the practice continued.[30] So, although the Bay Colony continued to treat with the Native Americans until King Phillip's War, their dominance in the area was growing, allowing them to ignore the rights and the very existence of the Native Americans to a larger and larger extent.[31]

Along with the continuing, harsh repression of dissent, there were other repercussions from the trials in the churches. Church leaders were carefully scrutinized, to attempt to build uniformity. Darret Rutman states that after Hutchinson's trials "the ministers set about firming up the foundations of their religious house."[32] The ministers of the colony also "entered an intensive period of institutional self-examination that would continue throughout the colonial era" in response to the Hutchinson affair.[33] They went on "continual" visits to their congregants, "endeavoring to heal the hurts these false deceivers had made."[34] Further, some of their English brethren had some uncomplimentary things to say about the way that the Massachusetts Bay Colony dealt with differences of opinion. Those in England who were watching the "city on a hill" voiced their concerns,

either in sympathy, or, more frequently, in criticism, of the godly community. John Cotton had been uneasy about this aspect of the situation in
1636, when he asked some of the colonists who were returning to England
to report to those back home that the differences were merely semantic,
reflecting disparities in beliefs as to whether God was moving toward
people, or people were moving toward God. Although Cotton's attempt to
smooth things over with those back in England who had power to replace
the governor if they so chose reads almost like a pun or joke, he recognized that the situation was serious for the colony. They were anxious to
show themselves in the best possible light and thus it became evident to the
leaders of the colony that they had to delineate and defend their congregational system to those watching them from England. Church polity was
spelled out by both Thomas Hooker and John Cotton, and they defended
their methods of gathering churches and systematized their procedures so
that those in England who wished to criticize the new colony would be
unable to do so. Shortly before Cotton's death in 1652, Mr. Daniel
Cawdrey published a work that contrasted Hooker's *Survey of the Summe
of Church Discipline* with Cotton's works, *The Way of the Churches of
Christ in New England*, and *The Keys*. Cawdrey noted places in which
Cotton had changed his mind to agree with Hooker in his discussion about
excommunication policies of churches, and Cotton began writing a work
that would explain why he had changed his mind on the subject, but died
before he could finish the project. He stated in the work that he felt it was
perfectly appropriate for him to do an about-face, and could not understand why it should cause comment.[35]

It was perhaps one of the predictable results of the Hutchinson trials
that John Cotton's theology changed. He had been considered the fount of
her ideas—which no doubt he was—and the trials brought home to him the
need to conform to the kind of preparationism propounded by Hooker and
Shepard. After the trials Cotton therefore no longer insisted on the purity
of the covenant of grace as he had expounded it for Anne Hutchinson.
Although he defended his and the colony's treatment of Hutchinson in, *The
Way of the Congregational Churches Cleared*, and asserted that he had not
changed his thinking under pressure, but had (rather fortuitously, it would
seem) recognized the superiority of the theological position of the majority
of the clergy in Boston, it certainly appears that he felt forced to change his
theology to conform more closely to that of Hooker and Shepard. Cotton
cheerfully acknowledged that he had done a complete reversal in his thinking. He asserted that his differences with ministers Thomas Hooker and
Thomas Shepard had never really been theologically unacceptable, and that
the deviations were not substantial, in any case. He claimed that "they

sometime declare such works of Grace to be preparations to conversion, which others do take to be fruits of conversion."[36] Perry Miller says of this attempt, "his effort to drape the conflict in the robes of harmony was assiduously seconded by the other spokesmen for New England, their deliberate obscurantism indicating not only how wide but how dangerous the breach had been."[37]

After the Hutchinson trials, Thomas Hooker went back to Connecticut certain that his church and his colony should remain entirely separate from the Bay Colony. He discussed the possibility of a "confederation" among the colonies, but he may well have had some influence in the decision by the Connecticut magistracy to reject the suggested agreement.[38] After this time as well Hooker intensified his insistence that good Christian citizens obey the secular as well as church leadership. His biographer, Frank Shuffleton, maintains that "after 1638 [Hooker] preached submission to the spiritual and civil powers."[39] Having seen that the possibility of a schism within a church would cause a split in a colony, Hooker was not at all averse to making explicit the need for good behavior. Citizens of the colonies would hear from him the responsibility they held to act as godly men and women, whether in church or in the secular arena.

Hooker's preparationsts' doctrinal stance became accepted in Massachusetts Bay as well as in Connecticut as "orthodox" after Hutchinson's trials. In this way Hooker, as a main proponent of the long period of preparation, strengthened his doctrinal posture. Although he and Shepard both went back to their respective towns outside of Massachusetts Bay, their doctrinal position made itself felt as the orthodox one in Massachusetts Bay as well. While he and Shepard and the rest of the clergy of the Massachusetts Bay Company taught before that time that a seeker after salvation could prepare his or her heart for the reception of God's grace, the statement that the act of seeking itself is proof of salvation was far in excess of what would have been claimed by any other minister. It came as a response to the Hutchinson trials, and represents an extreme position that Hooker felt he could—and should—then take. Shuffleton believes that "the crisis provoked by Anne Hutchinson and her followers fundamentally reshaped the religious life of New England, and it affected the content of nearly all of Hooker's preaching after 1637."[40] Hooker's sermons took on a more strident tone when he defended some of the teachings that had been the cause of the controversy. Some of his sermons, believed to have been given in Boston shortly after the affair, have passages in which he came out very strongly against the Hutchinsonians, and in support of the idea that the Christian must work for salvation. He admitted his doctrinal irritation with, "those Familists and Anabaptists, [who] think it is unprofitable for a believer to trouble himself for his sins, and to go up and down with his heart full of grief."41   Hooker used the first sermon of the series to stress the work that is necessary for a Christian. Quoting St. Paul in several places where work is mentioned as being necessary for the Christian, he says that we must "labor every day more and more to get from under that iniquity under which we are." He made clear to his hearers that it was necessary to strive for salvation rather than merely praying for it. As Bush notes, "The Christian life as described throughout Hooker's canon is full of striving, tensions, and paradoxes, all of which would be largely eliminated if Cotton's way prevailed."42   Other topics covered by Hooker in that series of sermons included: faith as an active venture for the Christian; God's power to do good works; Christ as the means through which the Christian has power to do God's will; faith causing fruitfulness in the converted person's heart; faith coming into the heart before justification; choosing one's teacher; and lastly, obedience to authority.43

He went even further in another untitled sermon that was published in 1638 and has internal evidence of having been preached shortly after the Antinomian crisis. That sermon states baldly, "he that doth worship God according unto the way which he hath appointed, that man shall be saved." This unequivocal statement is extraordinary in its claim that the person has control over his or her salvation.44 In one of his last sermons, *The Application of Redemption*, Hooker went so far as to discuss two graces that are received from God in the process of redemption. He discussed the reasons why humans are unable to come to Christ on their own, without God's help, but then makes the argument that when a person desires to come to Christ that very desire is proof that God has given the individual some grace. However, he believes that this grace having been received is not enough to do the whole job. "When these persuasions are offered, there is still left an indifferency; there remains a freedom in the Will, to Refuse or Receive as she [presumably the will] sees fit."45 This idea demonstrates how far Hooker had moved from Calvinistic doctrine. Hooker recognized that the acceptance of this grace had not propelled the person far enough along yet, but that it was merely "the aim of this work to make way and room for the Habit of Grace...," so he then explained that a second infusion of grace was needed to complete the job. "And yet Grace cannot do it [when a person is in a natural state]; for then there should be Grace before the FIRST Grace. Grace is attended in a double Respect..."46 He had seen the obstacle in positing an ability in persons that would allow them to begin their own process of regeneration, and so now stated that this process was begun to be an infusion of grace, but that was not completed until a second infusion "so that it [the soul] may be united unto his Christ."47 His theology had become by this date late in his life so wholly opposed to Cotton's as to posit two infusions of grace in order to get the job done: one to allow the seeker after salvation to prepare his or her heart, and a second to finish the job, and ingraft Christ into the heart. The first of these infusions of grace, which came to be called, "prevening" grace, or "preventing" grace, later in the century was to become a standard orthodox part of Puritan thinking on the subject of preparation of the heart, and Cotton's strict Calvinist thinking was to disappear.

Besides being the one of the most outspoken of the ministers at Anne Hutchinson's ecclesiastical trial, and who seemed most eager to excommunicate Anne Hutchinson, Thomas Shepard was the presiding officer in the synod that questioned John Cotton. He was the one who never quite believed that Cotton had changed his thinking.[48] Shepard has been referred to as the "chief spokesman for Winthrop and the elders," and Shepard was adamant in his belief that the theological position held by himself and Hooker, as well as most of the rest of the clergy, was correct. Like Hooker, he was certain that sermons must be directed at those who were struggling for faith. He believed in the ability to strive for faith, and would not allow Cotton or Wheelwright, nor indeed Hutchinson, deny the seeker some solace. Shepard therefore preached in an evangelical way even when ostensibly directing his sermons to the converted. In his sermon titled, "The Saint's Jewel" published in 1655, and clearly directed at those who were believers, he was unable to resist addressing the one who is still searching in this way, "For thy comfort, I will come one step lower to thee: hast thou any will to it? Mark this place; if any place in the whole Scripture be for thee, here it is in the last words of this verse. 'And whosoever will, let him take of the water of life freely.' (Rev. xxii. 17)." He continues after more explanation sounding for all the world like a twentieth, rather than a seventeenth-century divine, "What say you: Are you willing upon these terms?"[49] Shepard had no doubt at all that God would—indeed had to—confer salvation upon those who sought after Him. In his work, "The Church-Membership of Children, and their right to Baptism" published in 1663, he states unequivocally, "the covenant runs not only this, viz., If thou believest, thou shalt be saved, but also, I will enable [thee] to believe."[50] As McGiffert, editor of Shepard's autobiography, put it: "God's *promise* of salvation contained a binding guarantee that He would *perform* salvation."[51] It was this doctrine, promulgated most clearly by Hooker and Shepard, that held sway in the colony after Hutchinson's trials had annihilated any hope of Cotton's, and Hutchinson's, doctrines from taking hold among the people of the Boston church. It was a move away from the awful logic of Calvin's—as well as Hutchinson's and Cotton's—understanding of predestination.

In all, the Antinomian controversy had forced the colony to define itself. The community was separating itself from the mother country: drawing and endorsing its own "Body of Liberties" based upon a new conception of English common law and biblical strictures filtered through the new circumstances of the new country; making its own way into a conception of doctrine that would not be duplicated in any other country; settling its problems with the Native Americans on its own authority. Having gone through the annealing fire of the Antinomian controversy, the colony had entered into a new phase of the struggle to become the ideal community. It could no longer measure itself only by the yardstick of John Winthrop's "Model of Christian Charity." It had become necessary to search out its own essence, principles, and nature. The relationship of the clergy and the magistracy to the people changed, as well, as part of the organism of the society. Control of the populace by means of laws rather than by exhortations to Christian love were in order, within and without the church. Within the churches it was now necessary to preach good behavior, tying orthodox behavior to civil peace.

After Hutchinson's trials it was no longer possible for Winthrop and the rest of the colony to become a beacon for the people back home in England. The new land, for all the ordeals it would give to them, was now merely their earthly home and they would have to live with its—and their own—shortcomings.

One interesting development provides a fitting end to this study of the story of Anne Hutchinson. In 1989 the United Church of Christ, which counts itself as successor to those Puritan congregational churches of Boston and the surrounding area, held a solemn ceremony. The president of the United Church of Christ, Avery Post, burned the writ of excommunication for one Anne Hutchinson, reinstating her membership, and proclaiming that she was never a heretic at all. The name of the pastor who took her back into the church was John Wilson, pastor of the congregation at Newport, Rhode Island.[52]

Notes

1. Battis, pp. 90-91, 177-180.

2. Cyclone Covey, *The Gentle Radical: A Biography of Roger Williams* (New York: Macmillan, London: Collier-Macmillan, 1966), pp. 225-6.

3. Hall, *Antinomian*, pp. 279-281.

4. Battis, p. 270; Mary Caroline Crawford, *St. Botolph's Town: An Account of Old Boston in Colonial Days* (Boston : L. C. Page & Co., 1908), p. 128.

5. Williams, *Divine*, p. 185.

6. Battis looked into the question of what sort of miscarriage Hutchinson had delivered. For his discussion of the situation, see Appendix VII, pp. 346-348.

7. Williams, *Divine*, p. 190.

8. Thomas Weld of Roxbury, quoted in Williams, *Divine*, p. 192.

9. Winthrop, *Journal*, vol. 1, p. 330, n.

10. Ibid.

11. Augur, pp. 272–4.

12. Winthrop, *Journal*, vol. 2. p. 40.

13. Ibid., p. 39.

14. *Anne Hutchinson and Other Papers* (White Plains, NY: Westchester County Historical Society), pp. 5, 10–11.

15.Edward Johnson, *Johnson's Wonder–Working Providence: 1628–1651*, ed. J. Franklin Jameson (New York: Charles Scribner's Sons, 1910), p. 186, Winthrop, *Journal*, vol. 1, pp. 138, 276, 77.

16. Battis, pp. 247-248.

17. Winthrop, Journal, vol. 1, pp. 291, 279.

18. Ibid., pp. 283, 4.

19. Ibid., p. 285.

20. Lyle Koehler covers the aftermath of the Hutchinson trials in chapter eight of *A Search for Power: The "Weaker Sex" in Seventeenth-Century new England* (Urbana: University of Illinois Press, 1980), pp. 218–237.

21. Ibid., p. 229.

22. Winthrop, *Journal*, vol. 1, p. 282.

23. Ibid.

24. Koehler, pp. 228, 229.

25. Hutchinson, *Papers*, p. 71.

26. Winthrop, *Journal*, vol. 2, pp. 45–49.

27. Haskins, *Law and Authority*, p. 129.

28. Koehler, p. 230.

29. Winthrop, *Journal*, vol. 1, pp. 275–7, 328.

30. Yasuhide Kawashima, *Puritan Justice and the Indian: White Man's Law in Massachusetts* (Middletown, CT: Wesleyan University Press, 1986), pp. 228–231.

31. Ibid., pp. 229, 30.

32. Rutman, p. 107.

33. Stout, p. 26.

34. Johnson, pp. 182,3.

35. Ziff, *Cotton*, pp. 248-250; Cotton, *The Way Cleared,* p. 307.

36. Cotton, quoted in Miller, 'Preparation', p. 274.

37. Miller, 'Preparation', p. 274.

38. Shuffleton, *Hooker*, p. 274.

39. Ibid., p. 253.

40. Sargent Bush, Jr., *The Writings of Thomas Hooker: Spiritual Adventure in Two Worlds* (Madison: University of Wisconsin Press, 1980), p. 238.

41. Frank Shuffleton, Thomas *Hooker: 1586-1647* (Princeton: Princeton University Press, 1977), pp. 77- 83.

42. Bush, *Writings*, p. 83.

43. Ibid., pp. 83-93.

44. Everett Emerson, ed."A Thomas Hooker Sermon of 1638," in *Resources For American Literary Study*, vol. 2, 1972, p. 80.

45. Hooker, *Application*, p. 351.

46. Ibid., p. 355, emphasis in the original.

47. Ibid., p. 350.

48. Morison, *Builders*, pp. 122, 124.

49. Thomas Shepard, *The Works of Thomas Shepard, First Pastor of the First Church, Cambridge, Massachusetts, with a Memoir of His Life and Character* (New York: Ams Press, 1967), p. 293.

50. Shepard, *God's Plot*, pp. 13, 14.

51. Ibid., p. 13.

52. *The Christian Century*, vol. 105, Mar 22-29, 1989, pp. 304-5.

BIBLIOGRAPHY

Adams, Brooks. *The Emancipation of Massachusetts: The Dream and The Reality.* Boston: Houghton Mifflin Co., 1919.

Adamson, J. H. and Folland, H. F. *Sir Harry Vane: His Life and Times (1623-1662).* Boston: Gambit, 1973.

Ahearn, Marie L. *The Rhetoric of War: Training Day, the Militia, and the Military Sermon.* New York: Greenwood Press, 1989.

Allen, David Grayson. "Both Englands." In *Seventeenth-Century New England*: A Conference Held by The Colonial Society of Massachusetts, June 18 and 19, 1982. Boston: The Colonial Society of Massachusetts; Distributed by The University Press of Virginia, 1984.

Ames, William. *The Marrow of Theology.* trans. and ed. John D. Eusden. Durham, NC: Labyrinth Press, 1968.

Anderson, Virginia De John. "Migrants and Motives: Religion and the Settlement of New England, 1630-1640." *New England Quarterly* 58 (1985): 339–383.

"Anne Hutchinson's Refuge in the Wilderness." *Anne Hutchinson and Other Papers.* White Plains, NY: Westchester County Historical Society, 1929.

Augur, Helen. *An American Jezebel: The Life of Anne Marbury Hutchinson.* New York: Brentano's, 1930.

Bailyn, Bernard. *The New England Merchants in the Seventeenth Century.* New York: Harper Torchbooks, Harper and Row, 1955.

———. *The Peopling of British North America: An Introduction.* New York: Alfred A. Knopf, 1986.

Barry, John Stetson. *The History of Massachusetts: The Colonial Period.* Boston: Phillips, Sampson, and Company, 1857.

Battis, Emery. *Saints and Sectaries: Anne Hutchinson and the Antinomian Controversy in the Massachusetts Bay Colony.* Chapel Hill: University of North Carolina Press, 1962.

Beardsley, Charles Wareing. *Curiosities of Puritan Nomenclature.* London: Chatto & Windus, 1897.

Bercovitch, Sacvan. *The American Jeremiad.* Madison: University of Wisconsin Press, 1978.

———. *The Puritan Origins of the American Self.* New Haven: Yale University Press, 1975.

———— ed. *Typology and Early American Literature*. Amherst MA: University of Massachusetts Press, 1972.

————. "Typology in Puritan New England: The Williams-Cotton Controversy Reassessed" *American Quarterly* 29 (1967): 166–191.

Bible, Geneva Translation. Incomplete. 1577 edition.

Bickerman, Elias. *Four Strange Books of the Bible: Jonah/ Daniel/ Koheleth/ Esther*. New York: Schocken Books, 1973.

Billias, George Athan, ed. *Law and Authority in Colonial America: Selected Essays*. Barre, MA: Barre Publishers, 1965.

Black, Robert C., III. *The Younger John Winthrop*. New York: Columbia University Press, 1966.

Bolton, Charles Knowles. *The Real Founders of New England: Stories of Their Life Along the Coast, 1602-1628*. Boston: F.W. Faxon Co., 1929.

Botein, Stephen. *Early American Law and Society*. New York: Alfred A Knopf, 1983.

Bowdin, Henry Warner. *American Indians and Christian Missions: Studies in Cultural Conflict*. Chicago: University of Chicago Press, 1981.

Bozeman, Theodore Dwight. *To Live Ancient Lives: The Primistivist Dimension in Puritanism*. Chapel Hill: University of North Carolina Press, 1988.

Brachlow, Stephen. *The Communion of Saints: Radical Puritan and Separatist Ecclesiology, 1570–1625*. Oxford: Oxford University Press, 1988.

Bradford, William. *The History of Plymouth Colony*. ed. George F. Willison. Roslyn, NY: Walter J. Black, 1948.

Breen, T.H. "Creative Adaptations: Peoples and Cultures". In *Colonial British America: Essays in the New History of the Early Modern Era*. Edited by J. P. Greene, and J. R. Pole, pp. 43–85. Baltimore: Johns Hopkins University Press, 1984.

————. *Puritans and Adventurers: Change and Persistance in Early America*. New York: Oxford University Press, 1980.

Bremer, Francis J. *The Puritan Experiment: New England Society from Bradford to Edwards*. New York: St. Martin's Press, 1976.

Brown, B. Katherine. "Freemanship in Puritan Massachusetts" *The American Historical Review* 59 (1954): 865–883.

Bruce, F. F. *The English Bible: A History of Translations From the Earliest Versions to the New English Bible*. New York: Oxford University Press, 1970.

Bush, Sargent, Jr. "Four New Works by Thomas Hooker: Identity and Significance" *Resources for American Literary Study* 4 (1974): 3–26.

————. "The Growth of Thomas Hooker's 'The Poor Doubting Christian'" *Early American Literature* 8 (1973): 3-20.

————. "John Wheelwright's Forgotton *Apology*: The Last Word in the Antinomian Controversy". *New England Quarterly* 48 (Mar. 1991): 22–45.

————. "'Revising what we have done amisse': John Cotton and John Wheelwright, 1640" *William and Mary Quarterly* 45 (Oct. 1988): 733–750.

————. *The Writings of Thomas Hooker: Spiritual Adventure in Two Worlds*. Madison: University of Wisconsin Press, 1980.

Bushman, Richard L. *King and People in Provincial Massachusetts*. Chapel Hill, NC: University of North Carolina Press, 1985.

Byington, Ezra Hoyt. *The Puritan in England and New England*. Boston: Roberts Brothers, 1896.

Caldwell, Patricia. "The Antinomian Language Controversy" *Harvard Theological Review* 69 (1976): 345–367.

Calvin, John. *A Reflection Book: Introduction to the Writings of John Calvin, By John Calvin.* Edited by Hugh T. Kerr. New York: Association Press, 1960.

———. *The Epistles of Paul The Apostle to the Romans and to the Thessalonians.* Translated by Ross Mackenzie. Edited by. David W. Torrance, and Thomas F. Torrance. Grand Rapids, MI: Wm. B. Eerdmans Publishing Company, 1961.

Campbell, Douglas. *The Puritan in Holland, England, and America: An Introduction to American History.* vol 2. New York: Harper & Brothers Publishers, 1892.

Canup, John. *Out of the Wilderness: The Emergence of an American Identity in Colonial New England.* Middletown, CT: Wesleyan University Press, 1990.

Carroll, Peter N. *Puritanism and the Wilderness: The Intellectual Significance of the New Enlgand Frontier, 1629–1700.* New York: Columbia University Press, 1969.

Chafee, Zechariah Jr. "Colonial Courts and the Common Law" *Proceedings of the Massachusetts Historical Society,* 68 (1952): 132–159.

The Christian Century 105 (March 22-29, 1989): 304–5.

Cliffe, J.T. *Puritans in Conflict: The Puritan Gentry During and After the Civil Wars.* London and New York: Routlege and Kagan Paul, 1988.

Cohen, Charles Lloyd. *God's Caress: The Psychology of Puritan Religious Experience.* New York: Oxford University Press, 1986.

Cohen, Ronald. "Church and State in Seventeenth-Century Massachusetts: Another Look at the Antinomian Controversy." In *Puritan new England: Essays on Religion, Society, and Culture.* Edited by Vaughan, Alden T., and Francis J. Bremer. New York: St. Martin's Press, 1977.

Colonial Society of Massachusetts. *Seventeenth-Century New England.* Boston: The University Press of Virginia, 1984.

Cooper, James F., Jr. "Anne Hutchinson and the 'Lay Rebellion' Against the Clergy" *New England Quarterly* 61 (1988): 381–397.

Cotton, John. *God's Mercie Mixed with His Justice: Or His Peoples Deliverance in Times of Danger.* Facsimile reproduction with an introduction by Everett H. Emerson. Gainesville, FL: Scholars' Facsimiles and Reprints, 1958.

———. "God's Promise to His Plantation" *Old South Leaflets* 53. Boston: Old South Works, n.d.

———. *John Cotton on the Churches of New England.* Edited by Larzer Ziff. Cambridge, MA: Harvard University Press, 1968.

Covey, Cyclone. *The Gentle Radical: Roger Williams.* New York, London: Macmillan Company, Collier-Macmillan, 1966.

Crawford, Deborah. *Four Women in a Violent Time: Anne Hutchinson (1591–1643): Mary Dyer (1591?–1660); Lady Deborah Moody (1600–1659): Penelope Stout (1622–1732).* New York: Crown Publishers, 1970.

Crawford, Mary Caroline. *St. Botolph's Town: An Account of Old Boston in Colonial Days.* Boston: L.C. Page & Co., 1908.

Cremin, Lawrence A. *American Education: The Colonial Experience, 1607–1783.* New York: Harper and Row, Harper Torchbooks, 1970.

Crenshaw, James L. *Ecclesiastes: A Commentary.* Philadelphia: The Westminster Press, 1987.

Cressy, David. *Coming Over: Migration and Communication Between England and New England in the Seventeenth Century*. Cambridge: Cambridge University Press, 1987.

Cronon, William. *Changes in the Land: Indians, Colonists, and the Ecology of New England*. New York: Hill and Wang, 1983.

Davies, Horton. *Worship and Theology in England: From Andrewes to Baxter and Fox, 1603-1690*. Princeton: Princeton University Press, 1975.

Deanesly, Margaret. *The Lollard Bible and Other Medieval Biblical Versions*. Cambridge: Cambridge University Press, 1920.

Delbanco, Andrew. *The Puritan Ordeal*. Cambridge, MA: Harvard University Press, 1989.

Demos, John Putnam. *Entertaining Satan: Witchcraft and the Culture of Early New England*. New York: Oxford University Press, 1982.

———. *A Little Commonwealth: Family Life in Plynouth Colony*. New York: Oxford University Press, 1970.

Dexter, Franklin B. "A Report of the Trial of Mrs. Anne Hutchinson before the Church in Boston, March 1638" *Proceedings of the Massachusetts Historical Society* 4, series 2 (1887-1889).

Dow, George Francis. *Everyday Life in the Massachusetts Bay Colony*. 1935. Reprint. New York: Benjamin Blom, 1967.

Dunn, Richard S. "John Winthrop Writes His Journal" *William and Mary Quarterly* 41 (1984): 185–212.

Earle, Alice Morse. *Home Life in Colonial Days*. 1898. Reprint. Stockbridge, MA: The Berkshire Traveller Press, 1974.

———. *Margaret Winthrop*. New York: Charles Scribner's Sons, 1895.

———. *The Sabbath in Puritan New England*. 1891. Reprint Williamstown, MA: Corner House Publishing, 1969.

Easton, Emily. *Roger Williams: Prophet and Pioneer*. 1930. Reprint. Freeport, NY: Books for Libraries Press, 1969.

Elliot, Emory. *Power and the Pulpit in Puritan New England*. Princeton: Princeton University Press, 1975.

Emerson, Everett. *English Puritanism from John Hooper to John Milton*. Durham, NC: Duke University Press, 1968.

———. *John Cotton*. New York: Twayne Publishers, 1965.

———. "Thomas Hooker: The Puritan as Theologian" *Anglican Theological Review*. 49 (1967): 190-203.

———. "A Thomas Hooker Sermon of 1638" *Resources for American Literary Study* 2 (1972): 75-89.

———. *Puritanism in America: 1620–1750*. Boston: Twayne Publishers, 1977.

Ernst, James. *Roger Williams, New England Firebrand*. New York: The Macmillan Company, 1932.

Eusden, John Dykstra. *Puritans, Lawyers, and Politics in Early Seventeenth-Century England*. n.p.: Archon Books, 1968.

Felker, Christopher D. "Roger Williams' Uses of Legal Discourse: Testing Authority in Early New England." *New England Quarterly* 63 (1990): 624–647.

Flaherty, David H., ed. *Essays in the History of Early American Law*. Chapel Hill, NC: University of North Carolina Press, 1969.

———. *Privacy in Colonial New England*. Charlottesville VA: University Press of Virginia, 1972.

Foster, Frank Hugh. *A Genetic History of the New England Theology*. Chicago: University of Chicago Press, 1907.

Foster, Stephen. "English Puritanism and the Progress of New England Institutions, 1630–1660." In *Saints and Revolutionaries Essays on Early American History*. Edited by Hall, David D, Mc Murrin, John M. and Tate, Thad W. New York: W. W. Norton and Co., 1984.

———. "New England and the Challenge of Heresy, 1630–1660: The Puritan Crisis in Transatlantic Perspective" *William and Mary Quarterly* 38 (1981): 623–628.

Frederick, John T. "Literary Art in Thomas Hooker's 'The Poor Doubting Christian'" *American Literature* 40 (1969): 1–8.

Goodman, Paul, and Gatell, Frank Otto. *The American Colonial Experience: An Essay in National Origins*. New York: Holt, Rinehart and Winston, 1970.

Greene, Jack P. and J. R. Pole, eds. *Colonial British America: Essays in the New History of the Early Modern Era*. Baltimore: Johns Hopkins University Press, 1984.

Gura, Philip F. *Glimpses of Sion's Glory*. Middletown, CN: Wesleyan University Press, 1984.

Habegger, Alfred. "Preparing the Soul for Christ: The Contrasting Sermon Forms of John Cotton and THomas Hooker" *American Literature* (1969): 342–354.

Hall, David D., ed. *The Antinomian Controversy, 1636–1638: A Documentary History*, 2nd ed. Durham NC: Duke University Press, 1990.

———. Mc Murrin, John M. and Tate, Thad W. eds. *Saints and Revolutionaries: Essays on Early American History*. New York: W. W. Norton and Co., 1984.

———. "Toward a History of Popular Religion in Early New England" *William and Mary Quarterly* 41 (1984): 49–55.

———. *Worlds of Wonder, Days of Judgement: Popular Religious Belief in Early New England*. New York: Alfred A. Knopf, 1989.

Haller, William. *The Rise of Puritanism: Or, The Way to the New Jerusalem as Set Forth in Pulpit and Press From Thomas Cartwright to John Lilburne and John Milton, 1570–1643*. 1938. New York: Harper Torchbooks, Harper & Row, Publishers, 1957.

Haskins, George. *Law and Authority in Early Massachusetts: A Study in Tradition and Design*. Lanham, MD: University Press of America, 1968.

———. "Law and Colonial Society" *American Quarterly* 9 (1957): 354–364.

Hatch, Nathan O. and Noll, Mark A. eds. *The Bible in America: Essays in Cultural History*. New York: Oxford University Press, 1982.

Heath, Peter. *The English Parish Clergy on the Eve of the Revolution*. London: Routledge and Kagan Paul, 1969.

Heimert, Alan, and Delbanco, Andrew. *Puritans in America: A Narrative Anthology*. Cambridge, MA: Harvard University Press, 1985.

Herget, Winfried. "Preaching and Publication: Chronology and the Style of Thomas Hooker's Sermons" *Harvard Theological Review* 65 (1972): 231–239.

———. "Writing After the Ministers; The Significance of Sermon Notes." In *Studies in New England Puritanism*. Frankfurt Am Main: Verlag Peter Lang, 1983.

Hilkey, Charles J. *Legal Development in Colonial Massachusetts: 1630–1686*. New York: Columbia University Press, 1910.

Hill, Christopher. *Change and Continuity in Seventeenth-Century England*. Cambridge, MA: Harvard University Press, 1975.

Hirsh, Adam J. "The Collision of Military Cultures in 17th Century New England" *Journal of American History* 74 (1988): 1187–1212.

Hoffer, Peter Charles. *Early American History: Homage to New England: Selected Articles on Early New England History 1637–1693*. New York and London: Garland Publishing, 1988.

———. *Law and People in Colonial America*. Baltimore: Johns Hopkins University Press, 1992.

Holliday, Carl. *Woman's Life in Colonial Days*. New York: Frederick Unger Publishing Co., 1922, 1960.

Hooker, Thomas. *The Application of Redemption by the Effectual Work of the Word and Spirit of Christ, for the Bringing Home of Lost Sinners to God*. 1657. Reprint. New York: Arno Press, 1972.

———. *The Soules Implantation Treatise: Containing, the Broken Heart, on Esay 57.15; The Preparation of the Heart, on Luk. 1.17; The Soules ingraffing into Christ, on Mal.3.1; spirituall Love & Joy, on Gal. 5.22*. London, Printed by R. Young, 1637.

———. *The Vnbeleevers Preparing For Christ*. London: Thomas Cotes for A n d r e w Crooke, 1638.

———. ed. Williams, George H. *Thomas Hooker: Writings in England and H o l l a n d , 1626–1633*. Cambridge, MA: Harvard University Press, 1975.

Howard, Leon. "The Puritans in Old and New England" in *Essays of Puritans and Puritansim, by Leon Howard*, ed. James Barbour and Thomas Quirk. Albuquerque: University of New Mexico Press, 1986

Hubbard, William. *A General History of New England: From the Discovery to MDCL-XXX*. Cambridge, MA: Massachusetts Historical Society: Hilliard & Metcalf, 1815.

Hull, N. E. H. *Female Felons: Women and Serious Crime in Colonial Massachusetts*. Urbana and Chicago: University of Illinois Press.

Hutchinson, Thomas. *The History of the Colony and Province of Massachusetts-Bay*, vol. 1., 2. ed. Lawrence Shaw Mayo. Cambridge, MA: Harvard University Press, 1936.

———. "Hutchinson Papers" *Publications of the Prince Society*. Boston: Burt Franklin: Research and Source Works Series #131, pp. 70–281.

Innes, Stephen. "Fulfilling John Smith's Vision: Work and Labor in Early America." In *Work and Labor in Early America*. Innes, Stephen, ed. Chapel Hill: University of North Carolina Press, 1988.

——— ed. *Work and Labor in Early America*. Chapel Hill: University of North Carolina Press, for the Institute of Early American History and Culture, 1988.

Johnson, Edward. *Johnson's Wonder-Working Providence 1628-1651*. ed. Jameson, J. Franklin. New York: Charles Scribner's Sons, 1910.

Jones, James W. *The Shattered Synthesis: New England Puritanism before the Great Awakening*. New Haven and London: Yale University Press, 1973.

Jones, Phyllis. "Biblical Rhetoric and the Pulpit Literature of Early New England" *Early American Literature* 11 (1976/77): 245–258.

Kawashima, Yasuhide. *Puritan Justice and the Indian: White Man's Law in Massachusetts, 1630–1763*. (Middletown, CN: Wesleyan University Press, 1986.

Kibbey, Ann. *The Interpretation of Material Shapes in Puritanism: A Study of Rhetoric, Prejudice, and Violence*. New York: Cambridge University Press, 1986.

Knappen, M. M. *Tudor Puritanism: A Chapter in the History of Idealism*. Chicago: University of Chicago Press, 1939.

Knox, S. J. *Walter Travers: Paragon of Elizabethan Puritanism*. London: Methuen & Co, 1962.

Koehler, Lyle. "American Jezebels" *William and Mary Quarterly* 31 no.1 series 3 (1974): 55–78.

———. *A Search for Power: The Weaker Sex in Seventeenth Century New England*. Urbana: University of Illinois, 1980.

———. *A Study of Rhetoric, Prejudice, and Violence*. Cambridge, MA: Cambridge University Press, 1986.

Kupperman, Karen Ordahl. "Errand to the Indies: Puritan Colonization From Providence Island Through the Western Design" *William and Mary Quarterly* 45 (1988): 70–90.

Labaree, Benjamin W. *Colonial Massachusetts: A History*. Millwood, NY: KTO Press, 1979.

Lang, Amy Schrager. *Prophetic Woman: Anne Hutchinson and the Problem of Dissent in the Literature of New England*. Berkeley: University of California Press, 1987.

Lang, Andrew. *Oxford*. London: Seeley and Co., 1906.

Langdon, George D., Jr. *Pilgrim Colony: A History of New Plymouth, 1620–1691*. New Haven and London: Yale University Press, 1966.

Law in Colonial Massachusetts: 1630-1800. Boston: The Colonial Society of Massachusetts, Distributed by the University Press of Virginia, 1984.

Lemon, James T. "Spatial Order: Households in Local Comunities and Regions." In *Colonial British America: Essays in the New History of the Early Modern Era*. Edited by Jack P. Greene, and J. R. Pole, pp. 86–122. Baltimore: Johns Hopkins University Press, 1984.

Levy, Babette. *Preaching in the First Half Century of New England History*. Hartford: The American Society of Church History, 1945.

Little, David. *Religion, Order and Law: A Study in Pre-Revolutionary England*. New York: Harper and Row, 1969.

Lockridge, Kenneth A. *A New England Town. The First Hundred Years: Dedham, Massachusetts, 1636–1736*. New York : W.W. Norton and Co., 1970.

Lowance, Mason I. Jr. *The Language of Canaan: Metaphor and Symbol in New England from the Puritans to the Transcendentalists*. Cambridge, MA: Harvard University Press, 1980.

Maclear, James F. "Anne Hutchinson and the Mortalist Heresy" *New England Quarterly* 54 (1981): 74–103.

Masefield, John, ed. *Chronicles of the Pilgrim Fathers*. New York: E. P. Dutton & Co., 1910.

Massachusetts Historical Society. *Proceedings 1914-1915*, vol. 48. Boston: Published By The Society, 1915.

Mather, Cotton. *The Magnalia Christi Americana: Or the Ecclesiastical History of New England; From its 1st Planting, in the Year 1620 unto the Year of our Lord 1698, in Seven Books*. "First American edition from the London edition of 1702." Hartford: Silas Andrus, 1820.

———. *Selections from Cotton Mather*. Murdock, Kenneth B. New York: Hofner Press, 1926.

Maurer, Oscar Edward. *A Puritan Church and Its Relation to Community, State, and Nation: Addresses Delivered in Preparation for the Three Hundredth Anniversary of the Settlement of New Haven.* New Haven: Yale University Press, 1938.

Mc Cusker, John J., and Menard, Russell R. *The Economy of British America, 1607-1789.* Chapel Hill and London: University of North Carolina Press, for the Institute of Early American History and Culture, 1985.

Mc Loughlin, William G. *Rhode Island: A Bicentennial History.* New York: W.W. Norton & Co., Inc., 1970.

Mc Mahon, Sarah F. "A Comfortable Subsistence: The Changing Diet in Rural New England, 1620-1840." *William and Mary Quarterly* 42 (1985): 26–65

Miller, Perry. *Errand into the Wilderness.* Cambridge, MA: The Belknap Press of Harvard University Press, 1975.

―――. The New England Mind: The Seventeenth Century, (New York: The MacMillan Co., 1939)

―――. and Thomas H. Johnson. *The Puritans.* 2 vol. New York: American Book Co., 1938.

―――. "The Marrow of Puritan Divinity" in *Puritan New England: Essays on Religion, Society, and Culture.* Edited by Alden T. Vaughan, and Francis J. Bremer. New York: St. Martin's Press, 1977.

―――. *Orthodoxy in Massachusetts: 1630–1650.* Boston: Beacon Press, 1959.

―――. "'Preparation for Salvation' in Seventeenth-Century New England" *Journal of the History of Ideas* 4 (1943): 253-286.

―――, ed. *The American Puritans: Their Prose and Poetry.* Garden City, NY: Doubleday Anchor Books, Doubleday & Co. Inc., 1956.

―――. *Roger Williams: His Contribution to the American Tradition.* New York: Atheneum, 1970.

Morgan, Edmund S. "The Case Against Anne Hutchinson" *New England Quarterly* 10 (1937): 635–649.

―――. *The Puritan Dilemma: The Story of John Winthrop.* Boston: Little, Brown and Company, 1958.

―――. *The Puritan Family: Religion and Domestic Relations in Seventeenth-Century New England.* 1944. Revised ed. New York: Harper & Row, 1966.

―――. *Roger Williams: The Church and the State.* New York: Harcourt, Brace & World, Inc., 1967.

―――. *Visible Saints: The History of Puritan Idea.* New York: New York University Press, 1963.

―――. "Miller's Williams" *New England Quarterly* 38 (1965): 513–523.

Morgan, John D. *Godly Learning: Puritan Attitudes Towards Reason, Learning and Education, 1560–1640.* New York: Cambridge University Press, 1986.

Morison, Samuel Eliot. *Builders of the Bay Colony.* Boston and New York: Houghton Mifflin Co., 1930.

―――. *The Founding of Harvard College.* Cambridge, MA: Harvard University Press, 1935.

―――. *The Intellectual Life of Colonial New England.* 2nd ed.1956. Reprint. Ithaca, NY: Great Seal Books, A Division of Cornell University Press, 1960.

―――. *The Puritan Pronaos: Studies in the Intellectual Life of New England in the Seventeenth Century.* New York: New York University Press, 1936.

Morris, Richard B. *Fair Trial: Fourteen Who Stood Accused, from Anne Hutchinson to Alger Hiss*. New York: Harper Torchbooks, Harper and Row, Publishers, 1967.

———. *Studies in the History of American Law: With Special Reference to the Seventeenth and Eighteenth Centuries*. New York: Columbia University Press, 1930.

Mullinger, J. Bass. *A History of the University of Cambridge*. New York: Anson D. F. Randolph and Co., nd.

Murrin, John M. "Magistrates, Sinners and a Precarious Liberty: Trial by Jury in Seventeenth-Century New England." In *Saints and Revolutionaries: Essays on Early American History*. Edited by David D. Hall, John M. Mc Murrin, and Thad W. Tate. pp. 152–206. New York: W. W. Norton and Co., 1984.

Nash, Gary B. "Social Development." In *Colonial British America:: Essays in the New History of the Early Modern Era*. Edited by Jack P. Greene, and J. R. Pole, pp. 233–261. Baltimore: Johns Hopkins University Press, 1984.

The Newe Testament of Ovr Lord Iesus Christ: Conferred diligently with the Greke, and Best Approued Translations. Geneva: Conrad Badius, Printer; 1577. A facsimile reprint, London: Samuel Bagster and Sons, n.d.

The New Testament Octapla: Eight English Versions of the New Testament, in the Tyndale/King James Tradition. Edited by Luther Weigle. New York: Thomas Nelson & Sons, n.d.

The New Testament of Our Lord Jesus Christ: Conferred Diligently with the Greeke and best approved translations in divers languages. [error: this is an edition of the entire Bible.] London: Deputies of Christopher Barker, 1589.

Norton, John. *Able Being Dead Yet Speaketh: A Biography of John Cotton*. 1658. facsimile. Dellmar, NY: Scholar's Facsimiles and Reprints, 1978.

Notestein,Wallace. *The English People on the Eve of Colonization: 1603-1630*. New York: Harper and Row, 1954.

Novvvm Testamentvm Graece. Oxonii: E Typographeo Clarendoniano, 1962.

Orten, Jon Dagfinn. "Elizabethan Puritanism and the Plain Style." Ph.D. dissertation, University of Minnesota, 1989.

Parker, David. "Petrus Ramus and the Puritans: The 'Logic' of Preparationist Conversion Doctrine" *Early American Literature* 8 (1973): 140–162.

Parker, Geoffrey, and Smith, Leslie M. eds. *The General Crisis of the Seventeenth Century*. London: Routledge & Kegan Paul, 1978.

Pearce, Roy Harvey, ed. *Colonial American Writing*. New York: Holt, Rinehart and Winston, 1964.

Pettit, Norman. *The Heart Prepared: Grace and Conversion in Puritan Spiritual Life*. New Haven and London: Yale University Press, 1966.

———. "Hooker's Doctrine of Assurance: A Critical Phase in New England Spiritual Thought" *New England Quarterly* 47 (1974): 518-534.

Polishook, Irwin H. Roger Williams, John Cotton and Relgious Freedom: A Controversy in New and Old England. Englewood Cliffs, NJ: Prentice-Hall, Inc., 1967.

Porterfield, Amanda. *Female Piety in Puritan New England: The Emergence of Religious Humanism*. New York: Oxford University Press, 1992.

Potter, Jim. "Demographic Development and Family Structure." In *Colonial British America: Essays in the New History of the Early Modern Era*. Edited by Jack P. Greene, and J. R. Pole, pp. 123–156. Baltimore: Johns Hopkins University Press, 1984.

Powell, Sumner Chilton. *Puritan Village: The Formation of a New England Town.* Middletown, CT: Wesleyan University Press, 1963.

Power, Susan M. *Before the Convention: Religion and the Founders.* New York: University Press of America, 1984.

Price, Ira Maurice. *The Ancestry of Our English Bible: An Account of Manuscripts, Texts, and Versions of the Bible.* 1906. 2nd revised edition by Irwin, William, and Wikgren, Allen P. New York: Harper and Brothers, Publishers, 1949.

Price, Jacob M. "The Transatlantic Economy." In *Colonial British America:: Essays in the New History of the Early Modern Era.* Edited by Jack P. Greene and J. R. Pole, pp. 18–42. Baltimore: Johns Hopkins University Press, 1984.

Pynchon, William. *Colonial Justice in Western Massachusetts (1639–1702): The Pynchon Court Record.* Edited by Joseph H. Smith. Cambridge, MA: Harvard University Press for The William Nelson Cromwell Foundation, 1961.

Rosenmeier, Jesper. "New England's Perfection: The Image of Adam and the Image of Christ in the Antinomian Crisis, 1634 to 1638" *William and Mary Quarterly* 27 (1970): 435–459.

———. "The Teacher and The Witness: John Cotton and Roger Williams" *William and Mary Quarterly* 25 (1968) 3rd series: 408–431.

Ross, Richard J. "The Legal Past of Early New England: Notes for the Study of Law, Legal Culture, and Intellectual History" *William and Mary Quarterly* 50 (1993) 3rd series: 28–41.

Rowe, Violet A. *Sir Henry Vane the Younger: A Study in Political and Administrative History.* Bristol, England: The Athlone Press, 1970.

Rugg, Winifred King. *Unafraid: A Life of Anne Hutchinson.* Cambridge, MA: Riverside Press, 1930.

Rutman, Darrett B. *American Puritanism: Faith and Practice.* Philadelphia: J. B. Lippincott, 1970.

———. *Winthrop's Boston: Portrait of a Puritan Town, 1630–1649.* Chapell Hill: University of North Carolina Press, 1965.

Seaver, Paul S. *The Puritan Lectureships: The Politics of Religious Dissent 1560–1662.* Stanford: Stanford University Press, 1970.

Schaper, Eva, ed. *Pleasure, Preference and Value: Studies in Philosophical Aesthetics.* New York: Cambridge University Press, 1987.

Schneider, Herbert Wallace. *The Puritan Mind.* 1930. Reprint. Ann Arbor: Ann Arbor Paperbacks, The University of Michigan Press, 1958.

Schweninger, Lee. *John Winthrop.* Boston: Twayne Publishers, 1990.

Schucking, Leven L. *The Puritan Family: A Social Study from the Literary Sources.* New York: Schocken Books, 1970.

Scobey, David M. "Revising the Errand: New England's Ways and the Puritan Sense of the Past." *William and Mary Quarterly* 41 (1984): 3-31.

Scott, R. B. Y., trans., ed. The Anchor Bible: Proverbs, Ecclesiastes. Garden City, NY: Doubleday & Company, Inc., 1965.

Seaver, Paul S. *The Puritan Lectureships: The Politics of Religious Dissent, 1560–1662.* Stanford, CA: Stanford University Press, 1970.

Segal, Charles M., and Stineback, David. *Puritans, Indians, and Manifest Destiny.* New York: G. P. Putnam's Sons, 1977.

The Septuagint Version of the Old Testament: With An English Translation, and With Various Readings and Critical Notes. Grand Rapids, MI: Zondervan, 1970.

Shepard, Thomas. *God's Plot, The Paradoxes of Puritan Piety: Being the Autobiography & Journal of Thomas Shepard.* ed. Michael Mc Giffert. Boston: University of Massachusetts Press, 1972.

———. *The Parable of the Ten Virgins Opened and Applied; Being the Substance of Divers Sermons on Matt. 25:1-13.* Reprint of Boston: Doctrinal Tract and Book Society; 1852. New York: Ams Press, 1967.

———. *The Works of Thomas Shepard, First Pastor of the First Church, Cambridge, Massachusetts, with A Memoir of His Life and Character,* vols. 1-3. New York: Ams Press, 1967.

Sheridan, Richard B. "The Domestic Economy." In *Colonial British America: Essays in the New History of the Early Modern Era.* Edited by Jack P. Greene and J.R. Pole, pp. 43-85. Baltimore: Johns Hopkins University Press, 1984.

Shipton, Clifford K. "The Laws of Authority in Colonial Massachusetts." In *Law and Authority in Colonial America: Selected Essays.* Edited by George Athan Billias, pp. 136-148. Barre, MA: Barre Publishers, 1965.

Shuffleton, Frank. *Thomas Hooker: 1584-1647.* Princeton: Princeton University Press, 1977.

Simms, Marion, ed. *The Bible in America: Versions that Have Played Their Part in the Making of the Republic.* New York: Wilson-Crickson, 1936.

Simpson, Alan. *Puritanism in Old and New England.* Chicago: The University of Chicago Press, 1955.

Smith, Joseph H., and Barnes, Thomas G. *The English Legal System: Carryover to the Colonies.* Los Angeles: University of California, 1975.

Solberg, Winton U. *Redeem the Time: The Puritan Sabbath in Early America.* Cambridge MA: Harvard University Press, 1977.

Stavely, Keith W.F. *Puritan Legacies: Paradise Lost and the New England Tradition, 1630-1690.* Ithaca, NY: Cornell University Press, 1987.

Stockham, Peter, ed. *Little Book of Early American Crafts and Trades.* New York: Dover Publications, 1976.

Stoever, K. B. *'A Faire and Easie Way to Heaven': Covenant Theology and Antinomianism in Early Massachusetts.* Middletown, CN: Wesleyan University Press, 1978.

Stone, Lawrence, ed. *The University in Society: Oxford and Cambridge from the 14th to the Early 19th Century.* vol 1. Princeton: Princeton University Press, 1974.

Stout, Harry S. *The New England Soul: Preaching and Religious Culture in Colonial New England.* New York : Oxford University Press, 1986.

———. "Word and Order in Colonial New England." In *The Bible in America: Essays in Cultural History.* Edited by Nathan O. Hatch and Mark A. Noll. New York, Oxford: Oxford University Press, 1982.

Sweet, William Warren. *The Story of Religion in America.* Grand Rapids: Baker Book House, 1975.

Thickstun, Margaret Olofson. *Fictions of the Feminine: Puritan Doctrine and the Representation of Women.* Ithaca, NY: Cornell University Press, 1988.

Toon, Peter, ed. *Puritans, the Millennium and The Future of Israel: Puritan Eschatology 1600–1660.* London: James Clarke & Co., 1970.

Treworthan, Glenn T. "Types of Rural Settlement in Colonial America" *Geographical Review* 36 (1946): 568-596.

Tuve, Rosemond. "Imagery and Logic: Ramus and Metaphysical Poetics" *Journal of the History of Ideas* 3 (1942): 365–400.

Ulrich, Laurel Thatcher. *Good Wives: Image and Reality in the Lives of Women in Northern New England, 1650-1750*. New York: Oxford University Press, 1983.

Vaughan, Alden T., and Francis J. Bremer, eds. *Puritan New England: Essays on Religion, Society, and Culture*. New York: St. Martin's Press, 1977.

———. *The Puritan Tradition in America: 1620–1730*. Columbia, SC: Univeristy of South Carolina Press, 1972.

Ver Steeg, Clarence L. *The Formative Years: 1607–1763*. New York: Hill and Wang, 1964.

———. and Richard Hofstadter, eds. *Great Issues in American History: From Settlement to Revolution*. New York: Random House, 1969.

von Rohr, John. *The Covenant of Grace in Puritan Thought*. Atlanta: Scholars Press, 1986.

Wakeman, Henry Offely. *The Church and The Puritans: 1570-1660*. New York: Anson D. F. Randolph and Co., n.d.

Walker, George M. ed. *Puritansim in Early America*. Boston: D. C. Heath and Co., 1950.

Walker, Williston. *Ten New England Leaders*. New York: Silver, Burdett and Co., 1901.

Walsh, Richard, ed. *The Mind and Spirit of Early America: Sources in American History, 1607–1789*. New York: Appleton-Century-Crofts, 1969.

Watkins, Owen C. *The Puritan Experience: Studies in Spiritual Autobiography*. New York: Schocken Books, 1972.

Weeden, William B. *Economic and Social History of New England: 1620-1789*. vol. I. Boston and New York: Houghton Mifflin Co., 1890.

Wendell, Barrett. *Cotton Mather*. New York: Chelsea House, 1980.

Wertenbaker, Thomas Jefferson. *The Puritan Oligarchy: The Founding of American Civilization*. New York: Charles Scribner's Sons, 1947.

Wescott, Brooke Foss. *A General View of the History of the English Bible*. Third edition revised and edited by Wright, William Aldis. London: Macmillan and Co., 1905.

White, Eugene E. "Master Holdsworth and 'A Knowledge Very Useful and Necessary'" *The Quarterly Journal of Speech* 43 (1967): 1–16.

Williams, Selma R. *Divine Rebel: The Life of Anne Marbury Hutchinson*. New York: Holt, Rinehart and Winston, 1981.

Willison, George F. *Saints and Strangers: Being the Lives of the Pilgrim Fathers and Their Families With Their Friends and Foes: & an Account of Their Posthumous Wanderings in Limbo, Their Final Resurrection & Rise to Glory, & the Strange Pilgrimages of Plymouth Rock*. New York: Reynal and Hitchcock, 1945.

Winslow, Ola Elizabeth. *Master Roger Williams*. New York: Macmillan Co., 1957.

Winthrop, John. *Winthrop's Journal: "History of New England," 1630–1649*. 2 vols. Edited by James Kendall Hosmer. 1908. Reprint. New York: Barnes and Noble, 1966.

Withington, Ann Fairfax and Schwartz, Jack. "The Political Trial of Anne Hutchinson" *New England Quarterly* 41 (1978): 226-240.

Wood, Gordon S. "Struggle Over the Puritans" *The New York Review* (Nov 9, 1989): 26–37.

Zaret, David. *The Heavenly Contract: Ideology and Organization in Pre-Revolutionary Puritanism*. Chicago: University of Chicago Press, 1985.

Ziff, Larzer. *The Career of John Cotton: Puritanism and the American Experience.* Princeton: Princeton University Press, 1962.

Zimmermann, Frank. *The Inner World of Qohelet.* New York: KTAV Publishing Company, 1973.